2 OCL

Hill, Lawrence Francis   E
AUTHOR   183.8
Diplomatic relations between B7
TITLE

the U.S. and Brazil   H56
    1970

E
183.8
B7
H56
1970

DIPLOMATIC RELATIONS BETWEEN THE UNITED STATES AND BRAZIL

Diplomatic Relations Between the United States and Brazil

By

LAWRENCE F. HILL, Ph.D.

*Associate Professor of History in
the Ohio State University*

GREENWOOD PRESS, PUBLISHERS
WESTPORT, CONNECTICUT

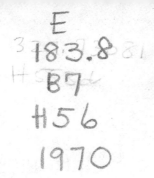

Originally published in 1932
by Duke University Press, Durham, N.C.

First Greenwood Reprinting 1970

Library of Congress Catalogue Card Number 70-109749

SBN 8371-4239-3

Printed in the United States of America

DIPLOMATIC RELATIONS BETWEEN THE UNITED STATES AND BRAZIL

To

HERBERT E. BOLTON

CONTENTS

FOREWORD

THE STUDY presented in the following pages represents an attempt to tell in comparatively brief space the story of the diplomatic relations between the United States and Brazil since the latter's independence. The plan of the work permitted the inclusion only of such material of a commercial and financial nature as seemed to have affected diplomatic intercourse.

The account is based primarily on manuscript material found in ministerial despatches (seventy-two large volumes to August, 1906), consular letters, instructions to American diplomatic agents, and communications between the United States foreign office and the Brazilian diplomatic agents at Washington. But it is also based in part on the publications of the two governments (such as *Foreign Relations* and the House and Senate documents of the United States and the *Relatorios* and the *Annaes* of Brazil), on contemporary newspapers of both countries, and on such monographs and special treatises as have appeared on topics which fall within the century covered. These sources, aggregating several hundred volumes, include all the official correspondence that passed between the Washington and Rio governments. The writer believes they contain sufficient material adequately to reveal official and public reaction to the issues considered from time to time. Foreign archives, some of which doubtless contain valuable material on the subject in hand, have not been examined for two reasons: they are not open for more than half of the period covered by the study and the writer does not consider the subject, as significant as it is, worth the endeavor of an entire lifetime. He invites those who may be inclined to criticise him for failure to utilize all the sources that the world may hold to comb the materials he has examined and others to be had in foreign archives and supplement the story. The writer himself has no time to pursue the task further. It is his belief that in the absolute sense there is no piece of work definitive in nature.

To some the present study may seem too critical of American agents and policy. By way of defense the writer claims that he followed only where the documents seemed to lead. Frankly, he made no effort to stick his head in the sand and refuse to see what was before him.

In the preparation of this work the writer became indebted to many for their helpful coöperation. For aid incident to the assembling of materials he is especially grateful to Dr. Tyler Dennett, Mr. D. A. Salmon, and Mrs. Maddin Summers of the Department of State, to Mr. and Mrs. Maurice H. Bletz of the Department of Commerce, and to the officials and attendants of the Library of Congress and of the Ibero-American Library. For assistance in the collection of material and for patience and sympathy throughout the writing he is more than grateful to his wife. He acknowledges the kindness of Dr. James A. Robertson for permission to reprint without much change portions of two articles which appeared in *The Hispanic American Historical Review*. Finally, he gives especial recognition to Dr. J. Fred Rippy of Duke University for reading the entire manuscript and for many suggestions for its improvement.

LAWRENCE F. HILL

The Ohio State University
October, 1931

DIPLOMATIC RELATIONS BETWEEN THE UNITED STATES AND BRAZIL

CHAPTER I

RELATIONS WITH THE PORTUGUESE COURT

A S A RESULT of Napoleon's ambitious program on the continent of Europe, the Portuguese royal family took flight to the Western Hemisphere near the close of 1807. Within a few brief days following the completion of the journey the political institutions of Portugal—generally known as the Court—had been set up on Brazilian soil. Immediately Thomas Jefferson took the initial step in the renewal of diplomatic relations, which had been suspended in 1801 for reasons of economy.[1] This action of the president was not taken because he suddenly discovered more money, but because of changed conditions. The grandiose plans of a Frenchman had almost overnight set in motion forces which seemed likely to result in the creation of an important American sister-state. What could give more promise for the success of Jefferson's recently conceived Pan-American policy![2]

The resumption of relations with the Braganza dynasty occurred on May 5, 1808, when Jefferson, learning of the arrival of Regent Dom John at Rio de Janeiro, availed himself of an opportunity to extend to the prince a cordial welcome to the New World. The greeting, sent through an American merchant, Henry Hill, who had just been invested with the title of consul, alluded to the friendly relations

[1] The Jefferson Papers (Library of Congress MSS), CXVII.
[2] On this Pan-American policy see an article by I. J. Cox entitled "Pan-American Policy of Jefferson and Wilkinson," in *The Mississippi Valley Historical Review*, I, 212-239.

which had always prevailed between the two countries, to the increased strength which they recently had acquired by the transfer of the young ruler's government to the new continent, and to the prospect of establishing "a system of intercourse between the different regions of this [the western] hemisphere" based on the principles of the peace and happiness of mankind. The northern republic was disposed to set this policy in operation at once.[3]

Upon arrival at Rio de Janeiro Consul Hill was given a cordial reception, and the message which he bore received prompt consideration. In a verbal response to Jefferson's approaches Prince John gave assurances that American citizens would enjoy in Brazil the commercial privileges of the most favored nation, freedom of private worship, the same rights as Portuguese subjects in the acquisition and disposal of property, and equality before the courts.[4] In the light of history, these proffers at first appear significant, for in general Portugal had maintained an exclusionist colonial policy in Brazil. Yet, in view of the fact that Brazilian ports had just been thrown open to the trade of all nations in amity with the Portuguese, serious reflection reveals little ground for rejoicing. The most-favored-nation commercial provision, considered the most important, was but in harmony with a general program of liberalization consequent upon the transfer of royal residence to the New World. It in no wise conferred a special concession. A knowledge of history might have indicated to the Americans that the British merchants would still remain their chief competitors. Notwithstanding the decree which had opened Brazilian ports to all friendly nations, the centuries-long English immunities were

---

[3] *Writings of Thomas Jefferson* (Washington, 1903), XII, 49-50.
[4] Secretary of state to Minister Sumter, Aug. 1, 1809, in Instructions to United States Ministers (Department of State MSS), VII.

to continue. Indeed, they had recently been confirmed and extended when Prince John acted upon the advice of Sir Sidney Smith and accepted passage across the Atlantic under convoy of a British fleet. But the fact that Brazilians purchased American goods to the value of almost $900,000 the following year (1809) was an announcement that the Yankees had entered the contest.[5] Diplomatic pressure would follow.

A period of ten months was insufficient time for Jefferson to complete the resumption of diplomatic relations with the house of Braganza, and the task fell to James Madison. Although Madison's Pan-American program was less ambitious than that of his predecessor, he did not lose all interest in the subject. One of the first things to which he turned his hand was that of the appointment of a minister to the Portuguese court. His choice fell upon Thomas Sumter, Jr., who, as secretary of the American legation at Paris, often had disagreed with his chief. Sumter was instructed to report on all important occurrences which might take place in South America as a result of the contest then in progress in the Iberian Peninsula and to start preparations for making the way easy for the establishment of harmonious relations with any form of government which might come into existence in the region. He was also requested to place his government in possession of such information of a commercial nature as would enable it to frame a treaty, though the negotiations were to take place on the Potomac.[6]

Because of a long delay in the United States the new minister did not present his credentials at Rio de Janeiro until the first of June, 1810. And soon after presentation

[5] Timothy Pitkin, *A Statistical View of the Commerce of the United States of America*, p. 232.

[6] Secretary Smith to Sumter, Aug. 1, 1809, in Instructions to United States Ministers, VII.

he found British influence dominant in diplomatic circles, though in his relations with the Portuguese officials he received cordial treatment. The three treaties entered into by Portugal and Great Britain a few months prior to his arrival were indicative of the prestige of the latter. While two of the treaties—one of friendship and alliance and the other for the establishment of a packet service between Brazilian and British ports—were not unusual, the third was somewhat out of the ordinary. It reduced the duty on British imports from twenty-four to fifteen per cent—three points less than the duty on goods from Portugal—and that without much reciprocation to Portugal.[7] This treaty deprived the Americans of their most-favored-nation status and for a time caused some anxiety. Nevertheless, American exports to Brazil for 1810 and 1811 were one hundred per cent greater than in 1809, despite the unfavorable discrimination.[8] The figures for the succeeding years seem extremely small, but this fact is explained by the second war with Great Britain which practically drove American shipping from the seas. After the close of the war Sumter pressed assiduously the topic of discrimination against American goods, and yet, though Prince John always appeared favorably disposed toward remedying matters, it was not until a quarter of a century later that a commercial treaty was wrung from Brazil. Finally, the American became discouraged with combating British prestige and almost ceased trying to secure the removal of the commercial discriminations against his countrymen. Instead he devoted a considerable portion of his time to furnishing his government information on the progress of the revolutions in Spanish America and on Portuguese connections with Platine affairs.

---

[7] Sumter to Secretary Smith, June 9, 1810, in Despatches from Brazil, I.

[8] The exact figures may be found in Timothy Pitkin, *op. cit.*, p. 232.

Unfortunately, Sumter found time to engage in an acrimonious controversy over court etiquette. Custom, which had become hardened into rules, decreed that all spectators should uncover and that all on horse-back should dismount upon the passage of one or more members of the royal family. While the American minister complied with the former requirement, he refused to recognize the latter. The prince was willing to overlook this irregularity but not so his more impetuous consort, to whom the act was a mark of disrespect. Princess Carlota exercised her authority and ordered the guard to oblige the American minister and the British minister, who was also recalcitrant, to unhorse upon appropriate occasion. Presently the guard did succeed in removing the Englishman from his saddle, but on approaching Sumter the latter drew his pistols and threatened to fire if touched. On a later occasion the American again resisted successfully and in the same manner.

It was natural that the princess regent should attempt to obtain official satisfaction for Sumter's flagrant insult. Luckily, the mild prince was unwilling to risk disturbing friendly relations with the United States in order to avenge this slight breach of etiquette on the part of her representative. While the minister was debating whether he should continue to pull his pistols or absent himself from court until receipt of instructions from Washington, Prince John, ignoring the protests of his wife, issued a decree exempting foreign ministers from observance of the obnoxious formality of descending from their saddles. After a time the tempest passed; and eventually the impulsive princess was found breaking her drives by stopping at the Sumter home and chatting with members of the family.

One can not measure accurately the effect of this stupid incident on the settlement of the diplomatic matters that came up for consideration from day to day, but surely the way was not made easier. It is known that it proved to be very embarrassing to the household of the American minister, for during the excitement the angry populace in Rio de Janeiro stoned Mrs. Sumter in public, and receipt of the news in Washington of Mr. Sumter's conduct produced a feeling of irritation against him at home. But Thomas Sumter was acting true to his argumentative reputation; and, unfortunately, he was creating a precedent for several of his successors.[9]

The air had hardly cleared when Prince John issued the decree of December 16, 1815, proclaiming Brazil a kingdom. Uninformed as to the real motives which had brought about the measure, Sumter thought the occasion opportune for bringing forward the American program. Thus he sought a private audience with the prince, extended to him warm congratulations, informed him that his recent decree had been expected by the American president for several years, and alluded to the more intimate intercourse between the two nations which should naturally follow. Stimulated by interjected remarks from the ruler, the American minister proceeded to accord a degree of justification for his ardor by saying "that the certitude now given of the independence of Brazil gave a new force and life to" his original instructions. The prince replied that the independence of Brazil was settled and signified a willingness to enter into negotiations for extending the commercial and political relations of the two countries.[10]

[9] For information on this incident consult a dispatch from Sumter to Secretary Monroe, Dec. 29, 1815, in Despatches, I; M. de Oliveira Lima, *Dom João VI no Brazil*, I, 268ff.; C. F. Adams, *Memoirs of John Quincy Adams*, IV, 339.

[10] Sumter to Secretary Monroe, Dec. 29, 1815, in Despatches, I. The communication can be found also in W. R. Manning, *Diplomatic Correspondence of the United States concerning the Independence of the Latin American Nations*, II, 696-700. Hereafter this collection will be cited W. R. Manning, *Diplomatic Correspondence*.

In the meantime, the Brazilian chargé, José Rademaker, and Secretary Monroe were exchanging notes on the same subject. And, paradoxically enough, the communications of the American secretary enunciated a policy not in entire accord with that proclaimed by Sumter at Rio. At any rate, Monroe's exchanges on the elevation of Brazil to the plane with Portugal and the Algarves were marked by a great deal less of enthusiasm, though he did assure Rademaker that his government looked upon the measure with great satisfaction, since it could not fail to promote the prosperity and strengthen the ties of friendship between the two nations.[11] It is believed that this difference was largely the result of the failure of the American government to keep its minister informed promptly on changing conditions. Partly because of the failure of the Braganza government to observe strict neutrality during the War of 1812, the friendship exhibited for Portugal in 1809, when Sumter received his instructions, had cooled considerably. But the infrequency of communications from his government kept the minister from appreciating the extent of this change. Nor did he know that the decree which elevated Brazil to a kingdom had been issued upon the advice of Talleyrand, who was desirous of establishing in the New World a monarchical counterbalance to the American Republic.[12] Yet, in spite of the difference in the ardor of her representatives, the step was welcomed by the United States, for, as Prince John said in his audience with Sumter, Brazilian independence was assured. That this new sister-state could revert to her old position as a colony was unthinkable; that she would soon find occasion to sever

[11] Secretary Monroe to Chargé Rademaker, June 5, 1816, in Notes to Foreign Legations, II.
[12] Oliveira Lima, *Dom João VI*, I, 519.

the slender cords which bound her to Europe was entirely probable.

But fate had decreed that the early relations of the two American countries were not to be altogether amicable. Several incidents, some important and others comparatively unimportant, were to play their part in making anything like a *rapprochement* impossible up to the time of the complete separation of Brazil from Portugal in 1822. One of the minor events which deserves some consideration at this point was the altercation between the officers of the *Congress,* an American vessel, and the public officials of Rio de Janeiro. Bearing the commission which the president had appointed to proceed to South America to gather information on the revolutionary movement, the frigate put in at Rio the last of January, 1818, for the purpose of delivering dispatches to Sumter. During the short stay in port several of the seamen on shore leave became intoxicated, as was quite customary. Among those who imbibed a little too freely was a seaman of Portuguese nationality. When he resisted the efforts of two frigate officers to take him on board, some of his countrymen extended aid and placed him under the protection of a port functionary. A little later the Americans returned, removed the seaman from his retreat, and forced him on board. Thereupon the Brazilian foreign minister, who alleged that the invasion of the office of a public official constituted a violation of Portuguese sovereignty, addressed a vigorous protest to Sumter demanding the release of all Portuguese subjects on board the vessel and a prompt apology for the offence of the American officers. The American minister, who was disposed to arrive at a friendly settlement if possible, induced Commodore Sinclair to offer an apology for the conduct of his subordinates, but the latter refused to release the seamen. The Brazilian minister then ordered the forts to prevent the *Congress* from leaving the harbor. Notwithstanding this order, the obstinate commander stationed men behind his guns and sailed out of port. Fortunately, he went unhindered.

Regardless of where custom or legality lay in this controversy, the procedure followed by the American commodore was bound to give serious offence. It was one of those small incidents which helped to ruffle feelings and render the solution of major problems extremely difficult.[13]

Chief among the major difficulties to disturb the good feeling of the two peoples during the period under consideration were those which arose from the subject of neutrality. During the War of 1812 the American government accused Portugal of extending aid to the British, while a few years later Portugal complained that the United States violated her neutrality by not restraining the privateers who left her ports under the flag of Artigas to prey upon Portuguese commerce.

Almost simultaneously with the outbreak of the conflict between Great Britain and the United States Sumter reported that a corvette had been loaned to the British fleet for operation in South American waters, though the action was immediately rescinded upon the recommendation of the British minister at Rio, who thought it important that the English armies in the Peninsula should continue to receive American supplies.[14] Following the resumption of control over the vessel came Portugal's proclamation of neutrality. But in actuality the declaration seems to have done little more than prohibit the disposal of belligerent prizes in Portuguese

[13] Accounts of this incident may be found in the April 29 and May 5, 1818, issues of the *National Intelligencer*. See also H. M. Brackenridge, *A Voyage to South America performed by Order of the American Government in the years 1817 and 1818 in the Frigate Congress*, I, 92ff.

[14] Sumter to Secretary Monroe, Sept. 30 and Oct. 1, 1812, in Despatches, I.

ports. When it was believed that American public vessels or privateers were lying off the shore waiting for their prey, British armed merchantmen were allowed to remain in Brazilian ports days after day. Furthermore, British men-of-war attacked American ships within Portuguese territorial waters, and Portugal furnished English merchant vessels with convoys as well. Needless to say the United States government entered vigorous protests against this unneutral policy. Yet there was little hope of obtaining satisfaction. Under the circumstances it should not be surprising that American commanders in their maneuverings often approached the verge of questionable conduct.[15]

At this point it may not be inappropriate to particularize by summarizing the history of the well-known *General Armstrong* incident. The *General Armstrong*, a privateer commanded by an American named Samuel C. Reid, entered the port of Fayal in one of the Azores toward the close of September, 1814, for the purpose of obtaining fresh water. Within a few hours after arrival a British squadron of three vessels also put into the harbor and cast anchor near the American vessel. The signals which passed from one enemy ship to another aroused Captain Reid's suspicions and caused him to essay a move to a position nearer the guns of the fort. While in the process of changing positions, the American officer was provoked to fire a broadside at three boats of armed men which had been dispatched for an attack. This infuriated Captain Lloyd of the British squadron and he began preparations for a fight. Meanwhile, the American consul at Fayal, John B. Dabney, called upon the Portuguese governor to fulfill the neutrality which the Prince Regent

[15] For verification of these statements see a communication from Sumter to Monroe, May 9, 1813, in Despatches, I; *American State Papers, Naval Affairs*, I, 290ff.; J. Barnes, *Commodore Bainbridge*, pp. 157ff.; A. Gleaves, *James Lawrence*, pp. 114ff.; J. Russel, *History of the War Between the United States and Great Britain*, pp. 212ff.

had promised to observe in his proclamation of August 18, 1812, by protecting him from the impending attack of the British commander. The governor complied to the extent of sending a note of protest to Captain Lloyd, but before an answer was received the anticipated attack had been delivered and repulsed with heavy losses to the British. Immediately following the encounter the British officer made reply to the governor's note in which he placed responsibility for the violation of the neutrality of the port on the Americans and gave notice of his determination to take possession of their vessel. The Portuguese executive then attempted to secure a suspension of hostilities until the antagonists could be brought together in a conference; but all was in vain.

Early on the following morning (September 27) one of the British brigs renewed the attack on the *General Armstrong* and, though temporarily repulsed, forced the Americans to abandon her and seek safety in the town, whence they soon retired before press gangs into the country. On the same day, after the British had pillaged and burned his ship, Captain Reid went to the American consulate, registered a protest with the Portuguese government for the failure to defend the neutrality of the harbor, and put in a claim for damages resulting from the loss of the vessel. Before the close of the year the matter had been brought before the Department of State at Washington where the wheels of diplomacy were immediately set in motion in behalf of the claimants. Sumter presented the claim at Rio de Janeiro, and the Portuguese government in turn made representations to the English government through the British minister at Rio and through the Portuguese minister at London. But in spite of the assiduity with which the case was pressed, the end of the year 1816 came without reparation. The following year witnessed no better results; in the spring of 1818

Secretary of State John Quincy Adams interviewed, both formally and informally, the Portuguese minister at Washington, Corrêa da Serra, on the subject, but the efforts of the secretary also proved futile, owing to the fact that Corrêa da Serra was at the time seeking indemnity for the capture of Portuguese vessels by Uruguayan privateers fitted out in American ports. The case was destined to drag on for many years.

Partly as a result of the unsettled condition of affairs in Portugal following the return of the court to Lisbon in 1821, the claim dropped into the background and did not receive serious consideration again until 1835, when it was resurrected as a consequence of a general rejuvenation of American foreign policy. It is perhaps sufficient to note that the Portuguese government had reversed its position completely by this time. Whereas it had formerly held the British as the aggressors, it now placed the responsibility for the beginning of the controversy on the precipitate action of the American commander, who fired the first shot. Thus the element of time alone was gradually winning a diplomatic victory for the British. Persistent pressure from the agents of the claimants, however, brought a momentary reconsideration from Secretary Upshur in 1844, though his successor practically neutralized the move by refusing to re-open negotiations. Except for one of the accidents of history Calhoun's indifference might have been the *coup de grâce*. But, as good fortune would have it, the principal heir to the claim, Samuel C. Reid, Jr., came to be a companion of General Taylor in the Mexican War; and, owing to American military-hero worship, Reid's companion became president in 1849. After taking office President Taylor remembered his comrade in arms, along with the promise he had made to him, and pressed Portugal for a settlement of his grievance.

The matter was pursued with such vigor that diplomatic relations were broken and the American chargé left his Lisbon post for the United States. But before he reached Washington the president died, and the case fell into milder hands. Secretary of State Webster accepted Portugal's arbitration proposal, a claims convention was concluded, and Louis Napoleon was chosen as arbiter. The Frenchman's decision, made on November 30, 1852, was against the United States, allegedly because the American commander accepted the challenge to battle before applying for Portuguese protection. Thirty years later, after prolonged debates and legal wrangling, the United States government paid the heirs to the claim the sum of $70,739.[16]

The *General Armstrong* is only one of many cases which might be narrated to show that Portugal did not enforce her neutrality during the War of 1812. In several other instances British commanders fired upon and captured American vessels within Portuguese territorial waters. In at least one case of flagrant violation of her neutrality, in the harbor of Porto Praya in the Cape Verdes, Portugal seems not to have troubled herself even to make a remonstrance; in other cases it may be doubted whether she employed her full energies to secure respect for her announced position.[17] But in defense of the Braganza government it may be said that it was usually a physical impossibility for it to carry out its declarations. Nevertheless, failure to do so partly accounts for the indifferent attitude which Washington officials were

[16] This summary is based upon accounts found in *American State Papers, Naval Affairs*, I, 493-496; J. B. Moore, *History and Digest of the International Arbitrations*, II, 1071-1132; *Sen. Doc.* 14, 29 Cong., 1 sess. (ser. 472), pp. 1-58; *House Ex. Doc.* 53, 32 Cong., 1 sess. (ser. 641), pp. 1-160; S. C. Reid, *The History of the Wonderful Battle of the Brig of War General Armstrong.*

[17] *American State Papers, Naval Affairs*, I, 405.

soon to take toward American privateers who used the Uruguayan flag to prey upon Portuguese commerce.

Occasional reference has been made to the counter complaints of Portugal against the United States over the subject of neutrality during the residence of the court at Rio de Janeiro. Perhaps this subject should now be treated in greater detail. During the revolutionary wars in Spanish America, there flared up afresh, with additional contestants, the centuries-long conflict which the two Iberian nations had been waging for Banda Oriental, the province situated east of the Plata River. One of the new entrants into the struggle was José Artigas, a native of the province, who attempted to play off one of the rival claimants against the other in order to bring about independence. Naturally the program of Artigas met with setbacks from time to time. In 1816 Portugal took advantage of confused conditions in the camps of her rivals, Buenos Aires and Spain, and laid siege to Montevideo by land and water. Powerless to cope with naval forces, the Uruguayan patriot sought to harass Portugal by commissioning privateers to prey upon her commerce, a method by no means novel, since France, Buenos Aires, Colombia, and Mexico had successfully resorted to it many times during the past quarter-century. The commissions were signed in blank and sold to adventurers of all nations, but American citizens, particularly those of Baltimore, were in a position to profit most by them.

As soon as the Portuguese minister at Washington, Corrêa da Serra, learned that instructions to cruise against his country's commerce had been issued to Baltimorean privateers, he declared his faith in the American government's disposition to deal with the adventurers, though he at the same time pointed out certain deficiencies in its existing neutrality laws and suggested the enactment of more adequate legislation. President Madison received the minister's communication favorably and sent it to Congress, which was then engaged in acrimonious debates on the necessity of strengthening the country's laws on neutrality. Whatever may have been the effect of Corrêa da Serra's recommendation, Congress passed the act of March 3, 1817. Framed to meet specific conditions then existing in the southern half of the hemisphere, the new law supplemented the old statutes of 1794 and 1797 by prohibiting cruising under commissions of "any colony, district, or people," terms calculated to include the unrecognized governments of Spanish America.[18]

Notwithstanding its specific nature, and the severe provisions for enforcement, the act failed to accomplish its purpose. Several reasons help to account for this, chief of which was the connivance at violations on the part of the public officials of Baltimore, the privateers' haven, where the federal judges, the collector of customs, the postmaster, the private attorneys, and the populace were culpable either because of selfish interests or incompetency.[19] In addition, the nature of privateering rendered legal action extremely uncertain, for in many cases, perhaps in a majority, the marauders simply transferred to their own vessels the goods of the captured ships and returned to Baltimore to dispose of them. Because of the facility of forging a set of covering documents it was indeed difficult to prove where the cargoes had been obtained.

After many vain efforts to secure convictions in the courts upon the mass of evidence which the Portuguese consuls had gathered from the four corners of the world, Corrêa da Serra decided to resort to other means, and presented to the American government a request for indemnity for the cap-

[18] *United States Statutes at Large,* III, 370.
[19] Adams, *Memoirs of John Quincy Adams,* IV, 164.

ture of three vessels. The reply denied the request, and suggested the competency of the American admiralty courts to deal with the outrages of which complaint was made. But, as the Portuguese minister no doubt suspected, the courts continued to be inadequate for the exigencies of the occasion, despite the assistance which the Department of State tendered Corrêa da Serra in order to make effective the prosecutions. The political appointments which President Monroe made to the judgeship of the Maryland district court and to the commandancy of Baltimore's revenue cutter more than counteracted all proffered assistance. With official aid and connivance the astute attorney William Pinkney was usually able to bring victory to the privateers.

Discouraged by its first attempt to secure indemnity from the American government, as well as by failure to bring about convictions in the American courts, the Portuguese government sought relief by presenting the subject of piracy to the Congress of Aix-la-Chapelle, which met in the autumn of 1818. Count Palmella, Portugal's representative at the meeting, offered a number of proposals for dealing with the evil. Among those adopted by the congress, was that which obligated all the powers represented at Washington to join in soliciting the American government to strengthen its laws sufficiently to obtain complete suppression as far as its citizens were concerned. France seems to have been the only power to carry out the agreement. United action was forestalled when Secretary Adams succeeded in convincing Great Britain that his government was doing what it could to withdraw its people from all participation in the evil.

Checked in its coöperative plan for putting an end to the ravages on the commerce of Portuguese subjects, the Rio de Janeiro government resumed negotiations with Washington on the subject of indemnity. On July 17, 1820, Corrêa da Serra presented a list of nineteen ships which had fallen into the hands of privateers fitted out in American ports and asked agreement on the appointment of a joint commission to examine resulting claims, which totaled $616,158. In an interview with the minister six weeks later John Quincy Adams rejected the proposal for a commission and again suggested the American courts as the only resort in such cases. The reply offended the old minister, and he sought solace in the hospitality of Monticello, where he had been a visitor many times before. Jefferson received his guest with marked kindness and even gave ear to the proposal which had just been rejected on the Potomac; but at the same time he told him kindly that his plan was impossible. He also told the minister that the Washington government looked upon privateering with abhorrence, and that it was using its best efforts to suppress it. Although Corrêa da Serra was unconvinced, and no doubt unconsoled, his farewell parting revealed a friendship as firm as ever.

When Adams made formal reply to the minister's request —it was almost a demand—on September 20, he stated that acceptance of the proposal would be inconsistent with the constitution of the United States and contrary to the practice of civilized nations. The secretary then pointed out once more the remedy which could be had in the American tribunals and offered every possible aid in facilitating court procedure. As Corrêa da Serra received this communication in New York on the eve of his departure for Rio de Janeiro, where he would assume the duties of a cabinet member, he gave it mere acknowledgment, with the remark that reply would be made after presentation to the Portuguese council of state. Although a sudden turn in the internal affairs of the Portuguese government changed the minister's destination to Lisbon, the council of state at Rio gave careful consideration to the American secretary's note. The response made a year later insisted on the creation of the claims commission and threatened commercial retaliation in the event that the proposal was again rejected. Nevertheless, it was rejected, along with a restatement of the former position. At various times during the next quarter-century the Portuguese government brought forward the subject of the claims, but perhaps it was usually to offset the demands made by the American government in defense of the *General Armstrong* case.[20]

The Pernambucan revolt of 1817 was another incident which vitally affected the relations between the United States and Portugal during the period under review. Influenced by the revolutionary spirit which was then exhibiting itself in so many parts of the world, the uprising was the first of a series to take place in northern Brazil.[21] The government's preoccupation with weighty matters elsewhere, particularly in Uruguay, and the prospect of getting assistance from the River Plate and the United States, lent encouragement to the leaders of the movement. On March 6, when the Portuguese officers attempted to apply disciplinary measures to some native troops, a disturbance ensued and on the day following a republic was launched. Following close upon the launching of the new government Antonio Gonçalves da Cruz was commissioned to go to the United States for the purpose

[20] This summary is based on *House Ex. Doc.* 53, 32 Cong., 1 sess. (ser. 641), pp. 161-208; *Annals of Congress,* 1824, pp. 3045-3051; Adams, *Memoirs of John Quincy Adams,* IV, 12, 23, 60, 85, 164, 306, 316, 327, 333, 342, 362, 372, 416, 417, 437, 445, V, 19, 63, 77, 93, 171, 180; *Writings of Thomas Jefferson,* XV, 262, 285-287, XIX, 224-228; W. P. Cresson, *The Holy Alliance, the European Background of the Monroe Doctrine,* pp. 81-82.

[21] See Oscar d'Araujo, *L'idée Republicaine au Bresil.*

of obtaining supplies and recognition, in return for which he was authorized to grant a favorable commercial treaty.[22]

About three weeks before Cruz's arrival in the United States an Englishman named Bowen brought the news of the Pernambucan outbreak. Although he called upon Richard Rush, the acting secretary of state, and gave him an account of events at Pernambuco, the visit was entirely unofficial in nature. Alarmed by newspaper reports which unfairly represented the Englishman as a diplomatic agent, Corrêa da Serra hurried from Philadelphia to Washington to counteract the influence of "Ambassador Bowen." When he called upon Rush, the day following Bowen's visit, he took occasion to characterize the happenings at Pernambuco as a transient and unjustifiable insurrection and to insist that they be given no cognizance by the Monroe government. Two weeks later, on May 14, the scientist minister returned to the office of the secretary to complain of the late departure from Baltimore of two ships loaded with arms intended for the rebels. Rush replied that trade in arms by American citizens was forbidden neither by international nor American municipal law. This statement was unsatisfactory, because it signified the recognition of the belligerency of the Pernambuco rebels, and drew from Serra the general retort that European nations looked upon the United States as a fomentor of rebellions anyway. Thereupon the American fired back the remark that if the nations of Europe held this view it was only because they were ignorant of our history. In spite of the minister's apology and its formal acceptance by Rush, the verbal cross-firing left matters in a bad way; nor were they improved by the appearance in the *National Intelligencer*, issue of May

[22] An excellent account of the revolution by a contemporary is that of Father Francisco Muniz Tavares, *Historia da Revolução de Pernambuco de 1817* (edited by M. de Oliveira Lima).

12, of a critical editorial which had been written under Serra's direction.[23]

Then appeared in Boston Gonçalves da Cruz with his explanation both of the motives which had inspired the revolt and of the democratic principles which had attended the launching of the new republic. When this news reached the ear of the Portuguese minister, it brought him almost to desperation. He hastened to insert in the *National Intelligencer*, under the caption "Official Notification of the Legation of Portugal," the notice that:

the Port of Pernambuco, and the adjacent coast, are effectually blockaded by the ships of war of H. M. F. Majesty. The American ships are therefore warned not to venture navigating to them, because the law of nations relating to strict blockades will be rigidly enforced.

The Portuguese Consuls in the Ports of the United States having been forbidden, in the King's name, by the Minister Plenipotentiary, to grant any Consular papers to ships directed to that port, as long as it shall continue in a state of rebellion, information of it is given to all persons to whom the knowledge of it may concern.[24]

Washington officials regarded this action as ill-considered. They had not been consulted; they had received no official notification of the blockade; they did not like the Genêt method of negotiation. When, through a further exchange of notes, it finally developed that the minister's notification was based on an assumption rather than on information derived from his government, the secretary of state released a reprimand which dealt specifically with the grave consequences likely to result from promulgating official communications through the medium of newspapers.

[23] Rush to Madison, June 14, 1817, in Monroe Papers (Library of Congress MSS), XVI. See also President Monroe to Madison, May 16, 1817, in Madison Papers, XIX.

[24] *National Intelligencer*, May 22, 1817.

Although it did not alter the need for the censure, it was subsequently learned that the Portuguese government had placed the blockade in effect.[25]

Although Rush wrote Sumter at Rio de Janeiro that "Mr. Corrêa's conduct was deemed irregular and unjustifiable," it was thought unnecessary to take any further notice of it. Yet one wonders if the incident did not play some part in changing the president's early esteem for the venerable scientist into his later coldness toward him. That it was not considered lightly by the administration is shown by the fact that a long defense of the course pursued was drawn up and dispatched to ex-presidents Madison and Jefferson, the other two members of the presidential trinity. Whatever may have been the motive for this procedure, President Monroe must have received some satisfaction in learning that his policy met the commendation of his closest friends.[26]

This was the state of the atmosphere about Washington when the representative of the new republic approached for an official interview. Granting that a personal conference with Cruz was regarded politic—which is extremely doubtful—the president's tour of the country made it impossible at the time. But it was significant that Ceasar Rodney, a pronounced partisan of the independence of the Hispanic peoples, was designated as the government's representative. Rodney met the visitor at Philadelphia on June 5 and soon convinced him that there was no want of sympathy for his cause, as well as for the cause of independence throughout

[25] Rush to Corrêa da Serra, May 28, 1817, in Notes to Foreign Legations, II, 229 (W. R. Manning, Diplomatic Correspondence, I, 40-41).

[26] See Rush to Sumter, July 18, 1817, in Instructions to United States Ministers, VIII, 142 (also in W. R. Manning, Diplomatic Correspondence, I, 41-42); Rush to Madison, June 14, 1817, and Rush to Monroe, July 20, 1817, in Monroe Papers, XVI; Madison to Rush, June 27, 1817, in Writings of James Madison (Gaillard Hunt, ed.), VII, 394; Adams, Memoirs of John Quincy Adams, IV, 12, 23, 327.

South America. But, largely because of English efforts at reconciling Spain and her colonies, it was believed that the United States should go no further than to extend to the new government the status of belligerent, with the privileges pertaining thereto, including the important one of purchasing armament and other supplies. It was reported that Cruz expressed entire satisfaction with this proposed stand.[27]

Although the Brazilian had been told that he probably would not want an interview with the president, about the middle of June he went to Washington, where he was accorded the treatment of an unofficial representative. Nevertheless, while in this capacity he secured the appointment as United States consul at Pernambuco of a certain Joseph Ray, who was a pronounced partisan of the revolution, and he dispatched supplies from Baltimore to his colleagues at home. But despite American sympathy and encouragement, expressed in both official and unofficial circles,[28] the rebellion failed and its instigators were executed—without as much as a protest from the Potomac. According to Father Muniz Tavares, the uprising miscarried because "Pernambuco deceived itself, when in the formation of its plans, it counted upon the decisive help of those governments which professed liberal principles, notably that of the United States of North America."[29] But, as it was, the Portuguese government was indignant at the policy pursued at Washington, one result of which was the arrest and imprisonment of Consul Ray for complicity in the conspiracy.[30]

The difficulties which arose from the Pernambuco ep-

---

[27] Rodney to Monroe, June 6 and 8, 1817, in Monroe Papers, XVI.

[23] For the attitudes of Jefferson and John Adams see letters from Jefferson to Lafayette, May 14, 1817, and Adams to Jefferson, May 26, in *Writings of Thomas Jefferson*, XV, 116-117, 123.

[29] Muniz Tavares, *op. cit.*, p. 155.

[30] Adams, *Memoirs of John Quincy Adams*, IV, 85.

isode, from the imprisonment of Americans at several Brazilian ports, and from the exchanges over the subject of neutrality brought the two countries almost to the verge of actual hostility. It was with the view of cooling this inflammation, and of bringing about a condition of commercial reciprocity and equality, that Secretary Adams, in the summer of 1819, secured the appointment of John Graham as Thomas Sumter's successor at Rio de Janeiro. Graham's membership on the special commission to South America was supposed to have fitted him peculiarly for the post. Yet his endeavors were so fruitless that he became discouraged, recommended that the rank of the legation be lowered to that of chargé, and departed for the United States with less than a year's service to his credit. Because of the return of the Portuguese royal family to Lisbon in the spring of 1821, Graham's successor took up his duties at the European capital.

The nature of our task, however, absolves us from the responsibility of attempting to pursue further the topic of Portuguese-American relations. Fortunately, only a few months elapsed after Graham's departure from Rio de Janeiro until American-Brazilian diplomatic relations were resumed. That the factors which governed Portuguese-American relations between the years 1808 and 1821 continued to influence American-Brazilian intercourse in subsequent years should become increasingly obvious in the following pages.[31]

[31] Joseph Agan, *The Portuguese Court at Rio de Janeiro*, the first of an announced five-volume series entitled *The Diplomatic Relations of the United States and Brazil*, has been of service in the preparation of the foregoing summary. But because of countless errors the work has been used with extreme caution. The little volume came from the press after the present writer had assembled most of his material.

CHAPTER II

AN INAUSPICIOUS BEGINNING

WHEN King John VI decided to accept the advice of the Portuguese *Cortes* and return to Lisbon, he appointed his son Dom Pedro regent of Brazil. As the father suspected, the separation of Brazil from the rest of the kingdom was near at hand. The liberalizing measures which came as a consequence of the hegira across the Atlantic in 1808 were the underlying causes of the separation; the reactionary policy of the Portuguese *Cortes* after the return of the royal family to the Old World in 1821 was the precipitating incident. From the vantage ground of the present, it is difficult to understand how the Lisbon government could have expected anything but independence when it attempted to reduce the young giant to the old status of a colony. Whatever may have been the anticipation, within less than eighteen months after his father's boat weighed anchor at Rio Dom Pedro declared Brazil independent. And the declaration, which came on September 7, 1822, was virtually equivalent to *de facto* independence, for the increasing anarchy in Portugal rendered almost futile any attempt to put down the revolt.[1]

The day following the Brazilian declaration of independence Condy Raguet, author, editor, merchant, and political economist of Philadelphia, arrived at Rio de Janeiro to assume the duties of an American consul. One of his earliest communications to the new government was a request for the

---

[1] J. P. Renaut, "Le Gouvernement Portugais à Rio de Janeiro," in *Revue d'Histoire Diplomatique*, XXXIII, 271ff. A longer and better account is in Oliveira Lima, *Dom João VI no Brazil*, I.

admission into her ports without certificates, which hitherto had to be secured from Portuguese consuls resident in the United States, of all American merchant vessels. In an immediate reply the Brazilian foreign minister granted the request and commercial intercourse got an early start.[2] But Raguet was not to remain long simply as a commercial agent, even if it had been intended that he should be merely that at the time of his appointment. Before he had been at his post two months the Philadelphian, alleging that he could not properly support his family on the income from a partnership in one of the principal American business houses in Rio and on the seven hundred dollar returns from consular fees, directed a confidential letter to his government in which he asked to be entrusted with other responsibilities, with additional compensation. The secretary of state replied that the government doubted the propriety of combining diplomatic and commercial functions in one agent, but that because of the peculiar circumstances the union would be made in the Brazilian case. Thus Raguet, on July 22, 1823, was appointed agent of the United States for commercial affairs in Brazil, a position distinct from that of consul. Though never made public, this anomalous creation carried a salary of $4500 and remained in existence until superseded by the familiar rank of chargé nearly two years later.[3]

In one respect it was unfortunate that the American representative was compelled to make a secret of his being more than a consul, for he needed all the prestige which his actual

---

[2] Raguet to the secretary of state, Oct. 1, 1822, in Consular Letters (from Rio de Janeiro), I. All citations to Consular Letters refer to manuscripts in the Department of State.

[3] Raguet to his government, Nov. 28, 1823, in *ibid.*, and reply of secretary of state, July 22, 1823, in Instructions to Consuls, II. Compare with W. R. Manning, "An Early Diplomatic Controversy Between the United States and Brazil," in *The Hispanic American Historical Review*, I, No. 2 (May, 1918), pp. 125-126.

position could carry. While the Brazilians, accustomed to the form and ceremony characteristic of the monarchies of the Old World, were not likely to lavish their hospitality on any agent of a republic, there was danger that they would not even take cognizance of a lowly consul. Yet, in spite of this love for ostentation, they gradually turned their eyes toward the United States, largely because it was the one nation from whom they might expect early recognition. This turning of Brazilian eyes toward the north was encouraged somewhat by a partial lifting of the censorship from the liberal papers which followed the dismissal of the Andrada brothers from the cabinet in the summer of 1823, but the greatest stimulus came early in the following year with the announcement that President Monroe's famous message had been received.[4]

While the excitement of the public mind over the December announcement was still at a high pitch, the Brazilian government appointed an agent, with the rank of chargé, to represent its cause in the United States. The introduction which Raguet gave Chargé José Rebello before his arrival at Washington was not flattering. He represented the Brazilian as an ultra-imperialist who had very little regard for either the people of the United States or the form of government which purported to represent their ideals, though he was willing to change his views in case they proved erroneous.[5] With this unenviable advance reputation, the Brazilian chargé presented himself at Washington in April, 1824. Immediately there arose in the cabinet a difference of opinion as to the wisdom of giving official audience to Rebello and thereby extending recognition to the Rio gov-

---

[4] Communications of Raguet to his government, Sept. 8, 1823; and Feb. 1, 1824, in Consular Letters, I.

[5] Raguet to the secretary of state, Jan. 20, 1824, in *ibid.*

ernment. It was true that several of the Spanish American states had been recognized; but these were republics, whereas Brazil was a monarchy. Some members demurred on the ground that an extension of recognition would encourage monarchy to gain a foothold on the continent; others favored immediate positive action in order to show the world that the United States was more concerned in the fact of independence than in any particular form of government.

At first the logic of events seemed to strengthen the opposition. Stimulated by the dissolution of the Assembly on November 12, 1823, a formidable separatist movement flared up in the principal towns of northern Brazil which raised serious doubt whether the organization at Rio de Janeiro were really a *de facto* government. In addition, the American representative at Rio, partly to check the vanity and pride which he despised in Brazilians and partly to secure all possible inducements, was counseling delay. On the other hand, the proponents from the beginning had the argument that recognition of Brazil was but part of the general program to foster the establishment in the Western Hemisphere of a large group of independent states. Furthermore, it was later reported that French influence was on the increase at the Brazilian court, one evidence of which was that French naval vessels had been used in the suppression of the republican revolt in the north. Was it not strange that one of the staunch members of the Holy Alliance should offer aid to a constitutional government!

Several members of Monroe's cabinet were suspicious, and these suspicions were nourished by the appearance in a number of the *Estrella* (a Brazilian paper which had been established for the purpose of promoting the commercial interests of France and the politics of the Holy Alliance) of the statement that the European monarchs regarded the emperor of Brazil as a "counterpoise to the democracies of North and South America." Was not Dom Pedro after all a sort of catspaw of the Holy Alliance? His dissolution of the Constituent Assembly and his delay in promulgating the liberal constitution drawn up by a council might be interpreted to mean this very thing. But if there were any hope of preventing the European agency of reaction from making of the young ruler its *point d'appui*, it lay in recognizing his government. Thus, on May 26, 1824, after he had been given assurances concerning the suppression of the slave trade, President Monroe formally received Rebello as Brazilian chargé.[6]

Rebello's reception at Washington created diverse impressions in different circles of Brazil. The chargé himself was the first to express gratitude that "the government of the United States" had "been the first to acknowledge the independence of Brazil," though Emperor Dom Pedro made a similar declaration upon receipt of the news a few weeks later. While most of the Brazilian public, unaware of Raguet's status, interpreted the event as only the first step toward recognition, celebrations were held in most of the provinces. On the other hand, the group known as the Portuguese party, practically every one of whom hoped for reunion with the mother country, indulged in bitter execrations, maintaining it was a disgrace for a monarchy to solicit patronage from a republic, especially one so insignificant in the scale of nations.[7]

At the time of his presentation Rebello suggested the formation of a "concert of American powers to sustain the

[6] See Raguet's letters of Sept. 8 and Nov. 10, 1823, and Mar. 8, 1824, in *ibid.* See also Adams, *Memoirs of John Quincy Adams*, VI, 280, 281, 283, 285, 308, 311, 314, 317, 328, 358.

[7] Raguet to the secretary of state, Aug. 2, Sept. 12, and Oct. 5, 1824, in Consular Letters, II.

general system of American independence." Although he received little encouragement on this initial overture, early in the following year (1825) he mustered courage to propose two treaties of offensive and defensive alliance. In the first, the United States was asked to pledge her aid in case any European power should assist Portugal in the resubjugation of Brazil. As the proposal was made only a few weeks before the close of the Monroe administration, it was not answered until shortly after the inauguration of the Adams régime. In his reply Secretary Clay, who had been for several years an enthusiastic advocate of South American independence, stated that, although the president adhered strictly to the principles set forth in the Monroe Doctrine, there was no occasion for the treaty, because it was unlikely that Portugal would be able to draw any other power to her side. To the second proposal, namely, that the United States should come to the aid of Brazil in case Portugal attempted to reconquer her unaided, a negative answer was also given. In this case, as in that between Spain and her colonies, the United States refused to interfere in a quarrel between the mother country and one of her dependencies.[8]

From the time of Rebello's reception by President Monroe Raguet hoped that his government would do away with his anomalous position by raising him to the rank of chargé. He believed that this would give the United States an influence in Brazil which it otherwise could never possess, since it was not only expected by the public but regarded by it as

[8] For the proposed treaties see Rebello's letters of Jan. 28 and Apr. 6, 1825, in Notes from Brazil, I; for the replies see Clay to Rebello, Apr. 13, 1825, in Notes to Foreign Legations, III. Consult also Adams, *op. cit.*, VI, 358, 475; W. R. Manning, "Statements, Interpretations, and Applications of the Monroe Doctrine, etc., 1823-1845," in *Proceedings of the American Society of International Law*, 1914, p. 35; W. S. Robertson, "South America and the Monroe Doctrine," in *Political Science Quarterly*, XXX, 83-105.

the consummating act of recognition. Nevertheless, the government delayed in sending the appointment to the Senate until March, 1825, and it was not until the close of October that the Pennsylvanian had the privilege of presenting his credentials as chargé. When the belated promotion did come, it brought with it additional responsibility. Perhaps most important among Raguet's new instructions was that requesting him to prepare the way for the conclusion of a convention to regulate commerce and navigation between the two countries, the negotiations to take place preferably at Washington. By way of preliminaries he was to say that the United States was entitled to equality of opportunity because she had been the first to acknowledge the Brazilian government and in her priority of recognition she had disregarded risks and overlooked anomaly in political form. Since the European powers had been tardy in granting similar favors, the United States was unwilling to see them "running off with commercial advantages which shall be denied to an earlier and more uncalculating friend," though she wanted no peculiar advantages for herself. In the next place, Raguet was to impress on Brazil the advantages to America of the principles of the Monroe Doctrine, as well as the importance of a strict adherence to them in all dealings with the European powers. Finally, the chargé was to express the solicitations of his government in the abolition of the Brazilian slave trade. While he was to use his influence to hasten the event, he was cautioned to act in a conciliatory and unoffending manner. He was to concede that the matter was under Brazilian jurisdiction entirely. Clay suggested that in case too much sensitiveness were encountered it might not be amiss "to have the new born zeal of Great Britain, in relation to the slave trade, to fret itself on the Brazilian government, as it is most likely that it will be exerted, in a manner not very acceptable." Such interposition might have the effect of checking in Brazil the undue influence of Great Britain, the greatest rival of the United States.[9]

Unfortunately, the American chargé was not permitted to devote his time to carrying out these instructions. Within two months after their receipt the government to which he was accredited found itself at war with the United Provinces of the Rio de la Plata over Banda Oriental, the region which emerged three years later as the independent republic of Uruguay, and he was forced to deal with more pressing matters. While the war was the result of conflicting interests, roots of which extended far back into colonial history, our purpose will be served by alluding to only a few events which crowded the years immediately preceding the outbreak of 1825. For a time after the beginning of the revolts in Spanish America, in 1810, Banda Oriental, the name given to the province of the viceroyalty of Buenos Aires which lay east of the Plate River, remained under the control of Spain. But the Spanish authorities were unable to control all individuals, and many revolutionary sympathizers escaped from the eastern province to Buenos Aires, among whom was José Artigas, an officer in the royal army.

Within a few weeks, however, Artigas was back on native soil with both a commission from the Buenos Airean *junta* and an army. Finally, in May, 1814, after three years of alternating success and failure, the royalist forces were driven from their stronghold of Montevideo.

But no sooner had the hilarity following the capture died away than Artigas, contending for a form of governmental organization similar to that of the United States, began to resist attempts of Buenos Aires to control the eastern province.

[9] Secretary Clay to Raguet, Apr. 14, 1825, in Instructions to United States Ministers, X, and Raguet to Clay, Nov. 12, 1825, in Despatches, IV.

During the prolonged strife between these rival factions of Spaniards, the Portuguese government reasserted claim to Banda Oriental as its Cisplatine province, and sent troops to make it effective. Although Artigas resisted the Portuguese forces as strenuously as he had those of Spain and Buenos Aires, they occupied Montevideo in 1817 and drove him from the country three years later. In 1821 the Portuguese authorities in the province convened at Montevideo a special congress, composed of representatives of all the towns, which declared the region incorporated with the united kingdom of Portugal, Brazil, and the Algarves. With the declaration of Brazilian independence the following year the Cisplatine province was united with the possessions of the new government. During the three years that it remained in the comparatively peaceable possession of the empire the region was administered by natives under the supervision of Brazilian functionaries.

Meanwhile, the government at Buenos Aires, never yielding its claim, awaited an opportunity to contest Brazilian possession. Accordingly, in September, 1823, a Buenos Airean commissioner was sent to Rio de Janeiro to offer proposals for a settlement. When the Brazilian government failed to answer his first communication within a reasonable time, he became restive and dispatched another, demanding a reply. The Brazilian foreign minister finally responded on February 6, 1824, but the long document was only a defense of the Brazilian claim and a refusal to enter into negotiations for the cession of the coveted region. The disheartened commissioner returned to Buenos Aires and reported the failure to his government. Although domestic difficulties necessitated a delay of several months, the matter was not forgotten. Early in the following year a few Uruguayan refugees residing in the city, stimulated by receipt of the news of the crushing defeat of the last royalist army in Peru and by the hope of assistance from the Buenos Airean government, organized the band of adventurers which has become immortalized in Uruguayan history as the famous Thirty-Three and crossed the river to free their native land from Brazilian dominance. Once upon Uruguayan soil, this little army under the leadership of Lavalleja increased by leaps and bounds. The numbers were swelled not only by the population, but by the desertion of soldiers and officers from the Brazilian army. Among those who joined the patriot cause, was General Rivera, whom Brazil had made chief executive of the province. As a result of this change of allegiance, Brazil lost quickly all of Cisplatina except Colonia and the capital city of Montevideo, the latter being saved only by the presence of war vessels in the harbor.

In July, 1825, the Brazilian government, certain that the United Provinces were supporting the insurgents in various ways, presented a strong note to Buenos Aires in which it requested a categorical explanation. Because Brazil attempted to treat through an admiral with a fleet at his back, the Rio de la Plata government at first refused to enter into negotiations, though later it sent a short reply denying that any official assistance had been given. Another communication of the Brazilian officer went unanswered and he returned home to report his failure. To a lengthy, argumentative protest, which the Brazilian foreign minister addressed directly to the government at la Plata the following October, came the answer that on the twenty-fifth of the month a general congress of the United Provinces, in conformity with the wishes of the people of Banda Oriental expressed through the medium of their representatives on the twenty-fifth of the preceding August, had declared the eastern province reincorporated in the territory of the republic and that the government would employ every possible means for its defense and security. Soon after receipt of this communication Brazil declared her intention to blockade all the ports belonging to the United Provinces and on December 10 issued a formal declaration of war. Argentina replied with a similar declaration and both governments authorized privateering.[10]

A week after receiving notice that Brazil intended to establish an immediate blockade of "all the ports" of a coast several hundred miles in extent, Raguet dispatched a long communication to the Brazilian government on the subject of the principles of blockade as viewed by the United States. The objects of the discourse were to remove at the outset all possibility of misunderstanding on the important subject and to modify the rigors which were bound to be disastrous to a rapidly growing American commerce. The necessity of making the representation was rendered the more imperious by the failure to secure indemnity, after a lapse of fifteen months, for the capture of an American ship for an alleged breach of the blockade of Pernambuco.[11] In discussing the history of the evolutionary doctrine of blockades the American chargé sought to give special emphasis to two principles

[10] This summary is based primarily on documents in *American State Papers, Foreign Relations*, VI, 1025; *House Ex. Doc.* 281, 20 Cong., 1 sess. (ser. 175), pp. 9-19; *British and Foreign State Papers*, XIII, 748-785. See also Raguet to Clay, Dec. 23, 1825, in Despatches, IV; V. G. Quesada, *História Diplomática Latino-Americana*, II, 67-103; I. Núñez, *An Account, Historical, Political, and Statistical, of the United Provinces of Rio de la Plata*, pp. 303-345.

[11] This was the case of the *Spermo*, an American vessel which entered the harbor of Pernambuco under stress of weather on August 11, 1824. Because of a revolt the harbor had been declared in a state of blockade some time previously; but the blockade had been lifted before the *Spermo* was forced into port. While there was a revival of the blockade on August 12, this was the day following the entry of the American ship. Nevertheless, the vessel was seized for violating the blockade and the case was taken to an inferior court, where the judgment was for acquittal with damages. But the captors appealed the case to the supreme military council at Rio. These long proceedings naturally caused the owners great expense and led Raguet to exert his influence in their behalf. Raguet to Clay, Dec. 23 and 31, 1825, in Despatches, IV.

held by his government; first, a blockade in order to be valid must be effective, that is, it must be confined to such ports as had sufficient forces stationed before them to intercept the entry of vessels; second, general or diplomatic notifications alone are invalid and no vessel, even though found attempting to enter a blockaded port, could be seized until she had been warned away from that port. These principles admittedly favored neutrals; but Raguet declared that it was only the benevolence of neutral powers which permitted blockades in any form. It was manifestly to the interest of all the new independent American states to adhere to these acknowledged principles of international law rather than to those broad principles which recent practices of certain European states had tended to establish.[12]

Whatever consideration may have been given to this famous dispatch, the reply of ten days later indicated acquiescence in one minor request; namely, that all neutral vessels in Buenos Airean ports at the beginning of the execution of the blockading decree should be granted fourteen days in which to clear with their cargoes.[13] Indeed, two days before the reply, on December 21, Admiral Lobo, who was charged with executing the blockade, had declared that "all the Ports and Coasts of the Republic of Buenos Ayres, and all those on the Oriental side [of La Plata] which may be occupied by the Troops of Buenos Ayres are from that date subject to the most rigorous blockade." This declaration of blockade, embracing an extent of maritime coast of more than twenty degrees, represented an ambitious program, for at first out of a navy of less than fifty vessels only five or six small ships could be spared for blockade duty. Later, after the Brazilian

[12] Raguet to the Brazilian foreign minister, Dec. 13, 1825, in *House Ex. Doc.* 281, 20 Cong., 1 sess. (ser. 175), pp. 9-14.
[13] Brazilian foreign minister to Raguet, Dec. 23, 1825, in *ibid.*, 15.

navy had doubled in size, the number was increased from time to time, though never sufficiently for the object to be served.

Raguet's efforts at Rio to secure acceptance of the American principles of blockade were ably seconded by the endeavors of other American representatives. Not long after Admiral Lobo's manifesto of December 21 John M. Forbes, the United States chargé at Buenos Aires, secured from the Argentine foreign minister a flag of truce, passed through the lines, and presented to the Brazilian commander his government's protest. Captain Elliott, as commander of the American squadron on the coast of South America, sought several occasions to reiterate the principles upheld by Raguet and Forbes, with the difference that he began his intercourse by employing the language of the militarist rather than that of the diplomat.[14]

But in spite of all the verbal protests—and the presence of United States naval vessels along the coasts of Brazil and Argentina to protect the interests of American citizens—the Brazilian government persisted in an attempt to carry out the blockade as announced. So drastic was the program of execution at first that Admiral Lobo even tried to prevent neutral war vessels from proceeding to Buenos Aires, one of the blockaded ports, though by early April, 1826, Captain Elliott of the public ship *Cyane* by a threat of resistance had settled satisfactorily this minor point as far as the United States was concerned.[15] A month later the Brazilian blockading commander yielded a more important issue when he agreed to limit the "rigorous blockade" to ports within the

[14] See several communications of the representative of the three governments in *British and Foreign State Papers*, XIII, 821ff.

[15] A short time before British and French commanders had determined the same issue for their governments. Consult an extract from the log-book of the U.S.S. *Cyane*, Apr. 3, 1826, in *ibid.*, pp. 826-827.

Rio de la Plata.[16] While relenting on the one hand, however, the Brazilian authorities were employing a new weapon in order to acquire strength on the other. When it was learned at Rio that an American schooner which cleared from Montevideo for the Pacific had eluded the blockading squadron and landed supplies at Buenos Aires, the imperial government issued a decree (January 21, 1826) requiring all merchant ships, both national and foreign, leaving that port to give bonds that they would not enter any ports of the Buenos Airean republic. This ruling worked a tremendous hardship on American traders. It practically prohibited the general practice of using the Brazilian ports for breaking up the cargoes of merchant vessels and reloading the unsaleable portions for reshipment to Pacific ports, since the limited acquaintance of the captains and supercargoes made it difficult for them to furnish the required bonds. Raguet and other United States representatives made frequent and vigorous protests against the obnoxious measure, though for a time these availed little.[17]

As the war progressed, the complaints of American citizens multiplied; and with the increase of complaints the American officials made longer and louder remonstrances. Position naturally decreed that the brunt of the diplomatic contest should fall upon Condy Raguet; and the American chargé was not disposed to shirk his responsibility. An experience of more than three years at Rio de Janeiro had primed him for the new encounter. Since arrival at the Brazilian capital in September, 1822, he had sent scores of dispatches in an attempt to secure redress for the grievances of his countrymen, some of whom suffered large pecuniary

[16] Admiral Lobo to Captain Elliott and reply, May 4, 1826, in *ibid.*, pp. 831-832.
[17] For the decree and much discussion concerning it see *House Ex. Doc.* 281, 20 Cong., 1 sess. (ser. 175), pp. 19-20, 138ff.

losses while others underwent the inconvenience of lying for days in filthy prisons only because of alleged breaches of petty port regulations. On the occasion of the imprisonment of a captain of an American ship in the summer of 1823 Raguet was provoked to the extent of suspending for two weeks his duties as consul, at the beginning of which he called for his passports. In reporting the incident to his government he stated that the whole difficulty was founded upon the most deep-rooted corruption in the custom-house and aggravated by the added fact that the courts and judges were destitute of moral principle.[18]

In the course of the war Raguet and his colleagues found it necessary to devote less of their time to the principles of blockade than to the grievances which arose from a disregard of those principles. One of the chief complaints was that American seamen were taken from United States merchant vessels and pressed into service on Brazilian war ships. This practice was not new, however; it had been resorted to while Brazil was winning her independence and during her difficulties with the northern provinces subsequent thereto. The records show that Raguet protested against the custom as early as June 4, 1823, when he reminded the Brazilian government that the United States had recently spent one hundred million dollars and offered up many thousands of her sons to secure its abandonment.[19] Although employed several times during the next two or three years, it was not a subject of serious complaint until the war with Argentina created the necessity for large numbers of seamen to man the

[18] The case was that of the American ship *Panther*. The difficulty arose because of an apparent error in the form of entry when the vessel entered the harbor of Rio on her return from a two year voyage in the Pacific. Raguet to the secretary of state, Aug. 7 and Sept. 8, 1823, in Consular Letters, I.

[19] Raguet to his government, June 4, 1823, Aug. 21 and Dec. 9, 1824, and May 12, 1825, in *ibid.*, I, II.

Brazilian navy. To meet the crisis various measures were employed by the recruiting officials. Sometimes American seamen were inveigled into service while intoxicated or were detained on absurd excuses after the expiration of their periods of enlistment; at other times they were mistaken for English deserters and pressed into service. On the other hand, many an unwary American broke his contract and escaped from a service he had entered voluntarily. But the latter class, however large their numbers, had no grievances, and consequently did not trouble the American chargé. It was from the so-called "impressed" class that there came the requests for relief; and as the requests multiplied, Raguet's patience dwindled and his protests to the Brazilian government became more vigorous.

Still stronger protests came from the American representative because of the treatment accorded the American seamen who manned the vessels detained as a result of the blockade. Against Raguet's insistence that they should be left on board their own vessels under the supervision of the prize crews, these men were frequently removed to the capturing ships and forced to endure insults, indignities, and privations not easily imagined. Sometimes they were deprived of their bedding and other personal property and placed on prison ships where the criminal surroundings were unsanitary and revolting. Occasionally when resistance or impertinence was exhibited, corporal punishment was inflicted. Conditions at the detention quarters on shore were not vastly better. It is not strange that Raguet's reclamations grew more acrimonious, especially in view of the fact that his reserve of patience was running low.[20]

It would be a mistake to think that the Brazilian government did nothing to meet the charges brought by Raguet and

[20] See especially Raguet to Clay, Sept. 1, 1826, in Despatches, V.

his colleagues. Its agents were busy drawing up refutations and presenting counter claims. They showed conclusively that some of the men for whom the American chargé had been making strong representations were only prisoners of war taken from Buenos Airean cruisers, many of which had been built, officered, and manned in ports of the United States. They produced much evidence to prove that the cruel treatment given some of the American seamen by the prize crews was a consequence of attempts on the part of the former to regain possession of their vessels while they were being towed into port for adjudication. But the Brazilian agents did more. For example, they protested strongly against the method employed by the Americans in securing the release of two of their countrymen who were being detained on board a prize vessel. Apprehensive that the two seamen would be forced into confinement on a notorious prison ship, a commander of a United States naval vessel, who was no doubt acting with Raguet's approval, sent an armed band aboard the prize and demanded their release. While force was not used—the commander later said he had no intention of using it—and the men were surrendered without resistance, the Brazilian government asked satisfaction on the ground that improper and offensive methods had been resorted to. But instead of surrendering the men, or offering substitute measures of satisfaction, the American government presented a counter claim.[21]

Frequent exchange of sharp communications over a period of several months had created a rather tense situation by the close of the summer of 1826. Failure to receive instructions from his government during a trying period, added

[21] Commander Biddle to Raguet, Sept. 6, 1826, and Raguet to Clay, Oct. 31, 1826, in *ibid.*, V; Chargé Rebello to Clay, Feb. 21 and Mar. 29, 1827, in Despatches from Brazil (Brazilian Legation), I; Clay to Rebello, Mar. 22, 1827, in Notes to Foreign Legations, III.

to the belief that his residence had been under espionage for a portion of the time, made the situation appear extraordinarily trying to Condy Raguet.[22] Then an incident suddenly arose to make matters still worse. It was the arrival at Rio, under convoy of a Brazilian war vessel, of the American brig *Ruth*, which had been captured about one hundred and fifty miles from land while en route from Gilbraltar to the River Plate. Upon learning that a portion of the crew and two of the officers of the brig had been treated with the greatest cruelty by the captors while they were conducting the ship into port, Raguet, after the hour of six in the evening, sought out the Brazilian foreign minister at a tea-party and under excitement of strong feelings told him

that the case was an urgent one, calling for immediate attention— that the question of liberty was the one which touched most deeply the sensibility of the government and people of the United States— that the liberty of a single citizen was valued by them at a greater price, than all property—and that if Brazil was desirous of avoiding a war with the United States, she must respect that liberty.

After he had been promised that the matter would be placed before the emperor on the following morning and assured that satisfaction would be given, Raguet returned home and on the following morning set out to make a thorough examination of particulars. Upon a visit to the prison ship, to which the Americans had been removed for safe keeping pending an investigation for the alleged attempt to recapture the *Ruth*, he received ocular proof of the horrible conditions which his countrymen had to endure. He said:

Upon the same deck with Mr. Budd (the supercargo), Capt. Jefferson, and his mate, were strewed a mass of wretched objects, prisoners, convicts, and *impressed seamen*, of all colors, some resting under

[22] Raguet to Clay, Feb. 14, 1826, in Despatches, IV.

the weight of their chains, some picking oakum, some gambling, and others, indifferent to their degraded condition, wallowing in filth, and indulging in obscene and beastly gestures. Mr. Budd had from the shore, just received a change of clothes, which enabled him to put off the suit he had worn for 17 days, in the den of filth and vice which he had just left, and to which he insured me this very *Prezi-ganza* [the name of the prison ship] was a palace. The crew of the *Ruth* had not yet been able to change their clothes, and they had had nothing to eat since they arrived on board twenty-one hours before, except what little they could obtain from their companions in misery. One of them told Midshipman Deas who accompanied me, that he would rather go ashore and be executed, than to remain ten days longer where he was.

Stimulated by what he saw on his brief tour of inspection, the American chargé returned to shore and proceeded to the Brazilian foreign office for another interview. Not finding the foreign minister at his desk, he took occasion to converse a half hour with the chief clerk, to whom he described the abhorrence which he "felt at the barbarous and inhuman conduct, of the Commander of the Brig Independencia ou Morte." He

pronounced it to be the greatest outrage upon civilization, that had ever been practiced in modern days, with the single exception of the crime lately committed by the Commander of His Imperial Majesty's brig *Emprehendedor*, who captured a Spanish vessel, off the coast of Africa, and *cut off the left ear of the Supercargo close by the head*, after threatening to hang him, from which he was restrained by his own crew.

Raguet then referred to the cruel commander, to whom he gave the appellation of barbarian and monster, and expressed astonishment that the Brazilian government had not made an example of him instead of sending him to sea to cut off the ears of other people. Finally, this was followed by a demand for the release of his countrymen who were held as prisoners, with the threat that if it were not immediately complied with he would go to the end of the world to prove the Brazilians "not to be a civilized people." These representations brought the release of the prisoners, but only after Raguet had promised to be officially responsible for their appearance at trial. Strangely enough, the replies of the Brazilian officials were usually couched in courteous and diplomatic language.[23]

Three weeks after the *Ruth* affair Raguet dispatched another strong communication to his government. In this he gave a general summary of the complaints for which he had sought redress during the past four years, and to which the Brazilian government had made only evasive and unsatisfactory replies, and expressed a keen disappointment over the failure of his government to send him a single instruction in seventeen months, despite the fact that in former communications he had urgently recommended a resort to decisive measures, the only sort that possibly could be efficacious with a people unacquainted with appeals to reason and justice. Still he took the liberty of suggesting for the consideration of the president the advisability of bringing the country's relations to Brazil before the public in his next message to Congress, for he believed a manifestation of displeasure from that source would be equivalent to volumes written by him and would have a powerful effect in restraining further abuses. He further recommended that he

be specifically instructed to make a formal demand upon this [the Brazilian] government for the immediate surrender with damages

---

[23] This account is based on Raguet's famous dispatch of Sept. 1, 1826, in Despatches, V. A badly edited form of the communication is printed in *House Ex. Doc.* 281, 20 Cong., 1 sess. (ser. 175), pp. 25–29.

of all vessels which have been, or may be captured in opposition to the laws respecting blockade, maintained by us, including the cases of the Spermo and Exchange—that I be instructed to require a total suspension of the practice of taking American seamen out of American vessels, and a formal public notification thereof—and to demand the satisfaction which is manifestly due for the aggressions, which have already been committed. Such instructions however should be accompanied by an order for my recall, in case the demand should be rejected, which I feel sure would not be the case, owing to the fear of this government, that the prospect of a breach, between the United States and Brazil, would give a moral strength to the Republic of Buenos Ayres, which might perhaps be fatal to the pretensions of the Emperor. *Now* is the moment to make *our* nation respected by *this*. *Now* is the moment to make this government *feel* the influence which we are destined to maintain in this Hemisphere of Liberty, and if it is desirable to negotiate a treaty of commerce, perhaps *now* is the moment, when the footing of the most favored nation, might be obtained as the price of reconciliation, particularly in case I should be obliged to proceed to the extremity of giving notice of my recall. Should the President approve of these suggestions, or resolve upon any other measures of a decided character, I would respectfully remark that, despatches sent by a fast-sailing public vessel, would produce an effect of the most important character. The *manner* in which a thing is done, is more regarded by these people, than the thing itself.[24]

While waiting for this recommendation to reach its destination and for his government to act upon it, Condy Raguet did not refrain from sharp epithets when communicating with the Brazilian foreign office. More than once his impatience got the better of his judgment. Although the foreign minister's notes continued to be characterized by politeness, to one of his replies to Raguet's bitter remonstrances was appended a regret for the acrimonious language of the latter

---

[24] Raguet to Clay, Sept. 23, 1826, in Despatches, V, or in *House Ex. Doc.* 281, 20 Cong., 1 sess. (ser. 175), p. 74.

and a hope for more moderation in the future. Just after receiving this, Raguet wrote Clay that the Rio government was highly incensed at his late correspondence, that he should not be surprised if he were notified of a refusal to hold intercourse with him, and that in case of such event he would leave the country immediately. But since the Brazilians were *not a civilized people,* the American chargé seemed indifferent about the matter.[25]

The last two months of 1826 and the first two months of the following year brought hope for a satisfactory adjustment of the difficulties between the two countries. This was primarily because of a conciliatory policy on the part of the high functionaries of the Brazilian government, who seem to have become convinced temporarily that it was dangerous further to incur the ill-will of neutral powers. Raguet believed that an increase in the strength of the United States naval forces on the southeastern coast of South America, together with the independence of the commanders and his own persistence in registering protests against aggressions, caused the imperial officials to suspect that the American government was on the verge of joining Argentina in the war. Whatever the degree of truth in this diagnosis, the Brazilian program for a time grew less severe. Toward the close of October the official paper carried notice of an order to Brazilian naval commanders to be careful not to impress foreign seamen, as well as another for the discharge of all who were then held against their volition. This was followed by a gradual relaxation of the blockade. The new instructions to the Brazilian admiral charged with enforcement were modified in such a way as to exempt all neutral vessels from

[25] Raguet to the Brazilian minister of foreign affairs, Oct. 13, 1826; the reply of the latter, Oct. 31, 1826; Raguet to Clay, Oct. 2 and Oct. 31, 1826. Except the October 2 document, which is in Raguet's Despatches, V, these communications are in *House Ex. Doc., ibid.,* pp. 56-58, 63-64, 53-55.

detention upon the high seas or while proceeding to Montevideo, even though their passports showed the ultimate destination to be the blockaded ports. Encouraged by this
indication of success, Raguet hastened to inform the Brazilian
foreign minister that the American government would regard
the step as an evidence of friendly disposition, inasmuch as
it not only removed the ground which had hitherto given
occasion for all the complaints but held out the assurance that
all captured American vessels would speedily be released
from detention. But the American chargé did more as a
result of his stimulation. Since he wanted to force Brazil to
acknowledge formally the principle in which she had merely
acquiesced as a special favor to the United States, he sent a
long dispatch to the foreign office in which he contended for
the former doctrine that no neutral vessel was liable to detention for a breach of blockade unless arrested in the attempt
to enter a blockaded port, after having been warned off by
the blockading force. In other words, he wanted to take
advantage of the momentum he had recently acquired to induce Brazil to forego her doctrine that a general notice of a
blockade by a belligerent was alone sufficient. The imperial
government, however, did not permit itself to be drawn into
a lengthy argument on this issue.

Nevertheless, throughout January and February of 1827
relations between the governments continued to improve.
The new Brazilian foreign minister gave prompt and conciliatory replies to all Raguet's communications; American
vessels captured as a result of attempting to enter the Buenos
Airean ports were conducted to Montevideo and promptly
released; and all American seamen reported that they were
receiving courteous and considerate treatment at the hands of
Brazilian officials. Raguet attributed this marked change in
policy to the effect produced by the new instructions which

his government had sent approving his conduct as well as by the receipt of President Adams's message to Congress the preceding December in which he alluded to the matter of the treatment of United States citizens by Brazil. The American chargé reported that all foreigners resident in Brazil, including the English and the French, whose governments had not given them much support, appreciated the endeavors which the American government had put forth to bring about a change of policy.[26]

Unfortunately, the pleasant relations which extended from October, 1826, through February, 1827, were but the calm which preceded a hurricane. On March 12 Raguet wrote Clay that it became his painful duty to announce that "one of the most deliberate and high-handed insults against our flag and national honor" had recently been committed by the express orders of the Brazilian government. The offense was all the greater because the foreign minister had recently advanced gratuitously professions of friendship for the United States and because Raguet believed it had been deliberately planned to give lustre to Brazilian arms and to stain the honor of a republic.

The case was that of the brig *Spark*, a privately owned vessel which had been purchased from the United States government by an American citizen. The brig arrived at Rio de Janeiro from New York toward the close of January, and, after conforming to the usual requirements, was entered in regular fashion. She had on board a short crew, a few passengers, and ten guns, only four of which were mounted. The owners intended to sell the vessel and were in search of a market in Brazil, which was understood to be in need of

[26] Raguet to Clay, Nov. 18 and 27, Dec. 4 and 22, 1826, and Jan. 9 and Feb. 7, 1827, in Despatches, V; Clay to Raguet, Oct. 22, 1826, in Instructions to United States Ministers, XI. Most of these communications with many of their enclosures may be found in *House Ex. Doc., ibid.*

ships of her description. A negotiation immediately got under way, but the captain and the Brazilian minister of marine failed to agree on the terms of purchase. An offer of the latter to purchase the guns without the vessel was declined, and the commander resolved to proceed to Montevideo. Before clearing for the new destination the captain accepted Raguet's advice and landed six of the guns, for the Brazilian government had intimated that the vessel would not be permitted to leave port with a larger number of guns than was expressed in her clearance papers. But while the guns were reduced in number the crew was increased from fourteen to twenty-seven; the excuse for the augmentation was that the rougher sailing in the south Atlantic necessitated a larger force than that required for the calmer regions of the north.

When the *Spark* was several miles out of harbor, she was seized by a public vessel of the Brazilian government which had been sent out in advance for that specific purpose and carried back into port amidst the *vivas* and plaudits of the populace. In the course of the seizure the American crew were not only told that they were pirates but were given the outrageous treatment usually accorded such lawless characters. Furthermore, wanton violence accompanied the search that was made of the vessel after her return—a search carried out in an attempt to find the Buenos Airean commission which was thought to be on board.

On the morning following the seizure—before the beginning of the search—Raguet wrote a short note to the Brazilian foreign minister politely requesting information regarding grounds for the *Spark's* detention. Two days later, shortly after the overhauling had begun, he received a reply in which an attempt was made to throw the *onus probandi* upon him, for he was asked for "explanations upon the true character of the said brig, which had been detained in strong suspicion of her being a privateer bound for Buenos Ayres, and destined to increase the number of those actually engaged in insulting the Brazilian flag, and interrupting the commerce of the empire." Raguet was told that the strong suspicion had been raised because the brig had "not exhibited the legal license for carrying a warlike armament" and because, "without a permit to go thus armed, she sought to increase the number of her crew to nearly double what it was." In answering this note, which he regarded as an official insult, Raguet briefly stated that had the imperial government "thought proper, before the sailing of the *Spark*, to have communicated to him its suspicions of any other destination than that expressed in her clearance at the custom-house, he would most cheerfully have lent his aid in causing those suspicions to be removed." But under the circumstances he declined to give any explanations. In replying to this curt note two days later (March 9) the foreign minister expressed a desire to maintain without interruption the friendly relations of the two countries and to avoid all causes of the slightest displeasure. To this end he attempted to convince Raguet of the correctness of his government in bringing the *Spark* back into the harbor and in asking for an official explanation of her conduct. Following this he alluded to the "negative and rude reply" which his government's request had drawn from the American chargé.

But the day before this communication was written Condy Raguet, feeling that there was no middle course between national dishonor and a close of his mission, called for his passports. He was no doubt stimulated to take this extreme measure by the clamors of resident American citizens, who, indignant at the epithets to which they heard their countrymen constantly subjected, radiated their indignation when they turned to Raguet for redress. The foreign minister's note, dated March 10, which informed the chargé that his request for passports would be complied with, expressed surprise at the American's action and warned him that he would be answerable to his government for the consequences. While waiting for an opportunity to take his leave, Raguet dispatched two long communications to Secretary Clay in which he essayed a full explanation of his procedure. In one of these he declared:

So strong and decided a measure as the one which I adopted as the *ultima ratio* of a people which sincerely desires to preserve the relations of peace with all the word, upon honorable terms, could not, as you may suppose, have been regarded by myself or others as an unimportant act. I am aware that I have taken upon myself a responsibility of no ordinary character, and am prepared to meet all the consequences, even though one of them should be my being offered up as a sacrifice at the altar of public good. What I have done, I have done deliberately; and so far from regretting the act, I should do the same thing to-morrow, were I placed in the same circumstances.

After receiving his passports, Raguet made his silent bow to the emperor on April 7 and nine days later left Rio for the United States. Long before he departed the captain of the brig had abandoned his ship to the Brazilian government rather than comply with the demands which were required as a guarantee against the vessel's sale to the enemy.[27]

At this point it may be well to note what view Washington officials were taking of Raguet's conduct. As late as October 22, 1826, Secretary Clay had written to the chargé

[27] Raguet to his government, Mar. 12 and 17 and May 31, 1827; communications between Raguet and the Brazilian foreign minister, Mar. 5, 7, 8, 9, and 10, 1827. All the documents are in Despatches, V, and all except the note of May 31 in *American State Papers, Foreign Relations*, VI, 1061-1066, and in *House Ex. Doc., ibid.*, pp. 96-108.

that President Adams approved his zealous exertions to prevent an abuse of the law of blockade, referred him to the correspondence with the European governments for the principles adhered to by his government, and instructed him to remonstrate promptly and firmly in every instance in which these principles seemed in danger of violation.[28] But this was before the receipt of the communications on the treatment of the officers and crew of the brig *Ruth*.

Not very long after the arrival of the violent dispatches on this case Adams and Clay decided that Raguet must be restrained. On January 20, 1827, Clay wrote him that a perusal of certain parts of his dispatches had "occasioned the President the most lively regret." He was told that the executive expected him to seek redress for injuries to American citizens growing out of the war in Banda Oriental "in a language firm and decisive, but, at the same time, temperate and respectful," that "no cause is ever benefitted by the manifestation of passion, or by the use of harsh and uncourteous language." He was told that the president, while approving of his zeal in behalf of the outraged crew of the *Ruth*, believed it would have been better if he had abstained from the use of some of the language which he employed in his interview with the chief clerk of the department of foreign affairs, for "no nation claiming to be civilized and Christian, can patiently hear itself threatened to be characterized as an uncivilized people." He was reminded also that one of the topics on which he had animadverted (that of the personal outrage inflicted by the commander of the *Emprehendedor* on the supercargo of the Spanish vessel *Escudera*) did not appertain to his official functions, but belonged to those of the Spanish representative, "to whose judgment and discretion, exclusively, it would have been most proper to have

[28] Clay to Raguet, Oct. 22, 1826, in Instructions to United States Ministers, XI.

left the conduct of it." To Raguet's free advice concerning the nature of the instructions which he hoped would be sent him, the following pertinent comments were returned:

With respect to the nature of instructions which may be sent to you, and of orders to the commanders of our public vessels, that must rest with the President, where the constitution has placed it. If those instructions or orders do not correspond in all respects with your wishes or expectations, you must recollect that he is enabled, at this distance, to take a calmer view of things than you are; that we have relations with other nations besides those which exist with the Brazils; and that, even if we had not, war or threats of war ought not to be employed as instruments of redress, until after the failure of every peaceful experiment.[29]

This instruction should have been sent immediately following the receipt of news that Raguet had resorted to violent language in his communications to the Brazilian government during the preceding September. But the delay of a month or two caused the reproof to reach its destination too late to prevent the rupture. The impetuous chargé must have felt some consolation in being able to tell the president and secretary of state on his arrival at Washington that in spite of his earnest pleadings for frequent instructions only two had been sent him during a period of almost two years. And it would seem just to allocate a considerable portion of the responsibility for the rupture to these high functionaries, though of course they were busy with other important matters, not the least of which was petty politics.

President Adams' reaction to Raguet's conduct is not devoid of interest. When the news reached him that the chargé had demanded and obtained his passports, he entered in his

[29] Clay to Raguet, Jan. 20, 1827, in *ibid.*, and in *House Ex. Doc., ibid.*, p. 108.

diary: "he appears to have been too hasty in his proceedings, and has made us much trouble, from which we can derive neither credit nor profit." A few days later, after he and the secretary had reviewed the correspondence, he said: "we concurred in the opinion that Raguet could not be sustained." Concerning the interview which Raguet had with Clay and Adams subsequent to his arrival in the United States the president declared: "I told him that my opinion of his integrity, patriotism, and zeal was unimpaired; that I was convinced of the purity of his motives to the step he had taken; but that I had thought it would have been better if he had, before taking that step, consulted his government." When the president reported to Congress on Brazilian relations in his annual message of December 4, 1827, he said that Raguet's conduct in withdrawing from his post had not been disapproved because his decision had been "dictated by an honest zeal for the honor and interests of his country." Although refusing to censure him in public, he told a Pennsylvania senator who later solicited another appointment for Raguet that "to replace in diplomatic service abroad a man of such a temper and want of judgment, who took blustering for bravery and insolence for energy, was too dangerous."[30]

The president's estimate of Raguet was both accurate and fair, though the latter should have had more counseling from his superiors. It is quite probable that the chargé had no intention of leaving his post when he called for his passports; it will be remembered that a similar request made almost four years earlier did not terminate so seriously. He may have believed that bluff would work again. Still it is unlikely that he was bribed by Buenos Airean agents to bring about a rupture between his government and that of Brazil,

[30] Adams, *Memoirs of John Quincy Adams*, VII, 270, 272, 354-357, 401.

as was alleged by a statement in a Brazilian paper after his departure.[31]

A bird's-eye view of Raguet's forty-three months' mission to Brazil reveals no outstanding accomplishments. He was unable to make any progress toward carrying out his instructions to prepare the way for a favorable commercial treaty, and he did not accomplish much toward inducing the Brazilian government to substitute American for European principles. With respect to the latter, however, something was undoubtedly achieved. It may be assumed that the courageous fight that was waged on the subject of the doctrines of blockade played a part in bringing about at a later time general acceptance of the American contention that a blockade to be binding must be effective. On the other hand, the other principle for which Raguet contended so strenuously, namely, that a general or diplomatic announcement of a blockade was in itself insufficient notification, was later abandoned altogether. But if achievements on this subject were meager, it need not occasion surprise, for the British representatives were at all times advocating exactly the opposite principles, in spite of the fact that English merchants were suffering vastly more than those of the United States. That British diplomacy was strong in southeastern South America at the time is shown by the fact that the terms of the treaty which brought the Uruguayan war to a close were dictated from London.[32]

[31] *American State Papers, Foreign Affairs*, VI, 864-865.

[32] Raguet to Clay, June 27, Sept. 2, and Dec. 22, 1826, and Jan. 9, 1827, in Despatches, V. For a scholarly treatment of this entire controversy see W. R. Manning's article cited in the early pages of this chapter. Dr. Manning based his account exclusively on printed sources.

CHAPTER III

SOME IMPROVEMENT

As soon as the Brazilian chargé at Washington learned
that Raguet had called for his passports preparatory to
bringing his mission to a close, he hastened to Clay and expressed the desire of his government to preserve and even
to extend the friendly relations with the United States. He
hoped the president would disapprove of Raguet's conduct
in suddenly calling for his passports and appoint his successor as soon as possible. While Clay did not go so far as
to express disapproval of the conduct of the American chargé,
he did say that his action had been without orders and that
no interruption of diplomatic relations was desired at Washington. He said also that a new representative would be
appointed, provided assurance was given that he would be
received in a manner comporting with his character and satisfaction was guaranteed for adjustment of the injuries resulting from the maritime war with Argentina. Rebello
felt himself authorized to give assurance that indemnity
would be afforded for injuries inflicted in contravention of
public law, and urged the immediate appointment of the
minister.[1]

About four weeks after the termination of this correspondence William Tudor, then American consul at Lima, Peru,
was appointed chargé to Brazil. He was asked to repair to
Rio de Janeiro immediately in order to assure the emperor
that the intention of the United States was to remain on

[1] Adams, *Memoirs of John Quincy Adams*, VII, 276; several communications between Clay and Rebello during the spring of 1827, in *American State Papers, Foreign
Relations*, VI, 823-825.

friendly terms and his instructions were to be sent directly to the Brazilian capital.[2]   Tudor

was selected in consequence of his known qualifications, his long residence in South America, and his intimate and thorough knowledge of the habits and usages of that portion of this hemisphere, and the commercial connexions existing between it and the United States. The personal knowledge which the President had of him, and his extensive and interesting correspondence with the Department of State, during his long residence in South America, pointed him out as eminently fitted for this station.[3]

But a year lapsed between the time of Tudor's appointment and the assumption of his duties at Rio.   During this time as well as during the two months between Raguet's departure and his successor's appointment, William Wright, American consul at the Brazilian capital, took care of diplomatic matters for the United States, with the official title of acting chargé.   While the *ad interim* functionary did not attempt to adjust any of the claims which had arisen under Raguet, he continued the remonstrances against the capture of American vessels and the impressment of American seamen.   For a brief period early in 1828 he found it necessary to employ his time framing protests against a revival of the decree requiring foreign vessels departing from Brazilian ports to give bonds conditioning their not entering any ports of Buenos Aires.   His patience and good judgment received a more severe test, however, when Rebello wrote him that he expected the newly appointed American chargé, William Tudor, to employ courtesy and politeness in attempting to deal with matters in controversy, niceties which United

[2] Secretary of state to William Tudor, June 28, 1827, in Instructions to United States Ministers, XI.

[3] Clay to the House of Representatives in a reply to a resolution, May 23, 1828, in *House Ex. Doc.* 281, 20 Cong., 1 sess. (ser. 175), p. 5.

States agents had more than once forgotten. This nasty and uncalled-for jab at American representatives, with whom Wright classed himself, was too much for the acting chargé, and he stooped to reply in kind. He told the Brazilian chargé that his remarks upon the deportment of United States agents were "presumptuous, and unfounded, and certainly not dictated by that courtesy and politeness" which he so strongly recommended.[4]

In view of the circumstances it seems fortunate that Wright did not long fill the office of chargé. On June 22, 1828, he turned over his diplomatic functions to Tudor, who had just arrived at Rio after a long journey around the Horn. The new chargé found his instructions, which had been issued eight months before, awaiting his perusal. From these he learned of the circumstances which had led to his appointment and of the program which he was supposed to follow. As to his program, he was informed of the solemn pledge—as solemn as if a convention had been entered into—on the part of the Brazilian government to make a satisfactory adjustment of the claims originating from allegations of breach of blockade and from injuries committed by the public vessels of Brazil, and instructed to make preparations for their presentation. After reparation had been made for these claims, Tudor was to solicit the making of a treaty of commerce in order to remove the advantages which British and French goods had over those of the United States.[5]

Despite the tremendous labor involved in an examination of the details of the American claims, within two weeks Tudor had placed the most important cases before the Bra-

---

[4] The following are the dates of Wright's most important letters: May 7 and Nov. 30, 1827, Feb. 2, Mar. 4 and 21, and Aug. 27, 1828. Consular Letters (from Rio), III.
[5] Tudor's instructions, Oct. 23, 1827, in Instructions to United States Ministers, XII.

zilian foreign office. His first presentation document was strong and forceful, yet conciliatory and fair; and these attributes were to characterize practically all of his communications thereafter. They brought results, though for a time only in the less important matters. Several important obstacles made an immediate settlement difficult. Chief of these were the embarrassed state of Brazilian finances, the simultaneous pressure brought by the English and French in support of large claims, and the lack of harmony between the Brazilian executive and the assembly which often caused the latter to refuse to vote appropriations.

A mere mention of the term "claims" always arouses doubts and suspicions as to the justice which has prompted the claimants. There need be no surprise, therefore, that the validity of the claims under consideration was questioned. While Condy Raguet never stopped to raise a doubt, William Tudor was constantly wavering on the cases that came under his review. Shortly after he began his examination, he was moved to ridicule a statement in an American newspaper that United States citizens had been robbed of "millions" by the Brazilians, for he was convinced that American clamor had a real basis in only two or three flagrant injustices and that the documents would not support a total claim of more than a quarter of a million dollars. Two months thereafter the chargé scaled the amount down one hundred thousand more and said:

that a majority of these claims are more or less vitiated by the circumstances attending them, and though a case is drawn out and sworn to without hesitation, no impartial person would have a doubt that the intention was to break the blockade. Add to this that our countrymen have been so persevering in these small, hazardous speculations, and some of them who are claimants in these cases have been so notoriously doing everything in their power to aid the Buenos Ayreans, that the disposition to cavel at their demands is not unnatural.[6]

The Americans who rendered this aid to the enemies of the Brazilians did so by selling them vessels, cargoes, and flags through fraud and perjury. Tudor suggested the passage of a law placing penalties on any United States citizen who might dare to prostitute his country's flag, place in jeopardy the honest voyages of his countrymen, and involve his government in unpleasant and unnecessary disputes with foreign powers; but the suggestion was futile.

It would be mild to say that the amounts asked by the claimants were exorbitant; they were in many instances ridiculous. In order to make the figures appear as large as possible, unreasonable values were placed upon the captured vessels and cargoes and fictitious wages assigned to the officers and crews. In one instance the alleged owner of a vessel, who formerly had been employed in New York as a mere clerk, put in a personal service claim of three hundred dollars a month during the period of detention, a large part of which time he had spent attempting to run the blockade in another vessel.[7]

While Tudor's keen sense of justice would not permit him to present the cases of outrageous claimants, he made strong representations in behalf of those who had complaints supported by unquestioned evidence. Driven almost to the point of desperation because of the unsatisfactory answers to his remonstrances, on one occasion he assured the Brazilian foreign minister that he was presenting his last communication on certain cases he had pressed so long for consideration. In case the demand he was then making did not bring the

[6] Tudor's dispatch of Sept. 28, 1828, in Despatches, VI.

[7] Tudor's dispatches of July 14, Aug. 5 and —? (no. 102), and Oct. 22, 1828, in *ibid.*

desired reply, he intended to resort to the alternative of forwarding the correspondence to Washington and to wait in silence the result. Although not entirely satisfactory, the conciliatory reply of the foreign minister prevented the suspension of intercourse. After this, the commissioners charged with investigating the claims quickened their pace; but the embarrassed condition of Brazilian finances made immediate reparation impossible.[8]

Even though the government at Rio was unable to raise the funds with which to pay the indemnities allowed by the commissioners, the blockading squadron kept up its work to the end of the war. Just before the lifting of the blockade which accompanied the signing of the preliminaries of the peace of 1828, arranged through the mediation of Great Britain, seven American vessels were captured by the Brazilian squadron and sent into Montevideo for adjudication. These last captures brought just as strong remonstrances as had the first ones of two and a half years previous.[9]

The close of the war brought no cessation in the advocacy of the claims for illegal captures. Indeed, Tudor pressed the cases of American citizens with more assiduity, for he realized that the end of the conflict, inasmuch as it stopped an enormous expenditure, would soon relieve a part of the financial embarrassment which Brazil had so long experienced. Finally, in June, 1829, he reported that the Brazilian foreign minister had ratified the proceedings and awards of the commissioners in so far as the claims of American citizens were concerned. It was hoped that the Brazilian legislature would in its regular September session make ap-

[8] Tudor to his government, Aug. 25 and Sept. 28, 1828, with the enclosures, in *ibid.*

[9] The American chargé's communications of Sept. 11, Oct. 22 and 27, and Dec. 11, 1828, and their enclosures, in *ibid.*

propriations necessary for the payment of the indemnities allowed. But the hope was not to be fulfilled, for the legislature adjourned without passing any appropriations at all. Nevertheless, the emperor, who was exasperated at the legislators, soon issued an order in council authorizing the minister of the treasury to issue bonds for the purpose of taking care of the foreign claims which had been recognized by the government. Shortly thereafter three sets of bonds, which were to mature in six, twelve, and eighteen months respectively, were turned over to the claimants in thirteen cases. Including the allowances which had already been made to the owners of the brigs *Ruth* and *Ontario*, and the interest which had accumulated since the various claims were registered, the total amount paid was 427,000 milreis.[10] It is interesting to note that Tudor in the case of the *Ruth* did not exact the apology which certain American newspapers thought the national honor demanded. Indeed, the chargé thought that the claim would have had no basis at all except for the violent and offensive manner in which the vessel had been seized; for the fact that she had cannon in her hold not declared in her papers and that the captain had said publicly he would not sell to the Brazilian government but would go to Montevideo, obtain a commission from Buenos Aires, and cruise against Brazilian commerce, seriously vitiated the case.[11]

The American chargé deserved great credit for the claims settlement. He was more successful than the representatives of either France or Great Britain, whose governments were supposed to have had far greater prestige at the

[10] Because of the low value of the milreis at the time this was equivalent to about $250,000.

[11] Tudor's dispatches of Aug. 7 and Dec. 13, 1828, Apr. 18 and 30, June 24, Sept. 17, and Nov. 21, 1829, in Despatches, VI.

Brazilian capital. While the French minister arranged a settlement of the claims of his countrymen about the same time, the terms were less satisfactory than those secured by Tudor. In the case of Great Britain, whose minister backed claims to the extent of a half million sterling, no agreement was reached until some time later. Tudor's achievement appears the more impressive when we are reminded that he relied chiefly on persuasion, whereas the French and British ministers had their arguments flavored with costly diplomatic dinners and backed by imposing fleets. For once it seems that the simpler methods of a republic were more successful than the ostentatious procedure of monarchies.[12]

Thus far in our review of American-Brazilian relations during the period of the Uruguayan war attention has been confined to the complaints championed by the Washington government. But there were grievances on the other side also, most of which were related in one way or another to the general subject of neutrality. Notwithstanding the fact that the United States government had declared neutrality at the outbreak of the war, the conduct of many of her citizens seemed to Brazilian officials hardly in accord with the professed position. Toward the close of 1827, after the conflict had been in progress almost two years, the Brazilian chargé complained of the attitude of all the editors of American newspapers, who invariably rejoiced at the success of Buenos Airean arms. He alleged that nothing except contempt for monarchy could account for this unfriendly conduct, since American commerce with Brazil was four times that with la Plata. Whatever the reason, it could not be denied that the editors were sympathetic toward the cause of Brazil's enemies. But it was puerile to request interference

[12] Tudor to his government, July 18 and Dec. 13, 1828, and Apr. 30 and Nov. 22, 1829, in *ibid.*

by the United States government, for the conduct complained of in no way violated the country's laws on neutrality.[13]

Chargé Rebello was much more reasonable when he protested against the course which Buenos Airean privateers were allowed to follow in the ports of the United States. In December, 1827, upon receiving news of the arrival at New York of a Buenos Airean privateer with a Brazilian prize, he notified the Washington government of his expectations that the captors would be made to conduct themselves in accordance with the laws of nations. Clay replied that he had reminded the public officials of New York to be on their guard, though he knew it was unnecessary, as they would have performed their assigned duties anyway. At the same time, however, he told Rebello that the privateer would be given the same hospitable treatment as any other belligerent vessel as long as nothing was done to place in jeopardy the neutrality of the United States. Shortly after this correspondence on general principles Rebello was able to present a specific example in which he claimed the neutrality laws of the United States actually had been violated. The case was that of the Buenos Airean privateer *General Brandizen*, which was alleged to have replaced five members of her crew, who were either unwilling to serve or prevented from serving because of sickness, by citizens of the United States. In a note demanding satisfaction Rebello averred that a Brazilian privateer would not have been permitted to violate American neutrality in the same fashion and attributed the difference to "republican intolerance" for his government because of its form. Clay showed the note to President Adams. There was agreement that its language was "highly offensive" and that it must be modified before offi-

[13] Rebello to Clay, Nov. 14, 1827, in Notes from Brazil, I.

cial acknowledgment. As a result, the secretary was instructed to return the communication with suggestions for certain changes. If these were refused, the note was to be returned and a demand made for the chargé's recall. Fortunately, within a few days the offensive document was taken back and a milder one was sent in its stead. To the new communication Clay finally replied that every precaution had been taken, according to an investigation conducted by the port officials of New York, to prevent the violation of his country's neutrality laws and that he was convinced no ground for complaint could be found, though he did not deny the charge that substitutions had been made in the crew of the privateer. Before closing, the secretary wanted the chargé to assure his government that the policy of the government of the United States had not been influenced in the least by the nature of the internal institutions of the belligerents and that any effort to interject the subject into the discussion was only to becloud the issues involved. Yet one wonders whether Adams and Clay were themselves pursuing a policy conducive to an open settlement. The correspondence would indicate that the refusal to receive the so-called undiplomatic note of Rebello was no more than a sort of counter irritant to the Brazilian charges against the behavior of Condy Raguet.[14]

The Brazilian chargé not only complained of the augmentation of the crews of the privateers; he also protested against repairing the vessels and recruiting their physical equipment in American ports. In early March, 1828, he notified Clay that the privateer *Mayflower* was being repaired in the port of Baltimore in a way which violated the

[14] Rebello to Clay, Dec. 17 and 31, 1827, in *ibid.*; Clay to Rebello, Jan. 29, 1828, in Notes to Foreign Legations, III; Adams, *Memoirs of John Quincy Adams*, VII, 354-357.

laws of nations respecting neutrality. The Kentuckian ordered an immediate investigation through the district attorney of Maryland and within a short time sent Rebello papers which purported to show that the nature of the repairs did not constitute a breach of the nation's obligations. But the documents failed to satisfy the Brazilian, who said he would ask his government to make demands on the United States for reparation. In the course of the interchange of communications on the case he admitted that sea damages could be repaired legally, but he denied that the vessel should have been permitted to double her bulwark and increase her military strength in such way as to better prepare her for war.[15]

Although it is inexpedient to give the details of any other specific cases, the Brazilian chargé carried on a lively correspondence with the Department of State on the same subject for more than a year longer. Unfortunately, his arguments lost force as he shifted his ground from time to time. Upon one occasion he took the position that any act committed in the United States which increased the naval power of Buenos Aires was contrary to our declared neutrality. Clay, of course, took an early opportunity to deny the correctness of this stand. He told the chargé that building and fitting out vessels, as long as they were not permitted to depart from American ports when in a warlike condition, and as long as both belligerents were given like treatment, was a legitimate business for United States citizens. Since Brazil had entered into several contracts with American ship-builders during the war in which she was then engaged, Rebello was forced to admit the right, with the provision, however, that the ships could not be sent directly to a belligerent. Clay

[15] Rebello to Clay, Mar. 4 and 15 and Apr. 3, 1828, in Notes from Brazil, I; Clay to Rebello, Mar. 12 and Apr. 8, 1828, in Notes to Foreign Legations, III, IV.

was unwilling to concede the proviso, for he said the vendor could not assume responsibility in the matter. Thereupon Rebello countered with the argument that a distinction should be made between wars for independence and wars waged by two wholly independent nations. The American secretary would not concede that there was any principle in public law requiring such discrimination on the part of a neutral.[16]

Rebello was also called upon to demand indemnity for direct damages suffered by Brazilian subjects. In one instance property belonging to Brazilians was taken off an American vessel after she had been captured by a Buenos Airean privateer. Later, however, the privateer was made a prize by a United States sloop of war and carried to Pensacola for adjudication. Rebello, basing his argument on two facts, namely, that the privateer had left the port of Buenos Aires after the signing of the treaty of peace between Brazil and Argentina and that the Brazilians in placing their property on the American vessel in the first place accepted the American principle that the flag covered the goods, claimed that his countrymen were entitled to payment for their losses. But in spite of the fact that redress was sought through the application of a principle for which the United States was strongly contending, reparation was not secured. The Brazilian claimants, ignorant of the method of procedure in the United States prize courts, had failed to register at the proper time a claim through their government's representative at Washington.[17]

In another instance reparation was asked of the United States government because of the losses incurred by Brazilian

[16] Rebello to Clay, Apr. 7, 1828, in Notes from Brazil, I; Clay to Rebello, May 1, 1828, in Notes to Foreign Legations, IV.

[17] The Brazilian chargé to the United States government, Jan. 15, Apr. 16, 1829, and July 16, 1830, in Notes from Brazil, I, II; replies of the United States government, Jan. 16, Apr. 22, and Sept. 8, 1829, in Notes to Foreign Legations, IV.

subjects who had gone on board two American vessels as
passengers. Most of the injured parties were legislators
who, in going from Bahia to Rio, confided in a principle
avowed and maintained by the United States and took passage on ships which they thought secure from pirates. Nevertheless, in the course of the voyages the Brazilians were
exposed to all sorts of insults and indignities and their baggage and effects were plundered by privateers whose vessel
bore the flag of Buenos Aires. Upon a request for reclama-
tion, which was again based on the good American principle
that the flag covered the goods, the United States government promised to instruct its chargé at Buenos Aires to
employ his good offices co-jointly with the Brazilian representative at the same place to demand of the Argentine
government reparation for the robberies committed on board
the vessel, though it absolutely refused to assume any responsibility for enforcing the demand. Furthermore, it
would not undertake to make good the damages sustained
by the aggrieved parties in case the government at Buenos
Aires failed to do so. The Brazilian chargé, now Ribeiro,
insisted that the initiative at Buenos Aires should be taken
by the American representative, but he failed to carry his
point.[18]

After failure to receive reparation in these cases, Brazilian officials must have reached the conclusion that the principles for which the United States was attempting to secure
universal sanction were invented to apply only when the interests of Americans were in jeopardy. The same functionaries could not have had too high an opinion respecting the
efficacy of United States laws on neutrality, unless they found

[18] Chargé Ribeiro to Van Buren, Sept. 17, 1829, and Jan. 4, 1830, in Communications from Brazil, II; Van Buren to Ribeiro, Dec. 29, 1829, in Notes to Foreign
Legations, IV.

consolation in the fact that they never had been enforced or in the presentiment that they never would be.

During the exchange of this correspondence at Washington William Tudor was not idle at Rio de Janeiro. As soon as the essentials of the subject of claims were disposed of, he turned his attention to the part of his instructions which required him to urge upon the imperial government the negotiation of a treaty of commerce, friendship, and navigation. The second task was not an easy one either. The goods of British and French merchants were subject in Brazil to a maximum duty of only fifteen per cent, whereas the merchandise from the United States bore twenty-four per cent. As a consequence, flour was about the only product of American manufacture that could meet the competition from across the Atlantic. Raguet had employed his best efforts in attempting to get the unfavorable discriminations removed, but all his arguments were unavailing. Tudor, who, of course, was in an advantageous position because of the pledges of the Brazilian government previous to his appointment, made some effective strokes in his early dispatches to the foreign minister by pointing out the discriminations which the British and French were showing in not purchasing large quantities of Brazilian coffee and by suggesting the probable retaliation by the United States congress at its approaching session unless assurances were given of a willingness to enter into a favorable treaty. At any rate shortly thereafter, on August 27, 1828, a treaty was signed which guaranteed the entry of American goods under the same conditions as those of the most favored nation, Portugal excepted. This "excellent treaty of commerce" was the second achievement of the tactful diplomacy of William Tudor. It is little wonder that President Adams and Secretary Clay could say, early in

1829, Tudor's services had been entirely satisfactory to both and that they deeply regretted his desire to retire. Yet because of a sympathetic interest in the chargé's health, which was rapidly succumbing to an enervating climate, they acquiesced in his wish and promised to appoint a successor as soon as one could be found.[19]

Unfortunately, a matter arose which caused the Jackson administration to request Tudor to remain at his post for a while. It grew out of a dynastic quarrel over the Portuguese throne. When, on March 3, 1828, the Brazilian emperor, for reasons of expediency, abdicated the Portuguese crown in favor of his daughter Dona María, he designated his young brother Dom Miguel as regent and lieutenant. But the ambitious partisans of Dom Miguel, most of whom had selfish interests to accommodate, refused to abide by the arrangement and set about to organize a government with the boy as king. They succeeded in doing this and dispatched representatives to the various nations of the world to seek recognition. To the United States came Torlade in the spring of 1829. Naturally the Brazilian chargé at Washington objected to the American government's giving official cognizance to an agent of Dom Miguel, who was considered the usurper of Dona María's throne. In fact, he suggested that his recognition might place in jeopardy the commercial and diplomatic relations between the United States and Brazil. This was the problem which confronted Van Buren when he sent the request to Tudor to remain at his post until further instructions could be sent him. Notwithstanding the fact that he had at the time of the receipt of the request al-

[19] Adams, *Memoirs of John Quincy Adams*, VIII, 224; dispatches of Raguet, Aug. 21, 1824, Sept. 15 and 23, 1825, Jan. 17, Mar. 20, and June 27, 1826, in Despatches, II, IV, V; dispatches of Tudor, Aug. 25 and Sept. 30, 1828, in *ibid.*, VI; instructions to Raguet, Oct. 22, 1826, in Instructions to United States Ministers, XI; instructions to Tudor, Oct. 23, 1827, Mar. 31, 1828, and Jan. 29, 1829, in *ibid.*, XII.

ready given up his house, paid visits to the various ministers, and completed other arrangements incident to leaving, Tudor yielded and delayed his departure. Although a definite policy had not been determined upon at the time Tudor was asked to prolong his mission, the United States was inclined to continue adherence to the principle of extending recognition to *de facto* governments. While appreciating the principle to which his government wished to adhere, Tudor attempted to convince Van Buren that it was both just and politic to make an exception in the case of Dom Miguel's government. In addition to the contempt he had for the monkish administration directed from Spain and supported by the reactionaries of London, Paris, and Vienna, was his knowledge of the very unpleasant effect it would have on the court at Rio de Janeiro.

The efforts of the American chargé in opposition to recognition of Dom Miguel's government by the United States were ably seconded by the endeavors of the Brazilian government. The latter made the argument that Dom Miguel was a usurper, that his government was only a product of the intrigues of the reactionary figures of Europe, and that the United States had always made a distinction between the principles applied to the recognition of American and European governments. But the argument of the Brazilian government was as unavailing as was that of Tudor. Andrew Jackson accepted the recommendation of the American representative to Portugal and on October 1, 1829, gave official audience to Dom Miguel's chargé. The Rio government was advised that the United States was only adhering to a principle which had been pursued for some time and that the delay of a year in recognizing Dom Miguel's government was due to the friendly feeling for Brazil. The policy of the United States met the disapprobation of Emperor Pedro and had its reflection in the relations of the two countries for several years.[20]

William Tudor remained in Brazil in order to help solve what his government believed might become a knotty problem. His response to the call of public duty proved to be at a great sacrifice. His recommendation on the Portuguese question was ignored. Furthermore, on March 9, 1830, he succumbed to a disease that was aggravated by prolonged residence in a debilitating climate. Although his stay at the Brazilian capital was less than two years in duration, his achievements no doubt surpass those of any of his predecessors or followers. He reached a satisfactory settlement of the chief claims issuing from the Argentine-Brazilian war over Banda Oriental, "which had been much aggravated by the rashness and intemperance of Condy Raguet"; he "negotiated an excellent treaty of commerce" for his countrymen;[21] and he gave his government expert advice on many South-American and European matters. His mission hardly became known in the United States, though Brazilians revered him for many years because of his fairness. If we had had more William Tudors in Brazil, our relations would be more pleasant to chronicle.

[20] Raguet to Clay, May 25, 1826, in Despatches, V; Tudor to his government, July 2 and Aug. 23, 1829, and Jan. 2, 1830, in *ibid.*, VI; instructions to Tudor, Apr. 22 and Sept. 4, 1829, and Jan. 22, 1830, in Instructions to United States Ministers, XIV; communications from the Brazilian chargé, Nov. 22, 1828, Apr. 21, and June 19, 1829, in Notes from Brazil, I; a memorial from the same, Sept. 11, 1829, in Communications from Brazil, II; United States Consul Wright to his government, March 15, 1828, in Consular Letters, III, and Apr. 10, 1830, in Despatches, VII.

[21] Adams, *Memoirs of John Quincy Adams*, VIII, 224.

CHAPTER IV

CONFUSION AND MISUNDERSTANDING

WITH the exception of the question of the African slave trade, which has been reserved for special treatment in the succeeding chapter, the period between the death of William Tudor (1828) and the outbreak of the Civil War in the United States affords the student of Brazilian-American relations very few outstanding topics upon which to hang an interesting story. Yet there are topics—let us hope some of considerable importance—which must serve such purpose, even though they almost defy classification. Before attempting to reveal the nature of these subects it may be well to take a glance at the functioning of the Brazilian government during these years.

As might have been expected of a people without experience in self-government, the Brazilians encountered many difficulties in the establishment of a satisfactory political organization. Emperor Pedro I, who began his reign in 1824 under brilliant auspices, soon found his path anything but rosy. He had hardly promulgated the country's first constitution before he considered it necessary to suspend the article guaranteeing personal liberty; and the members of the two houses of the first assembly quarreled among themselves over methods of procedure and with the emperor over the subject of prerogatives. Moreover, the acrimonious quarrel between the executive and the legislators encouraged the dissensions of the opposing factions in the country known as the Brazilian and Portuguese parties. Before long, revolts flared up in various quarters and it seemed as though the empire might be dissolved into a number of independent states. The state of affairs at the end of the decade, though to some extent attributable to factors beyond ordinary control, was partly the result of the waning prestige of the emperor, which was caused by the disastrous outcome of the war with Buenos Aires and his relations with the beautiful and voluptuous Marchioness of Santos. Exhausted by attacks from within and without governmental circles, deserted by many of the imperial soldiers, who went over to the Brazilian faction, and anxious to proceed to Portugal to protect the rights of his daughter Dona María against her uncle Dom Miguel, who had usurped the Portuguese crown, Pedro I abdicated on April 7, 1831, in favor of his five-year-old son.[1]

The abdication of Dom Pedro I cured none of the ills with which Brazil was afflicted. Indeed, the event ushered in the most turbulent decade in Brazilian history. Neither the triple regency, which lasted to 1835, nor the successive one-man regencies, under Father Feijó and Araujo Lima respectively, proved capable of coping with the anarchistic tendencies of the time. Insurrections, often assuming the proportions of formidable revolutions, rent the empire from Pará on the north to Rio Grande do Sul on the south. Not even the interior province of Matto Grosso escaped the convulsions. In many of the outbreaks, beginning with the April revolution of 1831, the imperial soldiers supported the cause of the insurrectionists. Although political alignments are hard to trace through this confused period, the liberal factions seem to have been most often responsible for the eruptions. As a concession to the spirit of particularism— evidently the source of much opposition to imperial authority

---

[1] This summary is based on J. Armitage, *The History of Brazil*, II; copies of the *Aurora Fluminense*, April 6 to 13, 1831 (the official paper of the Brazilian government); A. Rangel, *Dom Pedro I e a Marquesa de Santos;* United States minister to his government, Apr. 7, 16, and 26, 1831, in Despatches, VIII.

—the Brazilian constitution was amended in 1834 by the *Acto Addicional,* which abolished the unpopular council of state and substituted for the municipal councils provincial assemblies with considerable local functions. Unfortunately, this concession seems to have had little influence in checking disorders in the provinces or in curbing lawlessness in the army. The failure of this and other expedients to secure order in the various parts of the extensive empire resulted in the launching of a movement in 1840 for declaring the majority of young Pedro. The agitation started by the liberals quickly gathered momentum because of the hope of finding in the person of an emperor a symbol around which all elements of the country might rally, and, stimulated by the apparent successes of monarchial governments in the Old World, terminated successfully with an act of parliament passed July 23 of the same year.[2]

The parliamentary declaration proved to be a step in the right direction, though naturally several years were required before the youthful Pedro, who in 1840 was only in his fifteenth year, was able to take full control of the reins of government. Gradually, as he advanced in years, the sterling qualities of Pedro II revealed themselves in the shaping of the major policies of state. By the end of 1845 most of the disorders which had disturbed the provinces had been suppressed by imperial soldiers, and by the middle of the century the central government commanded respect both at home and abroad. Much of Pedro's success should be attributed to his own personal qualities. Virtuous in domestic

[2] One of the best accounts of the period of the regency is that by J. M. Pereira da Silva, *Historia do Brazil durante a Menoridade de Dom Pedro II.* For an excellent discussion of internal conditions of Brazilian politics during the period, as well as for an account of the events immediately preceding the parliamentary declaration, see dispatches of American Minister Hunter to his government, July 31, 1840, and April 21, 1841, in Despatches, XII.

relations—in marked contrast to his dissolute father—simple, modest, and tolerant, he received a measure of adulation from his people seldom accorded to rulers. Fortunately, this esteem, which was mutual between governor and governed, lasted through almost a half century with only a few brief lapses.[3]

It was inevitable that the anarchic conditions which prevailed in Brazil from the abdication of Dom Pedro I almost to the middle of the century should be reflected in the country's foreign relations. Obviously, the frequent changes of government during this period made impossible the establishment of a line of conduct known in diplomacy as a policy. Opportunism rather than principle was of necessity the rule of conduct for those responsible for foreign affairs. Equally as important were the facts that the various organs of government were so inarticulate and the state of the finances constantly so bad as to make impossible the execution of diplomatic agreements. Unfortunately, it seems that the foreign nations having relations with the young state were more inclined to take advantage of her foibles and irregularities than to exhibit their own patience and forbearance.

The domestic disorders which characterized the period following the abdication of Dom Pedro I were not always merely indirect in their influence upon the relations between the Washington and Rio governments, for in at least two of the insurrections American citizens became involved directly. One of the outbreaks was that which took place in the province of Rio Grande do Sul, at one of whose ports, namely Alegre, Isaac Austen Hayes was serving as American consul. Accused of having taken part in the insurrection, Hayes was removed from office and imprisoned by provincial offi-

[3] Benjamin Mossé [Rio Branco], *Dom Pedro II, Empereur du Brésil*.

cials. The two hours imprisonment, though galling enough, caused the consul less anxiety than the threats of assassination which kept him confined to his home for several weeks. As soon as the news reached Rio de Janeiro, the American representative requested an investigation. But before the inquiry had got under way, the deposed consul proceeded to Rio and thence to Washington for the purpose of adding his personal influence to the diplomatic pressure in his behalf. His efforts at the American capital at least appear not to have been in vain, for soon an instruction went forth revealing the dissatisfaction of President Van Buren with both the mild disavowal and the arbitrary procedure of the imperial government and demanding a more adequate examination into the case, with an unequivocal declaration of apology and appropriate pecuniary compensation in the event the facts failed to show culpability on the part of Hayes. The American representative carried out the instruction by pressing for a further investigation. But he was soon convinced, partly as a result of further investigation, that Hayes was not unneutral in his conduct toward the insurrection in the southern province. Papers which had fallen into the hands of imperial officials showed that Hayes and his Swiss partner Engerer were not only the paid agents of the insurgents but that Hayes's house became a rendezvous for disaffected leaders. Under the circumstances, Hunter felt indisposed to make the matter the subject of further controversy and it was crowded gradually into the background. A few years later, however, after the death of the deposed consul, a brother, P. Barry Hayes, made an attempt to resurrect the family claim. Although he went so far as to threaten a congressional investigation, his efforts appear to have been in vain. Interestingly enough, at one point in the case Hunter explained the consul's "indiscretion" by saying it was the result of American zeal for republicanism.[4]

The second insurrection in which American officials became involved was that at Bahia. Starting on November 7, 1837, and supported by all the imperial soldiers at the post, the insurgents were said to have been fighting for separation from the central government and the erection of a republic. Whatever their motive, they ousted the president and commander-in-chief of the province and substituted officials of their own liking. As soon as the American representative heard of the disorders, he ordered Captain Mayo of the United States navy to proceed to Bahia to protect the consul, citizens, and commerce of his country. About two months later, January 25, 1838, he received a communication from the Brazilian foreign minister complaining of the conduct of both Captain Mayo and the United States consul at Bahia. The latter had refused to coöperate with the president of the turbulent province, who, in order to deprive the insurgents of provisions of war and pecuniary resources, found it necessary to move the custom-house to the island of Itaparica, while Captain Mayo, paying no attention to the Brazilian brig performing patrol duty but offering to engage her in battle, had furnished convoy to an America vessel carrying supplies to the rebels. Furthermore, a report was circulated that the convoyed vessel had carried as passenger to Bahia the insurgent president, Rocha Galvão, and that her captain had fêted on board his vessel the rebel chiefs, thereby giving

[4] For this entire controversy see dozens of communications in Consular Letters from Rio Grande do Sul, I, but especially those of July 17, Sept. 16, and Oct. 18, 1836. Consult also communications from Hunter to his government, July 26, Aug. 29, and Oct. 18, 1836, Jan. 17 and Mar. 23, 1837, Oct. 13, 1838, and Apr. 29, 1840, in Despatches, X, XI, XII. Finally, see the secretary of state to Hunter, Apr. 4, 1837, in Instructions to United States Ministers, XV, 43-45.

encouragement to the idea that the great republican power of the north countenanced them and their cause.

In satisfaction for the alleged violation of port regulations and the law of neutrality, as well as for the insult to the Brazilian flag, the foreign minister requested, in addition to adequate reparation, the withdrawal from the empire of the offensive American war vessel and the replacement of the American consul at Bahia. Hunter refused to comply with the requests, at least immediately, and asked for a suspension of judgment until an investigation had been made. Meanwhile, he assured the imperial minister that his government, far from being sympathetic toward any rebellion or insurrection, had the utmost respect for the central government of Brazil.

A few days later the American chargé notified Washington of a sudden settlement of the difficulties growing out of the Bahia flareup. He stated that the Rio government had yielded after the receipt of communications which tended to explain and correct previous impressions, which had resulted partly from exaggerations of a clamorous press and gossip of political circles. But, interestingly enough, Hunter had admitted to his government that there "had been perhaps a little too much display on the part of our Captain— his conversation partook of the fervor of republicanism so natural in our citizens." The captain (Mayo) himself had become indignant at the imperial government because it had asked for his recall from Brazilian waters, though later, after the foreign minister expressed an apology and recalled the offensive note, he became reconciled.[5]

In addition to the complaints arising directly from the disorders that rent the young empire, there were others

[5] Dispatches of Hunter, Nov. 18, 1837, Feb. 12 and 22, and Mar. 7, 1838, with their enclosures, in Despatches, XI.

which had an indirect or remote connection. Among the latter were those resulting from commercial intercourse. One minor, yet annoying, grievance of the Yankee traders was against the Brazilian regulation that the work of unloading vessels might not continue beyond the hour of eight o'clock in the morning. Obviously, the restriction resulted in the requirement of much more time for discharging than was either customary or necessary. A similar complaint was in opposition to the requirement that the hatches of unloading vessels be closed at all times when the cargoes were not in the actual process of being removed. In this case, it was alleged that constant closing was not only harmful to the seals but also, by preventing the circulation of air, injurious to the flour.[6]

While remonstrance by the American representative led to abandonment of the inconvenient practice of closing and sealing the hatches of discharging vessels, the restriction as to hours for unloading continued for some time with little modification.[7] And, unfortunately, a strict enforcement of more severe regulations soon followed. An example is found in the case of the ship *Thule*, whose master attempted to conserve time by discharging a part of her cargo before the proper customs official had gone on board. Taking advantage of the law, the Brazilian official seized forty-one barrels of flour which had been transferred to a lighter, went before a prize court, and asked for their condemnation. Although the evidence seemed to be convincing that the master had no intention of avoiding payment of duties, the Brazilian government refused to interfere with the ordinary legal process

---

[6] Flour was the chief article of importation from the United States. Concerning these complaints, see Tudor to his government, Jan. 9, 1829, in Despatches, VI.

[7] Tudor's dispatch of Feb. 18, 1829, in *ibid.*

and the matter dragged on indefinitely, resulting in much inconvenience and expense to the owners.[8]

In several instances exasperating regulations were enforced because the certificates granted by Brazilian consuls in the United States failed to correspond to the passports given to vessels by American port officials. For example, an American vessel carrying a mixed cargo left Baltimore with the intention of going both to Brazil and to India. The clearance papers secured from the American port official at Baltimore stated the vessel's two destinations; but, either through mistake or design, the certificate issued by the Brazilian consul in the same city mentioned only Brazil as the destination. As a consequence, upon arrival at Rio de Janeiro the ship was forced to enter in "full" and not in *franquía,* which meant that all her cargo had to be discharged in the Brazilian capital, despite the fact that most of it had been intended for sale in India. With varying details, many other vessels were subjected to irritating and expensive regulations because the certificates of foreign consuls were given precedence over the passports of the country to which the vessels belonged.[9] On the other hand, there were many instances in which the passports of American ships were designedly indefinite on account of opportunities afforded for evading customs regulations of foreign countries.

American traders complained of hundreds of other port and custom-house regulations. They professed to see no excuse for the decrees requiring detailed information on the quality and quantity of articles included in bundles and boxes of merchandise; they objected to the fines and confiscations resulting from failure—sometimes accidental—to include

---

[8] Acting Chargé Wright to the American government, Aug. 12, and Sept. 28, 1830, in *ibid.,* VII.

[9] Wright to his government, Sept. 28, 1830, in *ibid.*

items in the ship's manifest; they protested against the collection of duties on vessels which had put into port on account of stress of weather. And in addition to the duties levied by the general government, were those required by some of the provinces. While the provincial duties were not excessive, they were vexatious, even when collected for charitable purposes.

These practices became more galling as the Yankee traders saw special privileges of one sort or another bestowed upon foreigners of other nations. They believed that the spirit of the treaty of 1828 prevented the granting of monopolies to other nationals, and they were not slow in making their views known. But, unfortunately, the provisions of the treaty of 1828, with the exception of two items of a general nature, expired in 1843, after which the vexations seemed to increase.[10]

Americans also found it necessary to remonstrate against Brazilian practices other than those connected directly with trade and commerce. For example, they complained loudly of the regulations enforced in the post offices. Up until 1830 masters of United States vessels arriving at Rio de Janeiro had been in the habit of delivering letters and newspapers to their consignees, by whom they were distributed to their proper addresses. Suddenly, however, the regulations were changed so that all letters and packets brought from the northern republic were taken possession of by the local authorities and deposited in the post office, where very high postage rates were demanded of those who called for them. Obviously, the postage on the letters was paid almost invariably, if for no other reason because they usually contained

[10] Several examples of these annoyances may be found in the following communications: dispatches of American ministers dated Feb. 9 and Dec. 31, 1835, Nov. 8, 1842, July 30 and Oct. 7, 1853, and May 14, 1854, in Despatches, X, XII, XX, XXI.

bills of lading and other pertinent documents; but at first the newspapers were rarely removed from the post office, for the rate on an average-sized American paper was eighteen or twenty cents. Later, however, the authorities forced the payment of postage on newspapers by the additional requirement that letters could not be removed as long as papers addressed to the same name lay in the office. The significance of the exactions can not be realized unless one is reminded that the Brazilian capital was, because of its geographical location, the distributing center in South America of mail from the United States. Moreover, the frequent visits of ʼAmerican naval forces to that port made it a place of deposit for official and private communications to commanders and other officers of our squadrons. The circumstances rendered it most desirable that all possible facilities should be afforded for the transmission of letters and newspapers. They also explain the strong remonstrances registered by the American representatives against the unreasonable exactions. Yet, in spite of the official protests, the restrictions were not removed for several years.[11]

As in the previous period, the United States representatives were called upon to make frequent protests against the impressment of American seamen into service in the Brazilian army and navy. In most instances the complaints were in behalf of persons who happened to be caught in the country under unfortunate circumstances, such as survivors of shipwrecks or deserters from American vessels; in other cases they were in favor of those who had mortgaged their services on account of Utopian promises or because of intoxication. In most instances diplomatic protests brought prompt and

[11] The most important phases of this controversy may be found in the dispatches of the American ministers of Aug. 12, 1830, July 26, and 28, 1836, in Despatches, VII, X. See also the American government's instruction to Minister Brown, Oct. 20, 1830, in Instructions to United States Ministers, XIV, 110-111.

favorable action from the Brazilian authorities, though occasionally an American was held for several years.[12]

In addition to the practices of a private nature of which American citizens complained, there were a score of others of a public nature. In the latter category may be placed the decree of the imperial government, issued in 1835, which required the payment of the same duties on all articles imported for the use of foreign vessels of war as were paid by private vessels. Since it reversed a policy begun two years before, the decree brought protests from all the foreign governments accredited to Brazil. As a consequence, the new regulation, just before it went into effect, was so modified that no duty was charged on goods intended for squadrons, provided the importing ships unloaded directly into war vessels. But in the event the imported articles were stored, a duty of one and one-half per cent was collected, provided they were not later sold for private consumption, in which case the regular duty of fifteen per cent had to be paid. Since the modified regulation received application throughout the empire, and since the duty was very small—especially compared to the fifteen per cent rate originally intended— it was not made the subject of complaint by the American government.[13]

None of these minor matters was serious enough to place in jeopardy the cordial relations of the two countries, but their accumulation in time stirred the diplomatic waters considerably. What was more important, they made difficult agreement on more significant issues. This in part accounts

[12] These statements are based on dispatches of June 18, 1831, Aug. 13, 1838, Apr. 16, 1839, and June 25, 1842, in Despatches, VIII, XI, XII.

[13] The crux of the controversy is contained in dispatches of Feb. 25, 1833, Feb. 9 and June 1, 1835, and Dec. 16, 1837, in Despatches, IX, X, XI. But see the secretary of state to Minister Hunter, ·Feb. 10, 1835, in Instructions to United States Ministers, XV.

for the delay in the settlement of several of the prize cases which remained from the Argentine-Brazilian war over Banda Oriental. Although William Tudor had secured a fairly satisfactory adjustment on the more flagrant of the cases resulting from that conflict, the American government stood strongly behind those whose claims were not allowed in the first instance. The American government, of course, pretended to be more concerned with the vindication of its principles governing blockades than with the clamors of individuals.

Many interesting points were brought out on both sides as this controversy dragged through two decades. Immediately subsequent to the Tudor settlement, in the late twenties, the United States boasted that her arguments had produced satisfactory results whereas the stronger methods employed by the European powers had failed; soon, however, the claims backed by the governments of England, France, and Sweden were settled while a deaf ear was turned to the further demands of the United States. This discrimination against the United States in the adjustment of cases that were exactly identical produced a state of exasperation in American circles. William Hunter, United States chargé to Brazil from 1835 to 1843, attributed the success of European diplomacy to the fact that it was backed by threats of a resort to force. He thought that this was particularly true of the British—to Americans the least liked of all foreigners—whose seamen had stood behind the arguments of their diplomats "with matches lighted."[14]

Just before Hunter's retirement from the Brazilian post he made a supreme effort to signalize his mission by a settlement of the prize cases. Before sending the regular communication recapitulating the arguments in support of the

[14] Hunter to his government, Nov. 25, 1839, in Despatches, XL.

claims, he directed an unofficial note which he hoped would prepare the way for the more formal document. In this he alluded to letters which he had received recently from several members of the United States Congress complaining about the policy of the Brazilian government in the adjustment of claims and suggesting a congressional inquiry at the approaching session, and strongly intimated that a serious turn in policy might be expected—perhaps the imposition of a duty on Brazilian coffee, which was then entirely exempt—as well as a withdrawal of the minister on the ground that he was useless or inefficient. This threatening and opportune document was followed ten days later, just at the time of the meeting of the council of state, by the more formal one in which, after a summary of the American view of the facts in the prize cases, the chargé made an appeal for an American policy. He said:

> Is it not proper and expedient by paying the small sum demanded to put an end to the complaints and criminations, as I understand already commenced in the legislature of the United States, and which may lead to consequences at least unpleasant, if not deplorable? Are there not some American sympathies between Brazil and the United States? Is there not something in the pretensions and practices of at least one overgrown European power that emphatically admonishes both Brazil and the United States not only to beware of dissention [sic], but to combine their counsels and their efforts, without, however, the formality of an alliance, for the protection of their national rights and the security of their property and peculiar institutions? [15]

Not one whit less interesting was the chargé's statement of the methods which had been employed in bringing negotiations so near to an apparently successful termination. In this connection he remarked:

[15] Hunter to the American government, Nov. 8, 1842, in *ibid.*, XII.

I am afraid the truth is that all the credit I can take to myself in this transaction is that of having dressed up a specious apology for the assent of ministers to the allowance of these claims. Their magnanimity, their love of justice, their friendship for the United States, have been inspired and sustained by weightier arguments than mine. Presents, percentages, etc., in all such transactions are here a matter of course. The machinery of this government is motionless unless smeared by corruption. The amount paid, however, does not come out of the claimants, but out of this government. The mode is to augment the amount of claims by the addition, in some way, of the amount of the stipulated douceur. I refer to this odious part of the concern not from any express knowledge. I am not permitted to know anything of these business transactions, nor do I wish to; and I refer to them solely for the purpose of accounting for the confidence of the agents of the claimants, and as tolerable proof that this protracted affair is at length about to be finally settled.[16]

Hunter's prediction that the claims of his countrymen were nearing a settlement was but a forerunner of his disappointment. The mutability of Brazilian politics prevented him from signalizing a mission which party politics in the United States was bringing to a close. The term of service of Hunter's successor, George H. Proffitt, was too short for any accomplishment; Proffitt's successor, Henry A. Wise, stimulated by repeated instructions from his superiors, pressed the American claims with great zeal. Indeed, it is suspected that the Virginian became so zealous in his presentation as to injure the cause he was endeavoring to promote, as, for example, by the hundred-page communication which he sent to the Brazilian foreign minister on February 1, 1847.[17] At any rate, an adjustment was not to come for two more years, and after Wise's retirement. Finally, on

[16] *Ibid.*

[17] This document was enclosed in Wise's dispatch to his government of Apr. 12, 1847. See *ibid.*, XVI.

January 27, 1849, David Tod succeeded in negotiating a convention which settled the long-standing controversy. Ratified in January, 1850, the agreement promised to place at the disposal of the Washington government, which was to act as distributor, the sum of 530,000 milreis in full satisfaction of the claims of all American citizens. While this amount fell far short of the aggregate requested, the claimants signified their satisfaction. In view of the fact that William Tudor, one of the fairest-minded diplomats who ever represented the United States at the Brazilian post, had dismissed most of the claims as ridiculous twenty years before, it is not surprising that the claimants expressed satisfaction.

The Brazilian Assembly of 1850 appropriated the money for carrying the convention into effect, a board of distributors sitting at Rio de Janeiro prorated the funds, and the agents of the American claimants took a much-needed rest.[18] American diplomacy had won, but the reviewer of the negotiations wonders at what cost. A partial answer to this query will be disclosed in the following pages.

American representatives confronted still other tasks, one of the most important of which was that of negotiating a new treaty of commerce. The first commercial treaty between the United States and Brazil, which became effective in 1828, was far from satisfactory to the former nation, particularly after discovery that its provisions were not so favorable as those granted European powers in similar documents. Moreover, the treaty of 1828, with the exception of two provisions of a general nature, came to an end toward the close of 1843, after which the trade of the Yankee merchants had a very uncertain footing, though the old rates were continued

[18] In addition to the dispatches cited, see those of Jan. 11 and 27, Aug. 23, 1849, and Sept. 17, 1850, in *ibid.*, XVII, XVIII. See also instructions to American ministers Wise and Tod, May 25, 1844, Dec. 2, 1846, and Jan. 1, 1850, in Instructions to United States Ministers, XV, 100-102, 133-135, 170.

with little modification. It was with the hope of placing our commerce, already grown to many millions of dollars and increasing at an encouraging rate,[19] on a surer basis that the American representatives were instructed to prepare the way for negotiations. Since the Brazilian treaty of commerce with the British did not expire until 1844, and inasmuch as it was thought inadvisable, if not impossible, to treat in advance of the London government, the Yankee negotiations had ample time for taking care of preliminaries.

After the termination of the Anglo-Brazilian treaty, which had guaranteed to the subjects of the European nation unusual privileges, Rio de Janeiro became a diplomatic battle-ground of all the commercial nations of the world. Every manufacturing power was "eager to clothe the broad back and fill the capacious stomach" of the South American country; every navigating power was "on the alert to bring supplies and be the carriers of her products." The American diplomats thought for a time that they occupied a strategic position in the fight. Their country, they believed, could offer terms far more advantageous to Brazil than England, France, or Holland, all of which had extensive tropical colonies whose interests must be protected by the exclusion of the products of other countries. In addition, the first of the European trio had to take care of her abolition societies and parliamentary interests, while the second must consider her growers of beet sugar.[20]

Notwithstanding the fact that the battle to secure favorable commercial treaties from the Rio government raged for

---

[19] By 1835 Americans invested annually nearly $7,000,000 in Brazilian coffee alone, and the figure increased at a rapid rate in the following years. To pay partially for this coffee Americans sold to Brazilians domestics, furniture, lumber, naval stores, screwed hay, sperm candles, bacon, and flour. See Hunter to his government, Dec. 10, 1835, and Nov. 8, 1842, in Despatches, X, XII.

[20] Hunter's dispatch of Dec. 9, 1842, in *ibid.*, XII.

a quarter of a century, the fight was in vain, at least so far as concerned the attainment of immediate objects. The officials of the imperial government steadfastly refused all overtures looking toward the conclusion of agreements such as were sought by all the foreign nations. Unpleasant and often embarrassing experiences resulting from her first treaties, particularly the one with the British in which advantages injurious to herself had been conceded, and the conviction that her coffee would be purchased regardless of treaties seem to have weighed heavily in causing Brazil to render an adverse decision.

Although their proposals had been rejected, the American representatives felt that they had cause for gratification. If their efforts had been unsuccessful, so had those of the British, their chief rivals both in commerce and in politics. Moreover, the British had failed to secure a renewal of their treaty in spite of the fact that they negotiated through a special agent with the rank of ambassador and a salary of twelve thousand pounds in addition to an expense allowance of five thousand pounds. British failure meant that the Yankee trader would be on the same footing with his British cousin —at least so far as concerned the import and export duties levied by Brazil—a position he had not enjoyed hitherto. In view of the equalization of the privileges of the two Anglo-Saxon nations, it was perhaps wise that the United States congress did not carry out the threat to lay countervailing duties on Brazilian goods.

Much interest attaches to the negotiations for the renewal of the commercial treaties because the American representatives believed that their efforts were in harmony with the general plan to establish in the South American country what they chose to call an "American" policy. They believed, or in their negotiations with the Brazilian officials professed to believe, that the European powers, especially France and England, not "entirely exorcised from the phantasy that America is but an experimental, and for them, colonial or quasi-colonial territory," were attempting to exact preferences and impose restrictions without equivalents; and they implored Brazil, as the champion of American rights in the southern half of the Western Hemisphere as the United States was supposed to be in the northern half, to turn a deaf ear to the representations of the Old World imposters. They labored consciously for the gradual relaxation and ultimate destruction of the restrictive system of Europe and for the substitution of a liberal American system therefor. Deploring the fact that the instability of the Spanish-American republics prevented their aid in the establishment of this system, they endeavored all the harder to induce Brazil to make a start. Failure of British diplomacy to renew the provisions of the Anglo-Brazilian treaty, and favorable replies of the imperial officials to American communications, gave heart to Yankee negotiators.[21]

Up to this point in our story the internal disorders of Brazil have often been used to explain the confusion and misunderstanding in her diplomatic relations with the United States. It is now time to turn the canvas, observe the other side of the picture, and discover that it is possible to attribute much of the discord to the frequent failure of American officials properly to observe diplomatic form and ceremony. As

[21] On the establishment of an American policy, see especially dispatches of United States ministers of Nov. 8 and Dec. 9, 1842, and Jan. 12, 1845, in *ibid.*, XII, XIII. For the entire subject of the treaty, see, in addition to the communications cited, dispatches of Nov. 8, 1842, Jan. 31 and Mar. 31, 1843, Jan. 5 and Dec. 14, 1844, Jan. 12 and May 1, 1845, Sept. 29, 1846, Aug. 23, 1849, May 1, 1851, Apr. 30, 1853, Sept. 7 and 15, 1854, Mar. 12, 1855, and Jan. 15, 1858, in *ibid.*, XII, XV, XVII, XVIII, XX, XXI, XXII, XXV. Also, see instructions of the United States government to her ministers in Brazil, Aug. 1, 1843, May 8, 1851, Aug. 8, 1853, and Sept. 15, 1857, in Instructions to Brazilian Ministers, XV, 87-93, 187, 215-220, 270-274.

was natural with citizens of a young republic, our representatives were often disposed to go to absurd extremes in ignoring pomp and ostentation. Some of those sent to Rio de
Janeiro, disregarding Brazilian tastes and traditions, even
made intentional displays of their informality and simplicity,
apparently in order to be in marked contrast to the representatives of the Old World monarchies.

But part of the responsibility for the simple and informal
method of diplomatic intercourse employed by our representatives must be placed upon the officials at Washington.
For many years the official rank and salary of the Brazilian
post were too low to invest the incumbent with any degree of
prestige and influence. Notwithstanding the fact that Brazilian officials had broached the question of raising the diplomatic rank as early as 1835, that the European countries had
taken similar steps, and that William Hunter for several
years had stressed the importance of meeting European competition, it was not until near the end of 1841 that the American government changed the status of the Rio post from that
of chargé d' affaires to envoy extraordinary and minister
plenipotentiary. For the first time the American agent felt
that his position enabled him to carry on official intercourse
in such a way as to enforce the opinions and vindicate the
policy and interests of his country.[22]

The foreign office at Washington was also negligent at
times in sending to Brazilian officials, upon occasions auspicious in the history of the empire, letters of felicitation and
congratulation. Realizing the importance of such communications, the American representatives frequently prodded

[22] See dispatches of American ministers, Dec. 10, 1835, July 15, 1841, and Sept.
4, 1845, in Despatches, X, XII, and XIV, as well as an instruction to Minister
Hunter, Sept. 21, 1841, in Instructions to United States Ministers to Brazil, XV, 73-74.

their superiors to attend to such apparently trivial matters. For example, William Hunter, in April, 1841, following the parliamentary declaration that the young Pedro had reached his majority, felt it necessary to say:

For the last three months [I have been] expecting the cabinet letter by which my government would notice the fact of the Emperor's accession—our acquiescence and congratulation. This to be sure is a mere formal affair, but it is necessary and proper, and the omission on our part (being the only one) may be felt as disrespectful and unkind. I explain it of course as being *accidental* owing to our immense distance and the probable loss of despatches.

Waiting another month without receiving the pertinent document, the minister again wrote:

From the new administration [the Harrison administration] I could hardly expect to receive a communication, but from the old I had some right to expect the formal and necessary letter congratulating the Emperor upon his assumption of power. This has now been done by every government except our own. The absence of this trivial but indispensable document was the occasion of some conversation between Aureliano [the Brazilian foreign minister] and myself when he was about composing the speech for the throne. He was easily convinced that he might with propriety, if not with equal truth, say that the Emperor had received congratulations upon the event from every foreign power.

Despite our minister's pleas, the congratulatory letter was never dispatched from Washington, Secretary Webster giving as an excuse the failure of the American government to receive any official notification of the occasion in Brazil. Fortunately, the tact and diplomacy of William Hunter, united with similar qualities of the Brazilian foreign minister, brought a satisfactory settlement of this incident; but, unfor-

tunately, many other incidents arose at times when concil-
iation was much more difficult.[23]

But the classic example showing the influence of the failure to observe proper diplomatic form and ceremony was the
controversy resulting from the arrest and imprisonment by
Brazilian officials of Lieutenant Davis of the United States
ship *Saratoga*. The difficulty between the officials of the two
countries arose at Rio de Janeiro the last day of October,
1846, while the American lieutenant was intervening in a
drunken brawl between one of his own men and two other
American sailors. Before Davis had settled the altercation
local officers interfered, seized the American sailors, and,
after inflicting a severe beating for resistance, marched them
off toward the Palace. The lieutenant, protesting vigorously
against the action of the Brazilian officers all the while, followed the patrol to the Palace, where he was arrested, dis-
armed, and placed in prison along with the sailors.[24]

Upon learning of the occurrence, American Minister
Wise, whose recall had been requested because of the use of
discourteous language in some of his communications to the
Brazilian government,[25] sent a protest to the imperial minister demanding the release of his imprisoned countrymen,
the disavowal of the outrage, and the punishment of the
Brazilian guard responsible for the offense. The Brazilian
government released Lieutenant Davis after two days confinement, though it held the three seamen for further inves-

[23] For this topic see Hunter's dispatches of Dec. 31, 1835, May 20, 1836, May 15,
and Oct. 26, 1841, in Despatches, X, XII, and Webster's instructions of July 3, 1841,
in Instructions to United States Ministers to Brazil, XV, 71-72.

[24] Based on official reports of both contestants. See Wise's dispatch of Nov. 16,
1846, with its many enclosures, in Despatches, XVI, or *Sen. Ex. Doc.* 29, 30 Cong.,
1 sess.

[25] Brazilian foreign minister to Lisboa, imperial representative at Washington, July
31, 1846, in Communications from Brazilian Agents, II.

tigation and defended the conduct of its patrol, even in the arrest of the American lieutenant.

This was but the prelude to a controversy that became more complex and acrimonious with the increase of communications, and that ended only ten months later with the departure of Henry A. Wise from the Brazilian capital. Interestingly enough, the principles involved in the quarrel were neither numerous nor the divergence of viewpoints great. Although the American minister insisted that the conduct of the Brazilian patrol, particularly in arresting and imprisoning the American officer, was a direct insult to the American flag, and the Brazilian government countered with the unquestionable claim of the right to preserve peace and enforce her municipal laws within her own sovereign jurisdiction, the course of the wrangle was determined largely by what should have been insignificant incidents. One of these trivial, yet far reaching, incidents occurred on November 15, 1846, when Commodore Rousseau, commander of the United States squadron in Brazilian waters, refused to fire a salute on the occasion of the baptism of the imperial princess. Exaggerated, perverted, and misinterpreted by the public press, the commander's action generated a strong feeling against both the officer himself and the American minister. It was interpreted as an insult from republicanism to imperialism. And the indignation aroused by this incident had not subsided when, on December 2, the birthday of the emperor arrived and another occasion for a salute was neglected by the same commodore.

The effects of these incidents were reflected immediately in the mirror of diplomacy. On the day following Rousseau's refusal to greet the baptism of the imperial princess, the Brazilian foreign minister dispatched his first note asking for the recall of Wise and Rousseau, saying that the former would never again receive an invitation to the Palace; and on the third day following the failure to recognize the emperor's birthday, the same official penned an instruction conveying the second request for Wise's recall. In both instances the American minister was held responsible for the breach of diplomatic etiquette. In a later instruction to its agent at Washington the Brazilian government signified a willingness to bury in oblivion the Davis episode, but insisted that Wise must be recalled as a mark of reparation due Brazil because of his attitude toward the events which took place on November 15 and December 2.[26]

As the American government approved of its minister's conduct in the Davis affair, and as it believed, perhaps erroneously, that the reasons given to support the request were subterfuges, it refused to recall Wise. Although the refusal may have been wise from the viewpoint of upholding a principle, the price our minister was forced to pay in humiliation was a dear one. For several months he was the subject of attack by the Brazilian press; he was never again invited to the imperial Palace; and he was not granted an audience to appear before the emperor to deliver in person a congratulatory letter from the president of his country. Some of these slights and rebuffs Wise, though inwardly sizzling, ignored for a time; others, unfortunately, immediately called from him caustic and undiplomatic remarks.[27]

While Wise and the Brazilian foreign minister were exchanging sharp words at Rio de Janeiro, Secretary Buchanan and Lisboa, the Brazilian minister to the United States, were discussing the same problems in more amicable fashion at Washington. Agreement on the subject of the imprisonment

[26] Brazilian foreign minister to the imperial representative at Washington, Nov. 16 and Dec. 5, 1846, and Mar. 31, 1847, in Communications from Brazilian Agents, II.

[27] Wise to secretary of state, Dec. 9, 1846, in Despatches, XVI.

of Lieutenant Davis and three American sailors was reached on February 1 after ten days of negotiations, during which time our commercial centers were clamoring for an adjustment. But the settlement of the question of Minister Wise's conduct and recall proved infinitely more difficult. To the request that the American government make a categorical declaration disapproving the conduct of its envoy and ordering his recall as a mark of reparation, Buchanan gave a negative reply, stating that compliance would be admission of the correctness of Brazilian authorities in the Davis affair. Impelled by instructions called forth by the episodes of November 15 and December 2, 1846, Lisboa, perhaps reluctantly, pressed the demands of his government with great persistence. Convinced that the demands grew out of the Davis affair, and refusing to take further responsibility, Buchanan submitted the matter to his chief. A week later, February 10, 1847, Lisboa was told that the president thought he could not recall Wise immediately without censuring his conduct in the Davis controversy, which he approved. At the same time, however, the Brazilian was assured informally that the offensive minister, who had previously asked to be relieved of his duties, would leave Rio de Janeiro in the spring. Subjected to bitter attacks at home, Lisboa several times requested Buchanan for formal notification that Wise would soon return to the United States; but the secretary was not disposed to modify the position taken by the president.[28]

Following immediately upon receipt of dispatches from Washington announcing Lisboa's *amende honorable* for the Davis affair, the Brazilian council of state convened and decided that the imperial representative should be called home.

[28] Buchanan to Wise, Mar. 2 and 29, 1847, in Instructions to Brazilian Ministers, XV, 136-137, 139-146.

A few days later (May 3) the emperor appeared before the Assembly, announced the recall of Lisboa, and stated that while the Davis incident was still in an unsatisfactory state it would be settled in a manner comporting with the national dignity.[29] The following day Minister Wise was notified that the diplomatic interruption between the two countries would continue because of the disapproval of Lisboa's conduct at Washington. Still the American minister had been instructed to stay by his post until his successor had arrived and presented his credentials. If the Washington government had known how unpopular its minister had become at Rio de Janeiro, surely it would not have insisted that he continue at his post. However that may be, the Virginian, in spite of repeated official rebuffs as well as insults from the press, now and then mustered sufficient courage to attempt to reopen negotiations. It is useless to say that his efforts were as futile as King Canute's commands to the waves.[30]

It is interesting to note that Wise's increasing obnoxiousness to the Rio government was partly the result of another of his numerous indiscretions. This time the imprudence consisted in a few uncomplimentary remarks made while delivering a speech on the occasion of the baptismal ceremonies which took place on board a United States frigate. The ceremonies were in commemoration of the birth of a child, Alta California Harris, who had come into the world while her parents were emigrating from the United States to Brazil. At the invitation of the officers of the frigate *Columbia,* on which the child had been born, and of the sloop *Preble,* Wise went aboard the former to make a speech at the presentation of a vase to Alta California. With the hope, as he professed later, of effecting discipline on board, and in order to make

---

[29] *Gaceta Official* (Rio), Apr. 26, 1847; *Jornal do Commercio,* Apr. 27, 1847.
[30] See Wise's communication of May 22, 1847, in Despatches, XVI.

the colonists appreciate the fact that they had been born under republican institutions, he undertook to deliver an inspiring speech, during the course of which he compared the plebeian birth of the Harris child to the birth of the imperial princess, which had taken place a short time before. Delivered the latter part of November, 1846, the contents of the speech were unknown in Rio until appearance in Portuguese translation in the March 28, 1847, number of *Jornal do Commercio*. The Brazilian publication had secured the speech from the New York *Sun* of January 27, which, according to Wise, had copied it from an Ohio paper.[31]

The effect of the appearance of this speech in the Rio papers may easily be imagined. Obviously the reaction of the public mind was similar to that of a bull facing a waving red rag. And the feeling was not allayed by Wise's statement that his remarks had been addressed to an exclusively American audience on board an American public vessel which lay entirely outside the territorial jurisdiction of the empire.

When Felippe José Pereira Leal was appointed successor to Lisboa at Washington, his rank was not that of envoy extraordinary and minister plenipotentiary, but chargé d' affaires. The reduction in official rank was for the purpose of emphasizing the dissatisfaction of the Brazilian government with the Buchanan-Lisboa settlement. While signifying a willingness to bury in oblivion the Davis incident, the new chargé's instructions required a categorical declaration that the United States government disapproved the conduct of Wise and ordered his recall as a mark of reparation because of his responsibility in the incidents connected with the baptism of the imperial princess and the emperor's birth-

---

[31] *Jornal do Commercio*, Mar. 28, 1847; New York *Sun*, Jan. 27, 1847; Wise to Buchanan, Nov. 3, 1847, in Despatches, XVI; Lisboa to Buchanan, Mar. 28, 1847, in Communications from Brazilian Agents, II.

day. In case the United States refused to settle on this basis, arbitration of the differences was to be suggested. But in any event the recently appointed American minister would not be received until satisfaction had been given.[32]

Following shortly upon his reception at Washington (August 3, 1847) Leal made known the content of his instructions. The American government refused to make reparation or to disapprove Wise's conduct in the Davis affair; nor would it permit itself to be drawn into a discussion concerning the conduct of American officials at events honoring the imperial family. At the same time, however, it admitted the right of Brazil to exercise jurisdiction over crimes committed in her territory by foreign sailors.[33]

Meantime, David Tod of Youngstown, Ohio, had accepted appointment and set out to relieve Henry A. Wise of his embarrassing duties. Although he was informed of the possibility of the disavowal by the Brazilian government of the settlement reached with Lisboa and of the minister's recall, Tod was told not to permit himself to be drawn into a discussion of the matter, but to attempt to alleviate the high diplomatic tension through an application of courtesy toward all imperial officials. Since Lisboa was held in esteem in the United States, and since his recall would disturb the public mind and thus interfere with an important American market, he might take occasion to speak in commendation of the maligned representative. But he was not to run the risk of doing more harm than good by interfering actively in his behalf.[34]

On arrival at the Brazilian capital early in August, Tod found himself in an embarrassing situation. Wise, who had

[32] Leal's instructions, Mar. 31, 1847, in Communications from Brazilian Agents, II.
[33] Buchanan to Leal, Aug. 30, 1847, in Notes to the Brazilian Legation, VI, 40-65.
[34] Secretary of state to Tod, Mar. 18 and June 11, 1847, in Instructions to Brazilian Ministers, XV, 139, 147-152.

received a sealed letter from the president of the United States to the Brazilian emperor announcing the termination of his mission, and who had been instructed to seek an audience though not to insist on it with the imperial executive, attempted to convince his successor that he should delay in presenting his credentials until the receipt of new instructions. The Virginian argued that the refusal of the emperor to grant him an audience to present the president's letter constituted an insult which could not be met by orders issued with reference to an entirely different problem.[35]

The time and energy Wise consumed in attempting to convince his successor that he should not ask for a presentation audience until he had received new instructions were spent in vain. After waiting a few days, during which he had received from the Brazilian foreign minister satisfactory explanations for the refusal to receive from Wise the letter from the president of the United States concerning Wise's recall and assurances that no offense had been intended, Tod decided to request an audience. The request was granted, the presentation took place on August 29, and cordial relations between the two countries were once more resumed. The new minister and his wife entered immediately into the social life connected with the many national holidays which marked their early residence at the Brazilian capital. On one occasion at a big ball Minister Tod danced with the princess and His Majesty "had the pleasure of dancing with Mrs. Tod."[36]

On September 1 the *Columbia* conveyed the cantankerous Virginian out of the harbor of Rio de Janeiro and the Brazilians gave no expressions of regret. After arrival in the United States the ex-minister avowed his intentions of taking

[35] Wise to his government, Aug. 26, 1847, in Despatches, XVI.

[36] Tod to the Washington government, Aug. 31 and Sept. 18, 1847, in *ibid.*, XVII.

the matter of his insult before Congress with the hope of vindication, though he appears not to have carried out his
threat.[37]

With a change of administrations in the United States
in 1849, Brazil replaced Chargé Leal by Chavalier Sergio de
Macedo, who had the rank of envoy extraordinary and minister plenipotentiary. While the restoration of the rank of
her representative at Washington was viewed as a good omen
for future relations, Macedo's instructions to reopen the
Davis case seemed to point in the opposite direction. Fortunately, the new administration in charge of the American
government was conciliatory and Secretary Clayton was authorized to say:

Friendly ministers have been interchanged, and while declining
now to open again an useless discussion, I take pleasure in stating to
you, that the President regrets the occurrences which unfortunately
led to a temporary misunderstanding between the two governments
and the more especially as he anxiously desires to cultivate with Brazil pacific and intimate relations, and cherishes toward the Constitutional Sovereign and the people of that great country, the most
respectful and friendly regard.[38]

This polite refusal on the part of the Taylor administration to reopen the old controversy settled the matter for
three years, and should have been final. But in 1852 American Minister Robert C. Schenck noticed in an issue of the
Jornal do Commercio of Rio de Janeiro judgment of a Brazilian criminal court sentencing Alonzo B. Davis, the American lieutenant involved in the dispute concerning the arrest
of his countrymen in 1846, to three years and four months
imprisonment with labor. Schenck addressed a communica-

[37] See B. H. Wise, *The Life of Henry A. Wise of Virginia, 1806-1876*, pp. 118-119.
[38] Secretary Clayton to Macedo, April 11, 1849, in Notes to the Brazilian Legation,
VI, 78-80. See also the note of Mar. 10, 1849, *idem.*, 78.

tion to the imperial government immediately expressing surprise at the judgment in a case which had been settled through diplomatic channels and requesting an explanation. As soon as the matter was brought to his attention, the emperor issued a decree saying that the penalty inflicted by the court should be without effect. The American minister was of the opinion that the action of the court was a mock-trial for the purpose of enabling the government to quote the decision at any future time as evidence that Brazil had not yielded or receded from any position heretofore maintained.[39] Considered in this light, the petty incident must be put in the same class with that which made our records show that Henry A. Wise was "recalled at his own request."[40] But for the explanation of certain types of diplomacy both would be too petty to justify inclusion in a study such as this.[41]

One experiences relief in turning from the petty diplomacy connected with the Davis episode to that which had for its goal the promotion of an "American" feeling in eastern South America. While the negotiations on all topics of every character were supposed to be colored by the omnipresence of this goal, those relating to the episodes in the region of the River Plate reveal the aim most clearly. Early in 1838 Dictator Rosas of Argentina, already engaged in wars against Bolivia to the north and against his numerous enemies at home, found himself in a crisis with France. Claiming inability to obtain satisfaction for a number of

[39] Schenck to his government, June 7, 1852, with its enclosures, in Despatches, XIX.

[40] See Wise's instructions of March 29, 1847, in Instructions to Brazilian Ministers, XV, 139-146.

[41] In addition to the manuscript materials cited for the Davis episode, one should consult the *Relatorio da Reparticão dos Negocios Estrangeiros Apresentado a Assembléa Geral Legislativa* (hereafter cited *Relatorio*) for 1847, pp. 8-12 and 1848, pp. 9-12, as well as Antonio Pereira Pinto, *Apontamentos para o Direito Internacional*, II, 391-395.

grievances, among which was that of forcing her citizens into service in the Argentine army, the European power broke off diplomatic relations and followed with a blockade of Buenos Aires and the adjoining coast. It is needless to say that the blockade created an economic crisis which taxed all of Rosas' numerous talents to counteract.[42]

The American minister at Rio, William Hunter, looked upon French action with deep suspicion. He interpreted the interference in La Plata as a counterpart to the bombardment of the Mexican coast and intervention in the Texas question. The meddling in the three cases was viewed as an attempt at the establishment of a monarchial scheme in the New World which would be subservient to French interests, as well as an endeavor to get revenge on the United States for President Jackson's insolence in the indemnity controversy. Since the blockading incident was viewed in this manner, it is not surprising that Hunter lent encouragement to a plan for offering the good offices of the Washington government in behalf of a peaceful solution. Although Rosas received the proffer from the northern republic with a gracious spirit, the dictator so modified the proposals that the French were unable to reach an agreement with him.[43]

The suspicions of American agents in Brazil, and indeed in all eastern South America, became more pronounced as the conflict in La Plata widened. The spread of the Platine difficulty resulted partly from Rosas' attempt to aid the Oribe faction in regaining control of the Uruguayan government from the Rivera group and partly from his attempt to defeat the alliance between the Argentine province of Corrientes and Paraguay by laying an embargo upon their commerce.

[42] Adolfo Saldias, *História de la Confederación Argentina*, III, 17ff.

[43] *British and Foreign State Papers*, XXXI, 790-801; Hunter to his government, Feb. 2 and Dec. 29, 1839, in Despatches, XI and XII.

The former attempt resulted in the blockade of Montevideo and the latter in the closing of the Paraná River to the world's trade. Against both of these acts the British and French governments protested strongly. Since the protests brought no relief, the two governments issued a joint declaration of blockade of the Rio de la Plata and sent fleets to enforce it. Anglo-French forces were likewise stationed at Montevideo and other points in Uruguay.[44]

From what has been said previously, it is easy to judge the reaction of the American minister, now Henry A. Wise, to the intervention of the European powers in La Plata. To him the conduct was nothing less than lust for dominion cloaked under a less offensive term. It was conduct which had for its object the command of the enormous trade of the interior of South America, the last great unexplored country upon earth. Since the Paraná and Paraguay rivers were the veins and arteries for the outlet and inlet of this great commerce, the intervening powers were endeavoring to secure control of them.

Inasmuch as Wise was a man of action, as well as a man of words, he collaborated with the other American agents in a program calculated to diminish the influence of the European powers. Before Anglo-French interference reached the stage of blockade, the Virginian and Brent, the American chargé to Argentina, sought to induce Brazil to offer mediation in the Uruguayan difficulty. After the crisis resulting in the joint decree of blockade, the objects were to keep down jealousy, and perhaps war, between Brazil and the Argentine Republic, to bring about a cessation of hostilities between Rosas and the Rivera faction in Uruguay, and to in-

---

[44] Saldias, *op. cit.*, IV, 178ff.; *British and Foreign State Papers*, XXXIV, 1266ff.; Minister Wise to his government, Aug. 24, 1845, in Despatches, XIV.

duce the Argentinian dictator to recognize the independence of Paraguay. The attainment of these ends would obviate the necessity of armed intervention of England and France and result ultimately in the collapse of their ulterior designs.[45]

With the exception of the last, all of these objects appear to have been achieved by the combined efforts of the American diplomats and naval commanders. An amicable settlement of the controversy between Rosas and Paraguay was considered so vital that the Washington government, acting upon the advice of ministers Wise and Brent, appointed a special agent to aid in carrying on the negotiations. The special agent, E. A. Hopkins, proceeded to Asunción, the Paraguayan capital, and began his mediatory services; but his efforts proved entirely vain. The failure was probably the result of the demands of President Carlos A. López of Paraguay, who not only asked for the recognition of his country's independence but for an unrestricted use of the Paraná and La Plata rivers for commerce, of British influence, which worked to secure a dominant place in the heart of South America, of a disagreement between Chargé Brent and Hopkins, and of the insane ambition of Rosas. But there was consolation in the knowledge that the European powers had failed at the same point, even though the failure was attributable in part to difficulties in another quarter of the world. Better still was the thought that the failure of the Old World meddlers was accompanied by a noticeable waning of their prestige. Probably American agents took unto themselves no less credit for having secured results through coöperation with a dictator whose methods were often autocratic and brutal. Alliance with autocracy and barbarism was

<hr>

[45] Wise to his government, July 31, Aug. 24, Sept. 6, and Dec. 16, 1845, in Despatches, XIV.

justified in steering an American program around a whirl-pool.[46]

With the overthrow of Rosas early in 1852, American policy experienced a change. Indeed, the events connected with the downfall of the dictator themselves may suggest the change, for Brazil was partner with General Urquiza, governor of the rich Argentinian province of Entre Rios, and an Uruguayan faction in the triple alliance which brought about Rosas' undoing. Inasmuch as up to this point it had been the policy of American agents to keep Brazil at peace with the governments in La Plata, there was either a change in program or failure in application. Neither of these interpretations alters the fact of a variation in American policy with the advent of General Urquiza, the successor to Rosas, though the variation was probably one in tactics rather than in objectives. At any rate, American representatives at Rio and Buenos Aires coöperated with British and French ministers in negotiating treaties with Argentina for the free navigation of the Paraná and Uruguay rivers. The Americans, in addition, entered into treaties of commerce, friendship, and navigation with Argentina, Paraguay, and Uruguay, all of which abolished certain inequalities affecting Yankee traders.[47]

It would appear that the American policy, which first sought to encourage Rosas in his dogged resistance to European interference and to keep peace among the contending factions in La Plata, and which later advanced to exact the

[46] Dispatches of Wise, Feb. 18, Apr. 14, June 19 and 27, 1846, *idem.*, XV and XVI.

[47] The American government to Robert C. Schenck, minister to Brazil, Apr. 29, 1852, in Instructions to Brazilian Ministers, XV, 199-205; Schenck to the Washington government, Feb. 14, Sept. 4 and 17, 1852, May 12 and Aug. 16, 1853, in Despatches, XIX and XX; John F. Cady, *Foreign Intervention in the Rio de la Plata, 1838-1850.*

same privileges extended to European rivals, gained certain distinct advantages in the contest with Old World powers. And happily the gains seem to have been accompanied by a friendlier feeling between the United States and the other American states involved.

CHAPTER V

THE ABOLITION OF THE AFRICAN SLAVE TRADE TO BRAZIL

O F ALL the subjects that fall within the century of American-Brazilian relations, the African slave trade is the most important. But not only is it the most important; it is also the most intricate in its nature and therefore the most difficult of accurate characterization. The intricacy results partly from the fact that several nations had a share in it. Since Great Britain played a leading rôle in the abolition of the traffic, an attempt at elucidation requires at least careful consideration of her activity.

Although not the first Old World power to take action, Great Britain responded to the agitation of Clarkson, Sharpe, and Wilberforce and passed the act of March 25, 1807, which aimed to prevent participation in the trade by British subjects. Seventeen years later this act was followed by another which made the crime piracy.[1] It was soon evident, however, that complete eradication of the evil must depend upon concerted action of all nations rather than upon the independent action of a few. Partly because of her prestige and power, Great Britain assumed leadership in the larger movement. The program evolved by her had two main phases, namely, the negotiations of treaties with both the civilized nations and the African tribes for the suppression of the traffic and the maintenance of forts upon, and cruisers off, the African coast to enforce these treaties.[2] The first phase of this program was remarkably successful, for by 1842

[1] *British and Foreign State Papers,* 1815-1816, pp. 195 *et seq.* and 292 *et seq.*
[2] *Parliamentary Papers,* Slave Trade, Number 35, 1850, pp. 3-8.

treaties had been entered into with all the European countries except Belgium, Greece, Hanover, and Oldemburg,
with all the American nations except New Granada and Peru,
and with six of the African chiefs.[3]   As might have been expected, the second phase of the program was much less successful.   It was one task to negotiate; it was quite another
to enforce the terms resulting from negotiations.

For our purpose it is sufficient to note the nature of British negotiations with Portugal, the nation out of which Brazil
arose.   The treaty of friendship and alliance, signed at Rio
de Janeiro February 19, 1810, contained a provision whereby
Portugal agreed not to transport Negroes from those parts of
Africa not belonging to her, though another provision of the
same treaty seemed to neutralize it.[4]   As a consequence, the
first provision was not carried into execution, and several additional treaties soon followed. One of the most important in
the last category was the document of July 28, 1817, by
whose terms the public vessels of either signatory were given
the right to search the suspicious merchantmen of the other
operating north of the line, and two mixed commissions—
one in Sierra Leone and the other in Brazil—were established for adjudicating all captures. Of almost equal significance was the additional article, signed September 11 of the
same year, which guaranteed that the provisions of the July
document should remain in effect for fifteen years from the
date of the passage of a Portuguese abolition law.[5]

Despite these treaties, the Portuguese trade in Africans
failed to show any decline for many years.   Indeed, in

[3] For a list of the treaties and their dates, see *Hansard's Parliamentary Debates*
(3rd series), LXXX, 482; for the content of the treaties, see G. F. de Martens,
Nouveau Recueil de Traités.

[4] Martens, *Nouveau Recueil de Traités*, I, 245.

[5] For the July convention and the additional article, see *ibid.*, IV, 438 and 478;
for treaties of January 21 and 22, 1815, consult other volumes of the series.

Portugal's most important colony—Brazil—the number of African importations increased every year during the remainder of the colonial period.[6]   Fortunately, only a few years elapsed before the independence of the South American colony paved the way for direct negotiations on the traffic; and the part played by Great Britain in the separation placed her in an advantageous position for negotiating with the new state.   The first article of a convention drawn at Rio de Janeiro on November 23, 1826, and ratified the following March, provided that within three years it should not be "lawful for the subjects of the Emperor of Brazil to be concerned in the carrying on of the African slave trade, under any pretext or in any manner whatever, and the carrying on of such after that period, by any person, subject of His Imperial Majesty, shall [should] be deemed and treated as piracy."   The remaining articles, by renewing verbatim the provisions of the British-Portuguese agreements of 1815 and 1817, granted the signatories the right to visit and search each other's merchant vessels, and established mixed commissions for adjudicating all captures.[7]

The announcement of this treaty caused great excitement in Brazil.   Most people believed that if it were carried out a shortage of slave labor would follow immediately.   Moreover, cutting off Negro importation seemed only a step toward the destruction of the institution of slavery itself, upon which the prosperity of the country was believed to depend. But the evil day might be postponed by taking advantage of the three-year period before prohibition by Brazilian law. Accordingly, many millions of additional capital were invested in the business of importation.   Statistics indicate that the redoubled efforts were not in vain.   The records for the

[6] R. Walsh, *Notices of Brazil in 1828 and 1829*, II, 178.

[7] Martens, *Nouveau Recueil de Traités*, VI, 1087.

province of Rio de Janeiro tell the tale; the importation figure of fifteen thousand for 1820 had doubled by 1827 and
trebled by 1829, the year preceding that in which the treaty
was to take effect.[8]

The Brazilian abolition law, which was not passed until
November 7, 1831, though the treaty had provided a date
not later than March 13 of 1830, declared free all persons
illegally imported, imposed heavy penalties on those convicted for importation, and rewarded those who assisted in
making captures.[9] Notwithstanding its apparently severe
provisions, evidence that the act failed to interfere seriously
with the slave trade is both plentiful and convincing. A
British consul to Brazil estimated that forty thousand Africans were smuggled into the province of Rio de Janeiro alone
in the year 1838, while a member of the mixed commission
at the Brazilian capital reported that sixty-four thousand entered the entire country in 1844.[10]

As a result of the vigilance on the part of British agents,
the London government was always informed on events connected with the Brazilian traffic. It was aware that vessels
were fitted out in Brazilian ports almost daily for the business
of transporting Negroes across the Atlantic, and that as frequently Africans were landed in the empire's capital city.
The London government did more than assemble information; it formulated plans on the basis of its information.
On several occasions during the decade beginning in 1835 it
suggested to the Brazilian government effective measures
for the suppression of the traffic. Whatever may have been

[8] Reports of American ministers to Brazil, May 30, 1829, and Jan. 22, 1835, in
Despatches, VI and X.

[9] An English translation of the law is in *House Ex. Doc.* 61, 30 Cong., 2 sess.
(serial 543), p. 86.

[10] *Parliamentary Papers*, Slave Trade, 1839, class B, p. 123; *House Ex. Doc.* 61, 30
Cong., 2 sess. (serial 543), p. 86.

the reasons, the Brazilian government did not act upon the suggestions from London.[11]

The year 1845 witnessed a turning point in Anglo-Brazilian relations on the slave traffic. On March 12 of that year the British representative at Rio was notified of the expiration on the following day of the abolition convention of 1826. But the London government, headed now by Aberdeen, refused to admit that the general provision of the document—that it should be unlawful for the subjects of the emperor to be concerned in carrying on the African trade under any pretext or in any manner whatever—had expired, or could expire until its purpose had been achieved. Although the position taken by the Aberdeen government was indefensible, if not absurd, it became the basis of an application to parliament for an effective measure. And parliament acted promptly on the measure introduced; on August 8, 1845, the Aberdeen Bill became a law. The act provided for the trial of all cases arising from the alleged violation of the convention of 1826 by British courts of admiralty and vice-admiralty instead of by the mixed commissions sitting at Rio de Janeiro and Sierra Leone, though the decisions of the latter were to be recognized up until September 13.[12]

Obviously, the announcement of the Aberdeen Act aroused great indignation in Brazilian circles. While opposition to the measure took many and varied forms, the official protest was summarized in a ten-page document drawn up by the Brazilian foreign minister and presented to the British representative at Rio de Janeiro. This protest stated that the British law, though "passed under the pretext of

[11] *British and Foreign State Papers*, 1845-1846, pp. 666 *et seq.*
[12] *Parliamentary Papers*, Slave Trade, 1845, pp. 1481, *et seq.*, 1846, class B, pp. 280.

carrying into effect the dispositions of Art. 1 of the Convention concluded between the Crowns of Brazil and Great Britain, on the 23rd of November, 1826," was not "based either upon the letter or the spirit of the said article." The protest pointed out further that the British measure violated "the most clear and positive principles of the Law of Nations" and constituted an infringement "upon the Sovereign Rights and Independence" of Brazil.[13]

While some Brazilians were engaged in protesting against the aggressive and unjustifiable policy of the London government, other Brazilians were setting at defiance both the Aberdeen Law and the abolition law of their own country. If the activities of the first group were unavailing, those of the second were amply rewarded. It is estimated that the importers landed on Brazilian soil from forty-five to sixty thousand Negroes during each of the five years following the passage of the Aberdeen Act.[14]

In spite of the vigorous opposition in Brazil to the Aberdeen Act, the British government resolved to attempt an even sterner policy. Thus, on April 22, 1850, it announced that thenceforth British cruisers would enter Brazilian territorial waters and capture any vessels suspected of illegal conduct. The new order carried feeling to a high tension, the reasons for which are not difficult to fathom. It was announced in the face of determined attempts to bring about the repeal of the indefensible measure that brought it into existence; it led to the seizure of innocent vessels engaged in port to port trade—perhaps enabling British bottoms to profit thereby; it resulted in the stationing of guard ships, upon which cap-

[13] A copy of the "Protest against an act of the British Parliament" was enclosed in a communication of the Brazilian minister at Washington to Secretary Buchanan, Feb. 2, 1846, in Communications from Brazilian Agents, II.

[14] David Tod to Secretary Buchanan, Oct. 16, 1847, and Jan. 1, 1850, in Despatches, XVII.

tives were kept, in the harbor of the capital city, before the eyes of all; it precipitated an occasional exchange of shots between the hated British cruisers and the forts along the coast; and in a few instances its enforcement resulted in the loss of the lives of Brazilian subjects. Little wonder that diplomatic relations approached the breaking point![15]

A break in Anglo-Brazilian relations was averted perhaps by the passage of the Brazilian law of September 4, 1850. This act made the slave trade piracy, required bond of masters and captains trading on the African coast that they would not transport Negroes, and rewarded prize crews with the proceeds of captured vessels.[16] As public sentiment was at first not strongly behind the statute, the imperial government encountered considerable difficulty with its enforcement. In fact, violations were so flagrant that the order to allow British cruisers to seize suspects in Brazilian waters, which had been suspended for a brief time, was restored early in 1851. But shortly after the turn of the century a change in attitude on the part of Brazilians, noted especially in public officials, made possible effective enforcement. Within a few years the trade ceased. Convinced that there would be no resumption, the British parliament repealed the Aberdeen Act in 1869. Whether the severe program of the British or the gradual strengthening of the central government in Brazil was the major influence responsible for suppression of the evil we need not stop to inquire.[17]

The above summary suggests that numerous obstacles

[15] United States Minister Tod to his government, Aug. 1, 1850, in Despatches, XVIII; *Parliamentary Papers*, Slave Trade, 1850, pp. 349 *et seq.*, 1851, class B, pp. 365 *et seq.*

[16] A copy of the law may be found with the United States minister's dispatch from Rio, Sept. 17, 1850, in Despatches, XVIII.

[17] *Parliamentary Papers*, Slave Trade, 1862, class A, p. 48, 1870, class C, p. 4. For the entire subject of the abolition of the Brazilian slave trade see an article by Jane Elizabeth Adams in the October, 1925, number of *The Journal of Negro History*.

made difficult the task of putting an end to the Brazilian
slave trade. To the chief of these obstacles we must now
turn our attention. At the base of the problem was the general fact of the long continuance of the traffic. Following in
the footsteps of their fathers, the Brazilians had begun importations from Africa in the sixteenth century and had continued them for almost three centuries. By the end of the
colonial period there were some two million Negro slaves in
Brazil, a number almost as large as the free population.[18]
As a consequence of the existence of such large numbers of
bondsmen, all the enterprizes of the nation had been built
completely upon slave labor, so much so at least that the
country's future prosperity seemed to depend upon its continuance. Obviously, to break up the trade in Negroes was
equivalent to drying up the source of labor supply. Moreover, it would lead eventually to the destruction of the institution of slavery itself, a fact admitted by British statesmen. No group of people has ever consciously placed in
jeopardy its economic well-being—particularly at the behest
of foreigners—without determined resistance; Brazilian capitalists were to be no exception.

Before continuing with a consideration of the more
specific obstacles to the break-up of the trade it may be well
to allude once more to the means employed for the attainment of the desired end. As already noted, the British policy was first to negotiate treaties with the various nations and
then to enforce these treaties. In order to make effective the
second and more important part of the program, Great Britain stationed cruisers off the coasts of Africa and Brazil for
the purpose of searching suspicious merchant vessels. For

---

[18] Statistics on the free and slave population in Brazil may not be highly accurate.
See A. Cochin in Laylor's *Cyclopedia*, p. 723; United States Minister Hunter to his
government, Jan. 22, 1835, in Despatches, X.

a time, only the vessels which had slaves aboard were captured and hailed before the judicial bodies called mixed commissions; after 1839, however, all ships possessing materials necessary for fitting out temporary slave decks were taken into custody.[19]   Operating usually from the distant Cape Verdes, though sometimes from bases on the dark continent, most of these cruisers patrolled the waters relatively near the West African shore.   The British squadron was small at the beginning, that is, just after the close of the Napoleonic wars; by 1840, it had increased to fourteen ships.[20]   Although various emergencies in widely separated parts of the world occasionally caused removal of some of the cruisers, during the period between 1842 and 1857 an average of nineteen ships, carrying a total of one hundred and forty guns, saw duty in the African service.[21]   And during the same time the British squadron was supplemented at times by small squadrons of the United States and France. Usually consisting of only a few inactive ships, the supplementary forces were agreed to by these two nations as a lesser evil than that of acquiescing in the British proposal of the mutual right of search on the high seas.[22]   To cope with the numerous and varied difficulties which had to be faced these combined naval forces were indeed too weak.

Both the extent and character of the coast lines which had to be guarded presented not the least of the problems for the squadrons.   On the west coast of Africa, where most of the Negroes were loaded for the Atlantic voyage, some three thousand miles required constant scrutiny.   The com-

---

[19] A. H. Foote, *Africa and the American Flag*, pp. 214-215.

[20] W. R. Greg, *Past and Present Efforts for the Extinction of the African Slave Trade*, p. 21.

[21] *Hansard's Parliamentary Debates* (3rd series), LXXXII, 154; *Sen. Ex. Doc.* 49, 35 Cong., 1 sess. (serial 923), pp. 11-16.

[22] Foote, *op. cit.*, pp. 215-216, 232 *et seq.*

manding officer of the American cruiser *Truxton*, writing in March, 1845, gave an accurate picture of the difficulty of capturing a slave trader on this coast when he said:

It is extremely difficult to get up these rivers to the places where the slavers lie. The whole coast is intersected by innumerable rivers, with branches pouring into them from every quarter, and communicating with each other by narrow, circuitous, and very numerous creeks, bordered on each side with impenetrable thickets of mangroves. In these creeks, almost concealed by the trees the vessels lie, and often elude the strictest search.[23]

Thus protected by nature, the crews of the trading vessels unloaded their purchasing materials, laid the temporary slave decks, and placed on board their cargoes. After this was accomplished, the loose blockade was run at an opportune moment, and the floating prisons were on their way to Brazil. If detected by cruisers, the fast-sailing vessels were often able to escape without capture.

Conditions on the east coast of Africa and on the coast of Brazil were even more favorable to the illicit trader. Long reefs paralleling many of the thousands of miles of the latter coast afforded sheltered landing places for the unloading vessels, while on both coasts the cruisers to be eluded were fewer than on the Atlantic side of the dark continent.[24]

The connivance at the trade by both the Portuguese and Brazilian officials also vastly complicated the problem of extinction. It was alleged that the only object of the Portuguese colonial governors in living on the unhealthful African coast was that of amassing a fortune from the trade. At any rate the only problem encountered by the slave traders when dealing with these officials was that related to price.[25]   In

[23] *Ibid.*, p. 241.
[24] *Parliamentary Papers*, Slave Trade, 1850, class B, p. 28.
[25] T. F. Buxton, *The African Slave Trade*, pp. 174 *et seq.*

Brazil likewise the sympathy of officialdom was usually on the side of the trader. Indeed, the slave vessels were frequently fully equipped with the open and avowed assistance of the public authorities. And in the few instances in which arrests were made with a view to prosecution for violation of Brazilian law it was extremely difficult to secure convictions in the courts. Yea, it was mockery to give to the Brazilian tribunals the power of trial, so great was the prestige and influence of the wealthy dealers over both the public and the judges! The influence which the rich traders had in governmental circles is aptly illustrated in the case of Manoel Pinto da Fonseca, who, though the most notorious slave dealer in all Brazil, went about the capital city in pursuit of his occupation entirely unmolested. Fonseca, in fact, was an intimate friend of senators, deputies, and ministers, and upon numerous occasions attended their *élite* social functions as an honored guest. It was not until about 1850, by which time the authority of the central government had been greatly increased, that matters took a turn for improvement.[26]

As already intimated, one of the greatest obstacles encountered by those who labored for the suppression of the nefarious trade was that of the purse. Although the estimates of immediate profits vary considerably, depending upon a variety of circumstances, there is general agreement that they were ample. The Englishman Buxton, who was usually very well informed on the subject of the trade, computed the profits to the dealer as ranging from one hundred to two hundred per cent in 1840. Considered conservative, this estimate was discouraging to many British officials, some of whom maintained that any illicit practice could not be sup-

[26] Communications of United States ministers to the secretary of state, May 25, 1842, Feb. 18, 1845, Oct. 16, 1847, Jan. 8, 1850, in Despatches, XII, XIII, XVII; *Parliamentary Papers*, Slave Trade, 1848, class B, pp. 155-157.

pressed by legislation where the profits exceeded thirty per cent.[27] In 1844, Henry A. Wise of Virginia, then United States minister to Brazil, informed his government that no loss was entailed by the owners when two slavers out of five succeeded in landing their cargoes. A little later the same official, figuring from a slightly different basis, estimated the profits of a trader at from six hundred to twelve hundred per cent.[28]

Although these obstacles were not easy to surmount, the most serious difficulty in the abolition of the traffic was the use made of United States vessels and the flag that they bore. In the early forties President Tyler, in answer to a Senate resolution calling for the circumstances leading to the insertion of the slave trade provisions in the Webster-Ashburton Treaty, called attention to the well-grounded suspicions that a few American vessels were engaged in the traffic to Brazil.[29] The president's information was either incomplete or else the use of American vessels increased very rapidly, for about a year later the United States minister to Brazil wrote his government that

It is a fact not to be disguised or denied, that the slave trade is almost entirely carried on under our flag and in American built vessels sold here, chartered for the coast of Africa to slave traders. Indeed the scandalous traffic could not be carried on to any extent were it not for the use made of our flag, and the facilities given by the chartering of American vessels to carry to the coast of Africa the outfit for the trade and the materials for purchasing slaves.[30]

After mentioning the case of the brig *Hope* as an exemplifi-

---

[27] Buxton, *op. cit.*, pp. 186 *et seq.*

[28] Minister Wise to the secretary of state, Dec. 14, 1844, and May 1, 1845, in Despatches, XIII.

[29] *Sen Ex. Doc.* 52, 27 Cong., 3 sess. (serial 414), pp. 3-4.

[30] Minister Proffitt to his government, Feb. 27, 1844, in Despatches, XII.

cation of the manner in which the United States flag was "used and disgraced by American citizens," the minister proceeded to tell the president that he had "been incorrectly informed as to the efficiency of the American squadron on the coast of Africa in suppressing the slave trade." In the latter connection, he remarked that

the slave traders laugh at our African squadron and more than one trader to the coast has openly avowed that he could sail round the Frigate Macedonian three times in three miles, that they would not care if there were twenty such Frigates on that coast, that they have never yet seen one of the American squadron although they have visited the coast for hundreds of miles and that the only cruisers they meet with are British, and to them they have but to display American colors.[31]

At this point we may inquire how it was possible for the slave dealers to employ American vessels and the Stars and Stripes in the prosecution of their infamous business. The chief explanation is found in the American practice of granting sea-letters to vessels sold in foreign ports by one American citizen to another. Passed as far back as 1792 for the purpose of encouraging shipbuilding, the statute permitting this practice limited neither the duration nor the destination of the voyages made after transfers to new owners. Thus, American citizens in Brazil could purchase ships from their countrymen and apply to United States consuls for permission to make voyages to the African coast. Since orders from Washington made the issuance of sea-letters peremptory, there could be no denial on the part of consular officials, regardless of any suspicions which they may have possessed regarding the nature of the proposed voyages.

Before the vessels acquiring sea-letters left Brazil, they

[31] *Ibid.*

were chartered, ostensibly, by Brazilian slave dealers to take merchandise, and usually "passengers," to the African coast. In case only merchandise, known widely as "coast goods," was on board, the vessels unloaded their cargoes in Africa, reloaded with such African goods and passengers as could be obtained, and returned to Brazil. But in case merchandise and "passengers" both were aboard for the eastern voyages, the procedure upon arrival in Africa was different. In this event the goods were landed, the American crews were replaced by new crews composed of the "passengers" carried over, the names of the vessels were changed by a few strokes of the paint brush, the Stars and Stripes were replaced by the Brazilian emblem, and finally Negroes were rushed onto the improvised slave decks. With these labors completed in the course of a few hours, the vessels sought an opportune moment and put out across the Atlantic to land their live cargoes on the Brazilian coast. On the western voyages the Brazilian slavers usually escaped capture by the British cruisers either because American vessels served as decoys or because the slavers themselves often hoisted the American flag when in danger. The American crews left stranded on the African coast usually found passage back to Brazil on ships of their own nationality, though occasionally they returned on Brazilian slavers rather than subject themselves for long periods to the dangerous fevers infesting the African coast.

It has been suggested that the American vessels securing sea-letters in Brazil were only nominally chartered for the purpose of conveying merchandise and "passengers" to the African coast. In truth, such vessels were usually purchased by the slave dealers with the condition, secured in the form of a charter party, that a part of the purchase price remain unpaid until the ships had made one or more trips to the coast of Africa under their ostensible American character.

After the fulfillment of the condition named in the charter party, the vessels were transferred to the slave dealers, or rather to their agents on the African coast.[32]

Perhaps a summary of the activities of three vessels which participated in the nefarious traffic may serve to supply a few details to the story just told in outline. One of these vessels was the *Agnes*, a United States merchant ship hitherto employed in lawful trade between Rio de Janeiro and Philadelphia. On a visit to the Brazilian capital in 1843 she carried among her papers a letter from her owners instructing her Rio consignees to procure an advantageous charter party for the vessel. As was customary, the consignees employed an English broker named Weetman, of the British firm Nobkirk and Weetman, to negotiate the charter party. According to the document the vessel was leased to Manoel Pinto da Fonseca, whose only business was that of the slave trade, and whose reputation was as notorious as any other fact in the Brazilian capital. The *Agnes* returned to Philadelphia, where the charter party was to begin, took on a cargo, and at the end of October sailed for Liverpool. While in the English city she disposed of her cargo and received a new one consisting of sundry drygoods, powder, muskets, bar and hoop iron, and other articles—all known as "coast goods." About the first of January, 1844, she sailed with this cargo for Rio de Janeiro, consigned to American merchants. As there was no intention of discharging any of her cargo, the vessel entered the Brazilian port in *franquía*. After remaining in Rio two or three days—long

---

[32] This summary is based on a study of hundreds of pages of correspondence between consuls and ministers with their official superiors, and on other documents. See especially President Tyler to Congress, Feb. 20, 1845, in *Messages and Papers of the Presidents*, III, 215-217; Consul Gordon to Buchanan, Sept. 18, 1845, in Consular Letters (Rio), XI; Lord Howden to Viscount Palmerston, Nov. 12, 1847, in *Parliamentary Papers*, Slave Trade, class B, pp. 229-230.

enough to take orders from charterer Fonseca—the *Agnes* cleared for Montevideo. But instead of going to the Uruguayan city she sailed direct for Cabinda, Africa, consigned to one Cunha, a known agent of Fonseca. During her stay of several months on the African coast the cargo of "coast goods" taken in at Liverpool was discharged, part at Cabinda and part on the Congo.

Meanwhile, another American vessel was engaged in similar activities. Toward the close of 1843 the brig *Montevideo* arrived at Rio de Janeiro, consigned to an American house other than that to which the *Agnes* was consigned, with instructions to charter her for the African coast trade. The consignees negotiated the charter party—again through the English broker—with the same notorious Fonseca. It stipulated that the *Montevideo*, in consideration of nine hundred dollars per month, should take in at Rio a cargo for the African coast, the charterer having the privilege of determining the nature of the cargo and of placing on board a certain number of passengers. On February 11, 1844, the vessel sailed for Cabinda with her "coast goods" and Brazilian "passengers." In due time the goods were delivered to Fonseca's agent, the "passengers" were put ashore, and the vessel returned to Victoria, Brazil, where she began preparations for a similar venture.

While the crew of the *Agnes* were fighting the fevers of the African coast, and the *Montevideo* was making her first voyage, a third vessel was playing a complementary part. This vessel, the *Sea-Eagle*, arrived at the Brazilian capital in the late spring or early summer of 1844 and was chartered through the same agents and under the same general terms as the *Montevideo*. In other words she was engaged by Fonseca to deliver merchandise and passengers to the African coast.   In the course of time the *Sea-Eagle*, in fulfillment of the terms of her engagement, was at Cabinda, Africa, where she found the *Agnes* still lying at anchor.   Immediately the announcement was made that a Captain Gray, who had come aboard the *Sea-Eagle* from Philadelphia, had sold the *Agnes* to Cunha.   Shortly after the transfer the *Agnes*, her temporary slave decks—devised from iron pipes, pieces of wood, and rush mats—jammed with over five hundred Negroes, and her American flag and papers replaced by those of Brazilian character, set sail for Brazil under the management of a crew composed of the "passengers" taken over by the *Sea-Eagle* and *Montevideo*.   A few weeks later she landed her live cargo on the Brazilian coast near Cape Frio.

Meanwhile, the *Montevideo*—which our story left at Victoria, Brazil—was assembling another cargo and sailing for Africa on a second voyage.   Upon arrival at Cabinda this time, both ship and cargo were delivered to Cunha, who, after transferring the American crew to the *Sea-Eagle*, and changing her flag, papers, and name, loaded the *Montevideo* with eight hundred slaves and started her on a return voyage in charge of a Brazilian crew whom she took over as "passengers."   The *Sea-Eagle*, which it will be recalled carried to Africa the Brazilian crew for the *Agnes*, likewise began her return voyage, though instead of having slaves aboard had the American crews of both the *Montevideo* and the *Agnes* —that is those who had escaped death—and a small quantity of African merchandise.

Ostensibly, both the *Agnes* and the *Montevideo* were sold on the African coast.   As a matter of fact, both vessels were sold before departure from Brazil, the charter parties making possible delivery on the African coast.   In the case of the *Sea-Eagle*, the bargain was also made in Brazil, though the charter party may have been genuine rather than complementary to a sale.[33]

The procedure of the slave importers in making the American flag serve their purposes was often more complex than that just described; indeed, it was such at times as to baffle every attempt at tracing, even by those expert at the task. Part of the complexity resulted from the fact that vessels bound for Africa cleared for all parts of the world— islands in the south Atlantic and Indian oceans, ports in Asia, Europe, and the United States—and part from the existence of two sets of papers for each vessel. However complex the procedure, the American flag protected practically all the materials used in the purchase and transportation of the Negroes to the New World. But it not only protected the materials until the moment before the Negroes were placed on board the transporting ships; it always gave indirect, and frequently direct, protection to the live cargoes themselves. Furthermore, American citizens, in the capacity of agents, captains, masters, or crews, must share with the subjects of other nations in the responsibility for the prostitution of their country's escutcheon.

At this point it may not be out of place to interject the remarks of two American ministers to Brazil, both of whom had unusual opportunities to view the various phases of the entire subject of the trade. Stimulated by recently conducted investigations, Henry A. Wise wrote these sentences in a dispatch to his government on February 18, 1845:

I beseech—I implore the President of the United States to take a decided stand on this subject. You have no conception of the bold

[33] The facts detailed in these cases are found in the depositions of the American masters and crews taken at Rio de Janeiro by United States representatives. See Gordon to Secretary Calhoun, Dec., 1844, and Jan., 1845, in Consular Letters (Rio), VII, VIII, and IX; see also a communication from Minister Wise, Dec. 14, 1844, in Despatches, XIII.

effrontery and the flagrant outrages of the African slave trade, and of the shameless manner in which its worst crimes are licensed here. And every patriot in our land would blush for our country, did he know and see as I do, how our own citizens sail and sell our flag to the uses and abuses of that accursed traffic in almost open violation of our laws. We are a "bye word among nations"—the only people who can now fetch and carry any and every thing for the slave trade, without fear of English cruisers; and because we are the only people who can, are we to allow our proudest privilege to be perverted, and to pervert our own glorious flag into the pirate's flag— the slaver's protection—the Brazilian and Portuguese and Spanish passport to a criminal commerce against our own laws and the municipal laws of almost every civilized nation upon earth? . . . Our flag alone gives the requisite protection against the right of visit, search, and seizure; and our citizens, in all the characters of owners, of consignees, of agents and of masters and crews of our vessels, are concerned in the business and partake of the profits of the African slave trade, to and from the ports of Brazil, as fully as the Brazilians themselves and others, in conjunction with whom they carry it on. In fact, without the aid of our citizens and our flag it could not be carried on with success at all. They furnish the protection; they are the commerce carriers; they sail over and deliver up to the trade, vessels as well as cargoes; they transport the supplies of slave factories, the food and raiment of the slave trade's agents, and the goods which constitute the purchase money of the slave trade's victims; they carry the arms and the ardent spirits which are the hellish agents and instruments of the savage wars of African captivity; they afford safe passage to Brazilian masters and crews intended for the slave vessels when sold, and for the American masters and crews who have manned these vessels over to the Coast; and they realize a profit in proportion to the risks of a contraband trade. In one word, the sacred principle of the inviolability of the protection of our flag, is perverted in the ports of Brazil into a perfect monopoly of the unhallowed gains of the navigation of the African slave trade. And for the reason of this inviolability, our flag, and vessels are sought and bought, and our citizens at home and here, sail them and sell them in the African slave trade to and from all the ports of Brazil. And in all those ports, and in this the metropolitan port of Rio de Janeiro, especially, our vessels are fitted out for the slave trade, and the most of the crimes of that trade, in violation of the laws of the United States, openly have their inception under the very eye of the Imperial Government; and in them all, and in this port, especially, the consummation of those crimes is sheltered, as of right, by the sovereign jurisdiction of this Empire.[34]

Equally as illuminating were the remarks of David Tod made five years later:

Citizens of the United States are constantly in this capital [Rio], whose only occupation is the buying of American vessels with which to supply the slave importers. These men obtain sea-letters, which entitle them to continue in use the United States flag, and it is this privilege which enables them to sell their vessels to the slave traders, deliverable on the coast of Africa at double, and sometimes more than double, the price for which they were purchased on the preceding day. The vessels take over slave goods and slave crews, under the protection of our flag, and remain nominally American property until a favorable opportunity occurs for receiving a cargo of slaves; and it is not infrequently the case that our flag covers the slaves until the Africans are landed upon the coast of Brazil.[35]

Data assembled by our consular staffs in Brazil seem to substantiate these accounts. During the five year period ending in 1845 sixty-four American vessels were sold in Rio de Janeiro alone. That most of these were employed in the slave trade can be little doubted. Furthermore, during the same period fifty-six American ships left the Brazilian capital for, and forty arrived from, Africa. Inasmuch as there was almost no legitimate commerce between Brazil and the

[34] Wise to the U. S. Government, Feb. 18, 1845, in Despatches, XIII.
[35] Minister Tod to the secretary of state, Jan. 8, 1850, in Despatches, XVII.

dark continent, these figures also are significant.[36] The figures for other Brazilian ports run high, particularly in the case of Bahia, but are much smaller than those for the capital. It would be futile to attempt even an estimate of the number of American citizens who served in one capacity or another connected with the trade; it is sufficient to say that it falls in the thousands. It is certain, however, that through the aid of the Yankees and of their flag several hundred thousand Negroes were transported from Africa to Brazil between 1835 and 1853.[37]

From the extent of American participation in the slave trade we may digress to consider its cruelty. In a debate in the British parliament in 1844 Robert Peel branded it as "the most iniquitous traffic that was ever carried on; that it ingenders more misery—that it stimulates more crime—than any public act every committed by any nation, however regardless of the laws of God and man." In the same discussion Palmerston used still stronger language when he said "I will venture to say that, if all the other crimes which the human race has committed from the creation down to the present day were added together in one vast aggregate, they would scarcely equal, I am sure they could not exceed, the amount of guilt which has been incurred by mankind in connection with this diabolical slave trade."[38]

The horrors of the trade did not begin with the trip across the Atlantic, but with the exterminating wars waged by tribal leaders in the African interior for the purpose of securing captives for prospective buyers. While there are no records to reveal the number of victims sacrificed in such conflicts, Lord John Russell estimated it as greater than the

[36] Consul Gordon to Buchanan, Sept. 18, 1845, in Consular Letters, XI.

[37] Many of the consular reports substantiate these estimates. See for example the last citation.

[38] *Hansard's Parliamentary Debates*, LXXVI, 930, 946.

number actually landed in the importing countries. Of the number captured in the interior, the calculation was that one-third perished in the overland journey to the coast, another third in the barracoons—where they were collected for transportation—and on the voyage, and only the remaining third lived to become plantation laborers.[39] Concerning the nature of the hardships which took such heavy toll on the overland journey practically nothing is known except that the victims were driven along under crushing loads of ivory and other products of the hinterland. Upon reaching the coast the beasts of burden were branded on their shoulders or breasts with hot irons for identification purposes and then confined in barracoons—wooden corrals or stockades constructed of upright timbers set in the ground and fastened together at the top—where disease wrought further havoc with their already decimated numbers.[40]

Although the mortality on the voyage across the Atlantic was estimated as lower than that on the overland journey, available materials give us a much more vivid picture of the water journey. This picture of a real situation is not surpassed in its horrors, if indeed it is equalled, by the imagination of an Edgar Allan Poe. One might suppose that self-interest would have encouraged the importers to take every precaution against methods that resulted in deterioration and partial loss of cargo. Unfortunately, the principle seemed to operate in a reverse manner. As a consequence, the slaves, chained in pairs with rivetted fetters, were packed in the transporting vessels like sardines in a tin. Furthermore, after the small, swift ships—the American-built clippers among them—were brought into use, many of the Negroes

[39] *Ibid.*, LXXXI, 1162.
[40] See Consul Gordon to the State Department, in Consular Letters (Rio), IX; Greg, *op. cit.*, pp. 7-8.

were crammed on to temporarily constructed platforms with insufficient overhead space for upright sitting. It is little wonder that the survivors of a thirty or forty day voyage were landed with their bodies in every conceivable state of distortion!

Among the numerous agonies in addition to those consequent upon overcrowding was that of thirst. Owing to the scarcity of the water supply each slave was sometimes allowed less than a pint a day, a quantity obviously insufficient under normal circumstances but almost negligible in the case of victims afflicted with burning fevers. Scarcely less was the suffering from want of fresh air, especially when it became necessary to keep the ships' hatches closed for hours because of squally weather. A visitor to a prize on its arrival at Sierra Leone saw the slaves "in a profuse state of perspiration and panting like so many hounds for air and water." The captors of another prize described the "headlong eagerness" of the Negroes when offered water in these words: "their heads became wedged in the tub and were with some difficulty got out; they madly bit the vessels with their teeth and champed them into atoms."[41]

The absence of fresh air and failure to observe ordinary rules of sanitation made conditions on all the slavers bad enough; but an accumulation of filth and afflictions of dysentery, fevers, and smallpox made conditions on some vessels terrible. Once more it may be well to admit the testimony of eyewitnesses. Captain Bell of the American cruiser *Yorktown* vividly described conditions on the *Pons*, which he had captured off the southwest coast of Africa while flying the Stars and Stripes:

[41] Quoted in W. L. Mathieson, *Great Britain and the Slave Trade*, p. 41. See also Minister Tod's letter to the American government, Oct. 16, 1847, in Despatches, XVII.

The stench from below was so great that it was impossible to stand more than a few minutes near the hatchways. Our men who went below from curiosity, were forced up sick in a few minutes; then all the hatches were off. What must have been the sufferings of those poor wretches, when the hatches were closed! I am informed that very often in these cases, the stronger will strangle the weaker; and this was probably the reason why so many died, or rather were found dead the morning after the capture. None but an eye witness can form a conception of the horrors these poor creatures must endure in their transit across the ocean.[42]

A fortnight later the *Pons*, her cargo further decimated through the death of a hundred and fifty captives, was delivered to the missionaries at Monrovia, Liberia. Upon her arrival the superintendent of missions, Reverend J. B. Benham, paid the captive a visit. In a letter to one of his brethren in America a few days later he described in these words what he had seen the preceding Sunday:

Such was the stench that we remained but a few minutes on board. Long enough, however, to see something of the indescribable horrors of the abominable African slave trade! It was supposed that a thermometer would range at 100 or 120 in the hole [hold]. Tho I did not go down, I saw that with few exceptions they were in a state of entire nudity. Several were in a dying condition and many others were so emaciated that their skin literally cleaved to their bones. Others again had worn their skin thro' producing putrid ulcers, which fed swarms of flies.[43]

It is interesting to note that the horrible effluvium of the slavers was often a means of detection. By navigating to the leeward it was impossible for the naval officers to err, even though the distance was several miles.[44] Some intimation

[42] Quoted in Foote, *Africa and the American Flag*, pp. 242-246.

[43] Rev. J. B. Benham, to "Dear Brother Burns," Dec. 17, 1845, in Wise's dispatch of March 6, 1846, in Despatches, XV.

[44] *Hansard's Parliamentary Debates*, CLXI, 952.

regarding the condition of the importing vessels is gained from the fact that upon arrival in Brazil they were often abandoned because of the great expense and labor involved in cleaning them for new ventures.

This phase of the subject may be concluded by allusion to two of the most horrible cases on record. In the first case five hundred slaves who had been crammed into the hold of a small vessel mutinied at sea. A Mr. Page, an Englishman aboard the vessel, described the method of subduing the rebellious in these words:

Some eight or ten of them were shot, with small shot, in the hold of the brig before they could be subdued. Some 30 or 40 of them were then brought on deck and two and two in irons, were hung up at the yard-arm, shot, their bodies let down, and then their arms and legs chopped off to get the irons off the corpses, and one woman was thrown into the sea before life was extinct.[45]

In the second case a slaver that was being pursued by a cruiser was set on fire before abandonment by her officers and her one thousand black passengers were burned alive.[46] While this is an extreme case, there are others in which from eighty to five hundred were thrown overboard in order to avoid conviction. Perhaps the author of *Moby Dick* is not far wrong when he tells us that "Sharks are the invariable out-riders of all slave-ships crossing the Atlantic, systematically trotting alongside to be handy in case a parcel is to be carried anywhere or a dead slave to be decently buried."[47] It does appear, however, that the sharks were not always so discriminating, for eyewitnesses say they also devoured live jettisons.

Finally, we may consider the attitude of the American

---

[45] Minister Wise to the American government, May 1, 1845, in Despatches, XIII.
[46] Wise's communication of Nov. 24, 1845, in *ibid.*, XIV.
[47] Herman Melville, *Moby Dick*, Chap. LXII.

government toward the Brazilian trade and then seek an explanation of this attitude. At the outset it may be admitted that the inquiry into these topics will fail to yield totally satisfactory results. In connection with the attitude toward the traffic it is well to remember that Congress had prohibited the importation of Negroes into the United States after 1808 and twelve years later had made participation in the trade on the part of American citizens piracy. The justice and wisdom of these laws was acknowledged by all classes regardless of locality. Nevertheless, down to the outbreak of the Civil War hundreds of American citizens participated in the trade, most of them practically without danger of governmental molestation. What was worse, they practiced their foul deeds enshrouded as it were in the Stars and Stripes. Perhaps this may be partial explanation for the readiness of most Americans to resent an insult to their country's escutcheon by a foreign foe!

Failure to prevent American participation in the slave trade may be accounted for in two ways, namely, non-enforcement of laws already on the statute books and unwillingness to enact and enforce other laws. In the former case responsibility obviously rested with the executive and judicial branches of government; in the latter, it rested largely with the legislature. But it may be of interest to go further in an attempt to allocate this responsibility, particularly in the matter of non-enforcement. By way of elimination, our official representatives to Brazil should be absolved from all blame. Ministers Proffitt, Wise, Tod, and Schenck, whose terms cover the period of most flagrant violation, kept their superiors supplied with detailed and accurate information on all phases of the traffic. No less diligent were the American consuls, who labored long and arduously in taking depositions and in assembling other pertinent information on the trade.[48]

Unfortunately, the executive agents at home were not quite as enthusiastic as those in Brazil. Nor is this surprising, for their duties were multifarious, and the iniquities of the African trade did not come directly before their eyes. Nevertheless, the chief executives themselves seem to have given considerable attention to the performance of the duties which devolved upon them in this connection. At any rate, during the decade between 1839 and 1849, the most active period of American participation in the evil, Van Buren, Tyler, and Taylor resorted to the presidential message to inform Congress of the true status of the subject and made positive recommendations for measures calculated to remedy the glaring abuses.[49] But this apparent enthusiasm was not shared by all whose positions came under the supervision of the executive branch of government. The secretaries of state all but ignored the desperate appeals of our ministers and consuls for counsel and advice on matters pertaining to their offices. Writing from Rio de Janeiro in 1845, Consul Gordon complained because he had received only four replies to his thirty-three letters on the subject of the slave trade; and more significant was Minister Tod's acknowledgment—no doubt in a sarcastic vein—five years later of receipt of his *first* instruction in answer to dozens of his dispatches on the same subject. When an occasional dispatch did find its way out of the foreign office, the information it contained was usually fragmentary and evasive. In an exceptional case, however, the content of an instruction was both full and ex-

[48] For typical communications see dispatches of Feb. 27 and Dec. 14, 1844, Jan. 8, 1850, and Apr. 26, 1852, in Despatches, XII, XIII, XVII, and XIX; also consular report of Sept. 18, 1845, in Consular Letters (Rio), XI.

[49] Richardson, *Messages and Papers*, III, 1755, 1836-37, 1903, 1930-31, 2215-17, IV, 2553.

plicit. It was when the American minister to Brazil was directed to reverse his policy of refusing to permit the granting of sea-letters to vessels whose destinations were obviously the African coast. While grounded on both precedent and legality, this instruction encouraged the illegal use of the American flag.[50] It is interesting to note that there was little or no variation in policy whether the Department of State was directed by Daniel Webster, James Buchanan, John C. Calhoun, or John M. Clayton—at least so far as the instructions reveal.

It is doubtful whether the policy pursued by the Department of the Navy was more conducive to the enforcement of American statutes. Impressed with the fact that large cruisers were not of the slightest practical utility for running behind islands and into creeks, coves, and inlets of the Brazilian coast, where the slave vessels went to take in supplies, to land their live cargoes, and to escape observation or pursuit, our consuls and ministers unanimously recommended that they be replaced by vessels of a lighter class.[51] But for some reason the "floating palaces" of the commodores, as the large cruisers were called, remained in service, to the great delight of illicit traders, and probably naval commanders.

If considerable responsibility for failure to enforce old statutes should be attached to the executive branch of government, even more should be attached to Congress for refusal to enact a new one. The *sine qua non* for putting an end to American participation in the African traffic was a law prohibiting the granting of sea-letters, except for voyages home, to American vessels sold in foreign ports. Such a law,

---

[50] Apparently no copy of this instruction was preserved. That the instruction was sent there can be no doubt. For reference to it see David Tod to Secretary Clayton, Jan. 8, 1850, in Despatches, XVII.

[51] For a typical recommendation see Schenck to Webster, Apr. 26, 1852, in Despatches, XIX.

with proper enforcement, would have prevented American crews from delivering slave vessels and "coast goods" to Africa and the employment of the American flag to protect the live cargoes on the western voyages. But notwithstanding the urgent appeals of all our Brazilian agents, and the numerous recommendations of the chief executives, Congress refused to give serious consideration to any effective measure.[52]

The American judiciary also had to take cognizance of the slave trade. As a result of the exertions of American representatives to Brazil, vast quantities of material implicating many persons reached the district attorneys of the Atlantic coast states. Although there were several convictions for violating the laws against the trade, the verdicts were more often for acquittal. When unfavorable verdicts were returned, the penalties were seldom severe. The fact that the first death penalty for violation of the piracy act came forty-one years after its passage is very significant. The laxity, however, is easily explained: the crime had its inception in a distant land and a conviction was in great measure dependent upon a chain of circumstantial evidence and an intimate familiarity with the mode of conducting the trade which could be obtainable only on the spot where the offense originated. As a consequence, it is not surprising to learn that a Captain Hiram Gray, commander of the noted slaver *Agnes*, was acquitted in the district court at Baltimore for lack of evidence. Although usually very diligent in attending to his duties, in this case Consul Gordon had failed to take some necessary depositions at Rio de Janeiro.[53] On the other

[52] Typical appeals of American ministers may be found in communications of Tod and Schenck, Jan. 8, 1850, and Apr. 26, 1852, in *ibid.*, XVII and XIX. The recommendations of the presidents have already been noted.

[53] Baltimore *Sun*, Sept. 3 and 4, 1845; Wise to Buchanan, Nov. 24, 1845, in Despatches, XIV.

hand, the captain and first mate of the brig *Montevideo*, another well-known slaver, were convicted of a misdemeanor by the same court. The captain drew twelve months imprisonment and a fine of $1,000, while the mate drew six months in prison and a fine of $500.[54] The district court at New York, in 1850, sentenced to the penitentiary for two years the mate of the *Martha*, a slaver captured off the African coast by the American brig *Perry*. Unfortunately, the *Martha's* captain, whose bail had been reduced from $5,000 to $3,000, escaped conviction by jumping bond.[55]

If American Minister Wise had had his way, the courts would have had more cases to adjudicate. Knowing that trial in the Brazilian courts was a travesty on justice, on one occasion he requested the Brazilian foreign minister to secure the arrest of four persons on board the notorious *Porpoise* so that they could be sent home for trial. While waiting for a reply, Wise, accompanied by the American consul, went on board the slaver to conduct a personal inquiry. Convinced that there was guilt in several cases, an American guard was placed on the vessel with orders not to permit the escape of any person. Unfortunately, the strict orders prevented Brazilians as well as Americans from going ashore. As a result, a wave of excitement seized the city populace that led to a demand for the release of the Brazilians. To avoid complications Wise was forced to yield. Encouraged by victory in the first diplomatic encounter, the Brazilian ministers of state and justice next insisted on the release of the American prisoners and the vessel as a condition precedent to deciding the question of extradition. Partly because of the stand taken by the American commodore stationed in Brazilian waters, Wise was finally persuaded to yield his position a

[54] *Parliamentary Papers*, Slave Trade, 1846, class D, pp. 132-33.
[55] Foote, *op. cit.*, pp. 287-90.

second time.   It is useless to state that the request for extradition was not granted.   The only compensation the American minister got for his dogged persistence was a strong rebuke from his government for going beyond instructions to advocate a principle which the United States had invariably opposed.[56]

Considered geographically, it is not so difficult to locate responsibility for American participation in the Brazilian trade.   Most of the vessels intended for sale to Brazilian slave dealers were built in New York, Providence, Beverly, Boston, Salem, and Portland, though some were launched as far south as Philadelphia and Baltimore.   The capitalists, along with others, knew very well the uses which these vessels were to serve.   The vessels were, in fact, built specifically for the traffic, and sold deliverable to the African coast. They were responsible for the abuse of the American flag, the emblem which afforded protection not only to the time of sale to the slave kings but often long thereafter.   The officers and crews who navigated these slavers to the African coast and who often became directly involved in the trade were naturally from the ship-building centers.   In defense of the crews, some of whose representatives were arraigned before American tribunals, it may be said that they were usually employed unaware of the illegality implicated in their engagements.   As usual in such cases, technicalities of the laws gave adequate protection to those most responsible for their violation.[57]

It is interesting to observe that the section of the United States which gave greatest support to abolition also gave

---

[56] For the entire controversy over extradition see Wise to Buchanan, Feb. 18, 1845, in Despatches, XIII. See also Instructions to Brazilian Ministers, XV, 119-125.

[57] On this general topic consult communications of Proffitt, Feb. 27, 1844, Wise, March 6, 1846, and Tod, March 18, 1850, in Despatches, XII, XV, and XVII, respectively.

greatest encouragement to the foreign slave trade.   Furthermore, the support accorded these apparently antagonistic
movements was at floodtide at about the same time.   While
it would be unreasonable to believe that many individuals
gave support to the contrary movements, at least at the same
time, a citizen of Maine earned for himself that reputation.
The owner of the Bangor *Gazette* preached abolition in the
columns of his paper at the same time he was engaged in
building ships which he knew were to be used in the illicit
trade.   The lucrative business of shipbuilding may account
for the New Englander's hypocrisy.[58]

A partial explanation—not a justification—of the American government's attitude toward the slave trade is found in
the disagreements of Washington and London officials over
a common policy for suppression.   Following close upon
separate movements in the two countries which resulted in
the abolition acts of 1807, the common program bore its first
fruit in the Treaty of Ghent, article ten of which obligated
the Anglo-Saxon powers to use their best endeavors to put
an end to the traffic.[59]   Apparently Great Britain was the
more aggressive in carrying out her obligation; at any rate
within a short time she had entered into treaties with several
of the continental nations looking toward extermination of
the trade.   These treaties, as already noted, provided for the
mutual right of search and for trial of all captures before
mixed tribunals.   Not content to confine her attempts to the
Old World, however, Great Britain soon approached the
United States to enter into a treaty providing for a similar
arrangement.   President Monroe objected to both the right
of search for non-piratical offenses and to trial of cases by
mixed tribunals, and suggested a counter proposal, the essen-

[58] Wise to Buchanan, Mar. 6, 1846, in *ibid.*, XV.
[59] William M. Malloy, *Treaties and Conventions*, I, 618.

tial feature of which was a provision to make the trade piracy. On March 13, 1824, after several months of discussion, a convention was signed. A compromise measure, the document not only declared the slave trade piracy, but it authorized the naval officers of the signatories "to cruize on the coasts of Africa, of America, and of the West Indies," the captures to be taken before the courts of the nation to which the vessels belonged. Notwithstanding his opposition to the principle of right of search, President Monroe urged the ratification of this convention. He professed to believe that the limited right of search granted would not be abused. But when the document came before the United States Senate, it encountered strong opposition, the attacks centering on the clause extending the right of search to the coast "of America." Although ratification was finally achieved, it came only after the attachment of several conditions and reservations. Great Britain rejected the convention as amended by the American Senate. Other proposals brought the two nations no nearer agreement. The right of search was invariably the insuperable difficulty.[60]

Inasmuch as the smoke of the War of 1812 had hardly cleared away, it is not surprising that the American nation under the administration of James Monroe and John Quincy Adams refused to acquiesce in any proposals which gave countenance to the principle of the right of search. Whether surprising or not, the same policy was continued up until the outbreak of the Civil War in the United States. Adherence to this policy is partial explanation of the refusal of the United States to become a party to the Franco-British treaty on the same subject a few years later. Nor was there devia-

---

[60] On the convention of 1824 see *American State Papers*, V, 360-362; *Parliamentary Papers*, Slave Trade, 1832, class B, p. 246; Richardson, *Messages and Papers*, II, 812-826.

tion from the same program in the negotiation of the Web-ster-Ashburton Treaty, the eighth and ninth articles of which pledged the signatories to maintain squadrons on the African coast adequate to carry no less than eighty guns for the sup-pression of the trade and to remonstrate against the contin-uance of slave markets wherever they still existed. It is true, however, that Lewis Cass, our minister to France, resigned his post and returned home in disgust because his govern-ment had failed to make fullest use of its opportunities in securing renunciation of the right of search by Great Britain during negotiations. Although Cass may have been sincere in his protest, there is little evidence that his government in-tended yielding its cherished principle.[61]

Whether Great Britain was actually making use of slave-trade suppression propaganda in order to get acceptance of her old principle of the right of search need not concern us here. In any event it was unfortunate that the principle lay at the heart of her proposals, for it made agreement on a common program impossible.

Equally as important in determining the attitude of the Washington government toward the trade was the rivalry of the United States and Great Britain growing out of attempts of each to secure a dominant position in Latin-American af-fairs. Beginning during the struggle of Latin America for independence, and becoming keen before the middle of the nineteenth century, this rivalry expressed itself in Texas, in Mexico, in Central America, and in South America.[62] No-

[61] Richardson, *Messages and Papers*, III, 1930-1931, 2068-2073; *Sen. Ex. Doc.* 1, 27 Cong., 3 sess. (serial 413), pp. 31-32, 107-110; *Sen. Ex. Doc.* 223, 27 Cong., 3 sess. (serial 416).

Since the completion of this chapter an article entitled "The British Right of Search and the African Slave Trade" by R. W. Van Alstyne has appeared in *The Journal of Modern History*, II, No. 1. It has not altered the conclusions in the present work.

[62] For the general topic of Anglo-American rivalry in Latin America see J. Fred Rippy, *Rivalry of the United States and Great Britain over Latin America (1808-*

where on the continent of South America perhaps did the rivalry express itself more fully than in Brazil. And in Brazil the clearest manifestation of the spirit was in the contest for the abolition of the slave trade. The United States government was not particularly anxious to coöperate in carrying out a program which British statesmen admitted had for its ultimate goal the extinction of the institution of slavery, and which at the same time seemed likely to enhance generally the power and prestige of its greatest rival in the Western Hemisphere.

That differences of viewpoint on the maritime principle of the right of search and rivalry resulting from attempts to establish national policies in Brazil affected the plan for the break-up of the slave trade there can be no reasonable doubt; that these factors determined in large measure the attitude of the American government toward the plan is quite probable. Furthermore, agitation over these dual factors caused many Americans to question both the motives and the methods of the British government in endeavoring to carry through its program. Some critics claimed that the British were more interested in securing for British merchants a monopoly of the African trade than in the welfare of the Negroes. This was the explanation for refusal to destroy the factories along the African coast where all the supplies used in the purchase and transportation of the slaves were stored, for the destruction of such stations meant the destruction of markets for English goods; it was the explanation of the numerous treaties, which were largely of a commercial nature, negotiated by the London government with the African chiefs; it supported the allegation that the British cruisers more fre-

1830). The same author also has an excellent article on the rivalry of these powers in Mexico entitled "Britain's Rôle in the Early Relations of the United States and Mexico," in *The Hispanic American Historical Review*, VII, No. 1, pp. 2-24.

quently made prizes of the slavers after the Negroes had been taken on board than before. Other critics attacked the British practice which permitted the Negroes liberated by the courts to be bound out to British planters in Guiana and the West Indies for periods of three to seven years. It was hard to see how this system of apprenticeship, which was occasionally extended to three consecutive terms, differed from outright slavery. Unfortunately, British policy encountered grave criticism at home also.[63]

Whether these criticisms of British policy were well founded will have to be determined by further research. But whether based on fact or myth they furnished some support for American policy. Together with the controversies over the right of search and the establishment of national policies in Brazil they determined American policy on the slave trade.

The question of the effect of the slave trade on American policy in Brazil lies largely in the field of speculation. Nevertheless, it is safe to say that this policy did not suffer more than the policy of Great Britain, its rival. It seems probable that there was a distinct net gain in favor of the former. The spoils, therefore, did not go to the victor.

[63] For much material on this topic see T. F. Buxton, *The African Slave Trade*, pp. 228 *et seq.*; Greg, *op. cit.*, pp. 10-15; American ministers to their government, Apr. 29, 1839, Jan. 7 and Dec. 14, 1844, Sept. 29, 1846, and Aug. 1, 1852, in Despatches, XI, XII, XIII, XV, XVIII.

CHAPTER VI

THE DIPLOMACY OF TWO NEW YORKERS

DURING William H. Seward's incumbency as secretary of state the United States was represented in Brazil by General James Watson Webb. An inhabitant of Tarrytown, Webb was appointed in consequence of a long and intimate friendship with Seward in New York state politics. No doubt the new envoy felt that his reward had been well earned; he had as editor—first of the New York *Morning Courier* and then of the *Courier and Enquirer*—supported Seward in both his state and his national ambitions. And while backing Seward he had also championed the cause of whiggery and republicanism in general. In fact, the editor laid claim to responsibility for having suggested the name "Whig" for the political opponents of Andrew Jackson—despite the fact that he had advocated his old commander's election in 1828—as well as for having played a conspicuous part in the formation of the Republican party. As a reward for service in the national campaign of 1848, he had received from Taylor the commission of "General" and the appointment as minister to Austria.[1]

General Webb accepted the Brazilian post on June 3, 1861, following his refusal to be "exiled" to Turkey on an inadequate salary.[2] The necessity for going via England to

---

[1] On Webb's career before appointment to the Brazilian mission consult General James Watson Webb, *General J[ames] Watson Webb, Late U. S. Envoy Extraordinary to Brazil*; James Watson Webb, *A Letter from His Excellency, J. Watson Webb, U. S. Envoy Extraordinary and Minister Plenipotentiary in Brazil, to J. Bramley Moore*; James Watson Webb, *Reminiscences of General Samuel B. Webb, of the Revolutionary Army*; Webb to Seward, March 9, 1864, in Despatches, XXX.

[2] Webb to Secretary Seward, June 3, 1861, in Despatches, XXVII.

secure desirable transportation accommodations postponed his arrival at Rio de Janeiro until October 4, and an argument over the content of the presentation speech delayed assumption of duties three weeks more.   This argument, which developed until it assumed the proportions of a controversy, was the result of Webb's insistence on replying to remarks made by R. K. Meade, his predecessor and pro-Southern sympathizer.   En route to Brazil Webb had an interview with Meade in London and learned that the ex-minister had discharged faithfully "his whole duty to the Union," notwithstanding his personal sympathy for the southern cause. But from the captain and officers of the *Tyne*, the steamer which took Meade to England and carried the new minister to Rio on her return trip, he learned that Meade had denounced the Lincoln government, had justified the rebellion of the Southern states, and on several occasions had "made proclamation that he and every true son of Virginia would sooner witness the return of that state to the colonial position it occupied before the Revolution than consent to its ever going back into the American Union."   Soon after arrival at the Brazilian capital Webb was told by Chargé Blackford, who had been secretary of the American legation under Meade and was to retain the same office under Webb, that Meade in his parting interview with the emperor had expressed sympathy for the Southern cause and predicted the continuance of the war in the United States for twenty years. This information on the conduct and attitude of the retiring minister was too much for the impetuous general.   He must as soon as possible reply to the remarks of the "secessionist and traitor" and attempt to show that he himself "represented a *Nationality*, willing and abundantly able to protect itself and to compel the respect of foreign powers."[3]

[3] Webb to Seward, Oct. 24, 1861, in *ibid.*, XXVII.

Webb decided that the occasion of his official presentation to the emperor would afford him his first opportunity. Accordingly, in the address which he prepared for delivery on that auspicious occasion he incorporated statements intended as replies to the remarks of his predecessor. For example, he undertook to refute the statement in Meade's presentation speech that the common institution of slavery was fixed and deeply rooted in the soil of the two countries and that this fact established "an affinity between them" and insured "for mutual defence a unity of action and feeling that" would "prove invincible in the future."[4] Webb insisted that the affinity between the United States and Brazil was not because of the institution of slavery, for, said he, slavery was not a national institution in the northern republic but the creature of local law. To Meade's assertion—made at the time of his official leave-taking—that the United States was engaged in a civil war that would last twenty years, Webb replied that the conflict was not a civil war but only a rebellion which would be entirely crushed by the approach of the following spring.

We are not concerned with the degree of accuracy represented in these statements and counter statements; obviously the remarks represented divergent viewpoints which had come about partly as a result of time and changed conditions. We are interested, however, in Webb's insistence on replying to his predecessor regardless of the fact that the Brazilian foreign minister had informed him that any reference to slavery would be embarrassing to the emperor, particularly on the occasion of a full court. Suffice it to say that this insistence was of no avail. The Brazilian government was equally insistent on its position, and after a long argument the New Yorker consented to omit the objectionable portion

[4] Meade to his government, Dec. 14, 1857, in *ibid.*, XXV.

of his address—everything from the third to the final paragraph—with the understanding that this portion might be presented in a private audience with the emperor. The formal presentation took place on October 21, but a few days later the Brazilian government again called on Webb to change the wording of the version of his speech which was submitted for public print. One naturally wonders what effect this persistence may have had on the general's long mission.[5]

Webb reported to Seward that he finally yielded on the content of the presentation address because he wished to take up with the Brazilian government the question of its attitude toward the Civil War in the United States. In view of the fact that the Brazilian emperor, following the European nations, had on August 1, 1861, announced a neutrality proclamation,[6] it appears that there should have been little occasion for discussion. As a matter of fact, the American government was indisposed at times to recognize Brazil's status as a neutral, while at other times differences arose as to the obligations and privileges of a neutral.

Five weeks subsequent to the neutrality decree the *Sumter*, one of Jefferson Davis' privateers, entered the port of Maranhão, where the governor of the province allowed her to take on a supply of coal and provisions over the protest of the American consul.[7] Webb was not disposed to wait for instructions to guide his procedure in dealing with this episode. Relying upon his professed knowledge of international law, as well as upon his convictions as to the course his government would desire to follow, he arranged for a per-

[5] In addition to the dispatches cited above see that of November 8, 1861, in *ibid.*, XXVII.

[6] Pereira Pinto, *Apontamentos para o Direito Internacional*, II, 401-402.

[7] American consul at Maranhão to the secretary of state, Sept. 15, 1861, in Consular Letters (Maranhão), II.

sonal interview with the Brazilian foreign minister. At this meeting, which occurred on the last day of October, the Brazilian took the position that his country's neutrality had not been violated by the treatment accorded the *Sumter*, inasmuch as the vessel was a "man of war." To this position Webb's reaction is best set forth in his own words: "I expressed my regret that I had not rendered myself acceptable to the government, as there could be no doubt the course he indicated a disposition to adopt would result in my recall, the suspension of diplomatic intercourse, and a resort to such measures as the wisdom of my government might suggest."

One consequence of this personal interview was that Webb presented the view of his government in a formal communication, which was on the following day. This document characterized the conflict in the United States as a rebellion which would be crushed with the coming of the winter frosts, declared the *Sumter* and other Confederate cruisers piratical, and alleged that coal was contraband of war. It also denied to every nation the right to treat the "rebels" as belligerents. In denying Brazil the right to recognize the Confederates as belligerents, Webb refused to her the status of a neutral. Yet, in spite of this fact, he asked the imperial government whether it disavowed the breach of neutrality represented in the treatment of the *Sumter*.[8]

When the foreign minister replied to this inconsistent communication five weeks later, he encountered little difficulty in demolishing its arguments. He said that the practice of European nations, the size of the Confederate armies, the policy of blockade maintained by the Union government, and the exchange of prisoners conferred upon the Confederates the status of belligerents. Furthermore, he asserted that

---

[8] A copy of the communication was enclosed in Webb's dispatch of Nov. 8, 1861, in Despatches, XVII.

his government in recognizing the belligerency of the Richmond government was but following a policy set by the United States with reference to revolting groups in the Western Hemisphere. Finally, he flatly denied that coal was contraband of war, or that the *Sumter* had been allowed to violate Brazilian neutrality inasmuch as she had been compelled to conform to all rules of international practice applicable to such cases.

The able reply of the Brazilian minister failed to baffle General Webb. On December 17 he responded with a fifty-two page letter in which he reiterated his former arguments with profuse elaboration. This lengthy epistle was dispatched to its destination without the change of a note, notwithstanding the fact that a French steamer had just arrived at Rio and announced that on her departure from England a Confederate privateer, the *Nashville*, was lying in dock at Southampton.[9] A less presumptuous representative could not have mustered the courage to argue further that the *Sumter* was a pirate and that the Confederates were not belligerents. The New Yorker, however, was not of this sort.

Despite the numerous communications that passed between the American minister and the Brazilian foreign office between the close of 1861 and the spring of 1863, neither side yielded substantial ground on the major issue involved —whether the Confederates were rebels or belligerents. Yet during this period Seward's instructions and Webb's methods of carrying them into execution varied considerably. Variations in the former are attributable in the main to European reactions to the Civil War; in the latter they were due in part to the whims and caprices of an erratic nature. On one occasion Seward told the general to admit no debate upon the legal status of the Sumter, while on another he said it was

[9] Dispatch of Dec. 23, 1861, in *ibid.*

"not thought necessary to dwell longer upon the unfortunate event," unless something new occurred "to disturb our intercourse with Brazil."   At one time Webb was willing to wait until the end of the rebellion to demand of Brazil an *amende honorable;* at another he attacked the integrity of the governor of the province of Maranhão in an attempt to secure his removal from office because of alleged responsibility for the friendly treatment of the *Sumter;* at still another he strongly insinuated that a part of the American fleet, then en route to Paraguay, might find it convenient to stop at Rio and bring Brazil to terms in case an agreement were not reached on the point in controversy.[10]

In the spring of 1863, while General Webb and the Brazilian foreign office were still exchanging communications on the status of the Confederacy and the *Sumter,* causes for complaint on the part of the American government multiplied.   In the first place news reached Rio that the Confederate vessel *Alabama* was receiving supplies from and using as a base of operations the island of Fernando de Noronha, a Brazilian possession lying northeast of the Pernambucan coast.   It was reported that the raider, with many victims already on her prize list, had just captured six American whaling vessels as they were returning from voyages in the South Atlantic.   Webb registered a protest in the Brazilian foreign office soon after receiving the news; and the foreign minister, who had already been informed directly on the vessel's activities, replied promptly, saying that the commanding officer of Noronha who was guilty of giving aid and countenance to the *Alabama* had been removed from office, that the raider had been ordered to leave Brazilian

[10] For the negotiations over this period see Seward's instructions to Webb, Nov. 13, 1861, March 18 and Sept. 27, 1862, in Instructions to Brazilian Ministers, XV, 308-310, 319-325, 352-354; Webb's dispatches, Jan. 23, Feb. 15, 22, July 5, and Nov. 7, 1862, in Despatches, XXVII, XXVIII.

waters, and that his country would continue to fulfill all the obligations of a neutral.[11]

Almost before the general got through congratulating himself on his achievement, reports came from the American consuls at Bahia and Pernambuco that Confederate vessels had been permitted to use those ports to secure provisions and dispose of their captures. The *Florida* and the *Georgia* had visited both Bahia and Pernambuco, while the *Alabama* had put in at the former port.[12]   It is needless to say that Webb registered a protest; indeed, he sent many communications to the Brazilian foreign office.   But in these communications, at least one of which was almost a hundred pages in length, no new note was sounded.   Most of the space was consumed in an attempt to convince the imperial officials that the Confederacy did not have the status of a belligerent, and that as a consequence no countenance should be given the vessels commissioned by her.   Some space, however, was reserved for an appeal to the necessity of maintaining in the Western Hemisphere a policy—an *American* policy—entirely distinct from that advocated by the nations of Europe.[13]

Nor was there anything new in the replies of the Brazilian foreign minister.   He again refused to deny to the Confederacy the status of belligerent, basing his arguments on the practice of European nations and the practice of the American government itself both preceding and during the war then progressing.   Since Brazil accorded the Confederacy the status of belligerent, he said her vessels would be given the same treatment as vessels of the Lincoln govern-

---

[11] Webb to his government, May 7, 1863, with its enclosures, in Despatches, XXVIII.

[12] See numerous letters from the consuls at Bahia and Pernambuco, in Consular Letters (Bahia, III; Pernambuco, VII).

[13] For a typical communication to the Brazilian foreign office see the enclosure, dated July 6, in Webb's dispatch of July 8, 1863, in Despatches, XXIX.

ment. He denied that the *Florida* and *Georgia* had disposed
of their prizes in Brazilian ports, or that they had been given
other privileges in contravention of international law. He
did, however, admit irregularity in the case of the *Alabama*
in her use of the island of Fernando de Noronha and issued
a formal order excluding her from further use of Brazilian
waters. Furthermore, he sent out a new circular to the governors of the provinces setting forth once more the rules and
regulations which the central government wished applied to
the use of its ports by either belligerent. It would seem,
therefore, that the imperial government was anxious to comply with international law, at least as it conceived it.[14]

Webb was clearly disappointed with the degree of success which had rewarded his efforts. He attributed the failure largely to British influence, which resulted not from the
love of Brazilians for arrogant Englishmen but from the
fact that Brazilian business enterprises were entirely dependent on British capital; yet he said it was partly due to
the absence of American war vessels from the Brazilian coast
to give strength to his arguments.[15]   Apparently it did not
occur to the general that reason and international practice
were operating against him and his government's contentions.

Though discouraged with results, Webb was spurred to
renewed efforts by further instructions from his friend and
political superior. These new instructions, made stronger by
successes of Union arms on the battle field, ordered him to
permit no discussion of the principle of belligerency and to
suggest that the Lincoln government would resort to laws of
self-defense in case its protests regarding the treatment of

[14] For the circular of June 23, 1863, see Pereira Pinto, *Apontamentos para o
Direito Internacional*, II, 407-408. The compiler has mistakenly dated the circular
June 23, 1862. A typical reply of the foreign minister to Webb may be found enclosed in the latter's dispatch of July 8, 1863, in Despatches, XXIX.
[15] Dispatches of June 7 and Dec. 6, 1863, in *ibid.*

privateers were not heeded.[16]   The orders bore fruit quickly. Webb's dispatch of early April, 1864, informed Seward that Brazil was prepared to see destroyed within her ports any Confederate vessel discovered there by an American war ship.   While express consent had not been secured for such procedure, Webb said the matter had been discussed repeatedly with the foreign minister, and he had never objected.[17]

An opportunity to test the new course came exactly four months later, when the *Florida* put in at Bahia once more for water and provisions and for repair of her machinery.   The governor of the province, over the protest of American Consul Wilson, gave the cruiser forty-eight hours to remain in port.   Before expiration of the time for departure, however, while the commander and several members of the crew were on shore, the American war ship *Wachusett*, Collins commanding, fired on, captured, and towed the *Florida* out of port under cover of darkness.   Consul Wilson, who no doubt feared the consequences of his violated word, escaped to the United States with the *Wachusett* and her prize.[18]

Excitement ran high in various parts of the Brazilian empire as reports of this incident spread.   At Bahia a frenzied mob assembled before the American consulate for the purpose of showing disapproval.   Finding that the consul had fled on the offending *Wachusett*, it gave vent to its feelings by pulling the national arms down from the building. At Rio de Janeiro, where the excitement was fed by professed sympathy for the Brazilian cause on the part of Eng-

[16] Seward to Webb, July 13 and Nov. 27, 1863, in Instructions to Brazilian Ministers, XVI, 27-29, 38-41.
[17] Webb to Seward, Apr. 6, 1864, in Despatches, XXX.
[18] For the facts on the episode see Brazilian Chargé Barbosa da Silva to Seward, Dec. 12, 1864, with its numerous enclosures, in Notes from the Brazilian Legation, IV; a letter of the American consul at Bahia, Dec. 21, 1864, with its enclosures in Consular Letters, III.

lish residents and by exaggerated newspaper accounts, citizen police were detailed to guard the residences of the American consul and minister against possible violence from the infuriated populace.[19]   If imperial officials had been disposed to listen to public clamors, matters might have taken a serious turn.   That they did not do so may be attributed as much to the fact that diplomatic relations between Brazil and England were severed at the time as to the calmness of imperial officials.

Shortly after the news of the *Wachusett's* attack on the *Florida* reached Rio de Janeiro Webb anticipated the action of the Brazilian government and hastened to the foreign office to assume the position of complainant.   He believed that this forehanded action would break the force of the complaint of his opponent.   He remonstrated against the mob assault upon his country's national arms and the cancellation of the exequatur of the American consul at Bahia by the governor of the province.   On the other hand, he claimed that the action of the *Wachusett* was unauthorized and expressed hope that the conduct of subordinates would not disturb the friendly relations of the two great nations of the Western Hemisphere.   Yet he made no unconditional apology; he claimed that Brazil should not have followed England and France in recognizing the belligerency of the Confederates in the first place.[20]

In his formal correspondence with the Brazilian foreign minister the New Yorker said his government would be grieved to learn that Commander Collins had captured the *Florida* without instructions and would make reparation for every just complaint.   He averred that the American gov-

[19] See various numbers of *Diario, Jornal do Commercio,* and *Correio Mercantil,* all Rio papers.
[20] Webb to Seward, Oct. 19, 1864, in Despatches, XXX.

ernment would be more prompt in its action than if one of her cruisers had committed the same act in a port of the most powerful nation of the world. But, said Webb, the *amende honorable* would be made under "protest" because Brazil had treated the "rebels" as belligerents.[21] The foreign minister replied that the proposal to make reparation under "protest" was neither pleasing to Brazil nor admitted by her. As to the question of recognition, he said that his government considered no further argument necessary. This may have meant that the Brazilian government considered it futile to negotiate further through Webb. At any rate at this point negotiations were transferred to Washington. Although the New Yorker summoned every possible argument in his repertoire in an attempt to induce his government to remand the case to Rio for settlement, he failed in his effort.[22]

Soon after the transfer, the Brazilian chargé, citing the demands which the American government had made upon France because of an attack on an English vessel in Delaware Bay in 1793, presented directly to Secretary Seward his government's demands for the violation of its sovereignty. These were a public declaration by the American government of surprise and regret for the attack on the *Florida* in Brazilian waters; rebuke and dismissal from service of Commander Collins; a salute of twenty-one guns in the harbor of Bahia; and liberation of all on board the *Florida,* with the return of the vessel to Brazil.[23] With the exception of the vessel's return to Brazil, which was made impossible by her sinking in Hampton Roads, Seward's reply was in sub-

[21] *Jornal do Commercio,* Oct. 14, 1864.

[22] The reply, dated Oct. 25, is with Webb's dispatch of Nov. 6, 1864, in Despatches, XXXI.

[23] Barboza da Silva to Seward, Dec. 12, 1864, in Notes from the Brazilian Legation, IV.

stance an agreement to comply with the demands. With reference to the salute, however, the secretary said the flag of Brazil would receive the honor customary on such occasions; furthermore, he disallowed the contention that the Southerners were lawful naval belligerents and claimed reparations for injuries consequent on harboring the piratical vessels.[24]

Upon receipt of the news of the close of the war in the United States, Brazil, without waiting to learn what action the European nations had taken, repealed the neutrality decree of August, 1861.[25] This practically brought to a close four years of controversy, though inexcusable delay in carrying into execution some of the provisions of the Seward-Barboza agreement caused a further exchange of communications. It has already been stated that the sinking of the *Florida* prevented compliance with the demand for her return to Brazil. Probably aware that the American minister had advised sending the raider to sea and sinking her *accidentally* to prevent return, imperial officials were rather insistent on having the documentary evidence which Seward had promised on the manner of the sinking. After considerable delay and reluctance, this was finally submitted. While it is improbable that it convinced the officials, it enabled them to satisfy a curious public, and brought the matter to an end.[26] The salute in the harbor of Bahia was not given until midsummer of 1866, more than eighteen months after the agreement. The delay was partly the result of the American government's disposition to take advantage of a technicality in the reparations settlement. Whereas Brazil had

[24] Seward to Barboza da Silva, Dec. 26, 1864, in Notes to the Brazilian Legation, VI, 173-178.

[25] Enclosure in Webb's dispatch of June 7, 1865, in Despatches, XXXI.

[26] See Seward to Webb, June 15, 1865, in Instructions to Brazilian Ministers, XVI, 115-116.

demanded a salute of twenty-one guns, Seward had promised that the Brazilian flag would receive the honor customary on such occasions. Finally, after an exchange of several
dispatches on the subject, Webb yielded and advised his government to comply with the Brazilian request in full. A
more magnanimous spirit would have yielded long before,
especially in view of the fact that the request concerning the
Florida could not be conceded and that a clamorous public
must be satisfied.[27] The imperial government exhibited its
magnanimity by acquiescing in the reinstatement of Captain
Collins in the American naval service and by removal of all
prohibitions against the offending *Wachusett* in the use of
Brazilian harbors.[28]

Reflection upon Brazilian-American negotiations during
the Civil War convinces one that the United States government, especially in denying Brazil's stand on neutrality, assumed a position contrary to the general practice of nations,
and even to her own practice. The measures which her officials authorized to maintain that position are so asinine as to
need no characterization.

Leaving the major topic of the Paraguayan War for
treatment in another place, we may continue this chapter by
briefly discussing a few proposals which General Webb presented for the consideration of his government. Although
rejected, these proposals are full of genuine interest; and
some of them had far-reaching consequences. The first, providing for the establishment of a colony of liberated Negroes
on the Amazon, was called to the minister's attention by
newspaper accounts of President Lincoln's suggestion in a
message to Congress of the probable necessity of acquiring

[27] On this incident see communications of Sept. 1, 1865, Mar. 3 and July 2, 1866,
in Despatches, XXXI, XXXII; Seward to Chargé Lidgerwood, Apr. 18, 1866, in Instructions to Brazilian Ministers, XVI, 142.
[28] Webb to Seward, July 21 and Aug. 21, 1865, in Despatches, XXXI.

territory for manumission purposes.[29]   Immediately the
thought struck Webb that suitable land lay along the Amazon; a little reflection convinced him that every factor
pointed toward this as the best spot in the world for such a
purpose.   The rapidly increasing value of Negroes in the
southern provinces of Brazil, due partly to the steadily advancing price of coffee and partly to the decrease of the entire
slave population, was fast depopulating the northern sections
and causing them to revert to the beasts and the natives; and
the North-American Negroes, largely because in their African home they had lived in a similar latitude, were exactly
fitted by nature to conditions along the Amazon.   Surely the
"finger of God" was pointing the way!

Webb's plan—or rather God's plan—provided for the
creation of a joint-stock colonization company, the liability of
every subscriber being limited to the amount of his subscrip-
tion.   The president of the United States was to appoint the
president of the company—who was of course to be General
James Watson Webb—as well as one-fifth of the directors.
For every dollar paid in by the subscribers the American
government was to loan the company at five per cent interest
an equal sum.   The company was to begin with a capital of
six million dollars, though the amount was to be increased
so as to take care of the demands made upon it.   Before
transportation to Brazil the manumitted Negroes were to be
transferred to the corporation; after arrival in their new
home, they were to render personal service to the corporation
for three years.   At the end of the apprenticeship period
each black, in addition to his freedom, was to receive certain
agricultural implements, a small sum of money, and not more
than twenty acres of land, of which at least five acres were
to be made fit for cultivation at the expense of the company.

[29] Richardson, *Messages and Papers*, VI, 54-55.

Besides their rewards in heaven, the company stockholders were to be the recipients of the proceeds from the sale of the unallotted lands—amounting to four-fifths of the total acreage appropriated by the Brazilian government—and of the labor of the Negroes during the three years of apprenticeship.

This scheme was to be applied to the Negroes as they were emancipated. Eventually, of course, it would have included all who lived in the United States. Although he had not worked out every detail, the promoter said,

It is quite impossible that in a case where the giver, the receiver, and the party or things bestowed, are all to be palpably and immensely benefitted—where injury cannot possibly result to either, and where there can be no rivalry or jealousy, and where good only, and the greatest good, must accrue to all—it is impossible, I say, that where such are to be the fruits of a project, to look upon its failure as within the scope of probabilities, or even possibilities.

In commenting further upon the plan, the New Yorker pointed out the advantages which would accrue to all when he said,

The United States will be blessed by his [the Negro's] absence, and the riddance of a curse which has well nigh destroyed her; Brazil will receive precisely the species of laborers and citizens best calculated to develop her resources and make her one of the great powers of the earth; and the miserable, ignorant, and down trodden slave, who is now a mere chattel, with body and soul alike uncared for, will have his shackles knocked off, be liberated, educated for freedom, and have bestowed upon him the great boon of personal liberty.

With many details still to be worked out, Webb submitted his scheme for the consideration of his government. In case of approval at Washington, he thought an appeal should be made to the philanthropists of the United States for financial aid. Encouraged by the hope that the Lincoln government would soon authorize him to negotiate a treaty by which the scheme could be carried out, he began to lay plans to make certain of its acceptance in Brazil. Consequently, while waiting for a reply from Washington he drew up a memorial entitled "On the necessity of supplying Brazil with labor, and the policy of procuring free black labor from the United States" and presented it to the Rio government. An early response from the Potomac made it unnecessary for the Brazilian officials to make known their attitude toward the project, though from comments made at a later time it seems that they were not favorably impressed. But the Utopian plan met its *coup de grâce* at Washington. President Lincoln, while undervaluing neither the motives which suggested the proposal nor the grave consideration which supported it, could not grant the request to negotiate the treaty, primarily because conditions then existing in the United States did not warrant such action. In this manner vanished the dream to settle eventually four million American Negroes on the Amazon. The American minister was discouraged, partly no doubt because of selfish reasons, though he was not hopelessly disheartened.[30]

At the same time the American minister was attempting to promote the Negro colonization project, he was also negotiating for the establishment of a line of steamships between the United States and Brazil. And defeat in the former apparently left him undaunted in his zeal for the latter and more important project. Fortunately, two solid arguments,

[30] Concerning this colonization project see *Diplomatic Correspondence of the United States*, 1862, pp. 704-715. But because of deletions and bad editing it is better to consult Webb to Seward, May 20, 1862, and Mar. 9, 1864, in Despatches, XXVII and XXX; Seward to Webb, July 21, 1862, in Instructions to Brazilian Ministers, XV, 340-349. See also an article by N. A. N. Cleven entitled "Some Plans for Colonizing Liberated Negro Slaves in Hispanic America," in *The Journal of Negro History*, XI, No. 1, 41-49.

one political and the other commercial, were at hand to support the proposal for a steamship line. Both arguments were used effectively upon the officials of the two governments; they were extraordinarily appealing to Brazilian officials because of the hatred of England which resulted from the inexcusable reprisals of British cruisers in Brazilian territorial waters and a break in the diplomatic relations of the two countries.

The political argument had no new features. Webb simply took advantage of Brazilian estrangement from England to express again a feeling that had sought expression for a half century, namely, that all the governments in North, South, and Middle America should unite in a bond of political fellowship. This political union was supposed to promote somehow a set of democratic principles that were antithetic to the principles perpetuated by the governments of the Old World. It would seem as though General Webb, as well as the American ministers who preceded and followed him, must have been advocating a union in the spiritual rather than in the practical realm, however, for all suggestions in the direction of a union made binding by treaty were invariably side-tracked.

A stronger argument—at least for Americans—for the establishment of the line was the commercial one. Webb found statistics which showed clearly the disastrous effects on American commerce of the establishment of steamship communication between England and Brazil in 1850. Whereas in the decade between 1840 and 1850 the Yankee merchant, because of the superiority of the clipper ships, had the lion's share of the trade with Brazil, in the following decade he witnessed his English rival wrest this from him and then establish almost a complete monopoly. Thus before the end of the Civil War the United States was sending from fifteen to twenty million gold dollars to London annually to pay for coffee and other Brazilian products. Instead of sending this money to the English capital she should have been sending twenty millions worth of her own manufactured products to Brazil. But American merchants could not be expected to compete with the English as long as the mail facilities favored the latter by fifteen to twenty days and as long as the latter knew the price quotations of the former. Besides favoring the trader the proposed line would also favor the traveller. Not only would there be a reduction in time from forty to twenty days by the direct voyage, but a reduction in fare from $400 to $150 as well.[31]

Taking advantage of the ill-feeling between Brazilians and Englishmen during their diplomatic controversy, Webb worked assiduously for many months to perfect a scheme for the establishment of the line. His experience with the American Congress in the sessions from 1855 to 1857 convinced him that no plan could be put through that body unless it were presented in finished form with the recommendation to take it or leave it. He not only held countless sessions with numerous imperial officials; he also wrote articles which he had published, at an enormous personal expense, for the purpose of popularizing his project. Finally, he secured from the executive officials approval of a plan which he had presented to the Brazilian legislature. It provided for a line of steamers from New York to Rio de Janeiro via the West Indian island of St. Thomas and the Brazilian ports of Pará, Pernambuco, and Bahia. The company taking the contract was to maintain a monthly service of high class steamers and was to carry United States and Brazilian mails free of charge. Each of the governments was in turn to

[31] See especially Webb's dispatches of Sept. 22 and 24, 1863, in Despatches, XXIX.

grant a subsidy that averaged five thousand pounds a round trip for a period of fifteen years, the time the contract was to run.   As presented to the Brazilian legislature, the concession was to be given to Robert S. Webb, a son of the American minister, though in its original form the proposal made J. Watson himself the concessionaire.[32]

With a bright outlook for approval by the Brazilian legislature, Webb turned his attention to making his plan acceptable at home.   Since the executive branch of the American government had approved of the establishment of a steamship line,[33] he expected his only opposition to come from Congress, which would be called upon to pass the measure providing for the subvention.   In order to meet this opposition, he called upon his friends in the United States, among whom were Parsons, late American consul at Rio, Reverdy Johnson, and Seward, to be prepared to rush to the rescue at the strategic moment.   The private letters which the minister sent to Secretary Seward, whom he addressed as "Dear Governor," in an attempt to convert him into a political henchman are indeed significant.   These revealed features of the proposed scheme which up to this time had not been known to the Lincoln administration.   Among the unknown features was that naming Robert S. Webb as the concessionaire.   The son, of course, was to assign his rights to his father immediately.   But, said Webb, was there anything wrong about this arrangement?   He had labored hard and long for a concession which nobody else could have secured.   To either country or to the public it mattered not who got the apple.   Why should it not go to one who had given long and faithful service to his country and party?   Who "would use more liberally, and with more considera-

[32] Webb to Seward, Oct. 8, 1863, with its enclosures, in *ibid.*

[33] Instructions of June 19, 1863, in Instructions to Brazilian Ministers, XVI, 24.

tion to his old and gray friends, the great patronage and power to do good, which I will receive from this line of steamers instead of giving it to a stranger?"

Although Webb had called upon other friends to aid, he placed upon Seward all responsibility for getting the measure through the United States Congress. The "Dear Governor" was warned to see that it was not defeated through the powerful influence of J. P. Morgan, who was at enmity with the general. He was told also to suggest that President Lincoln "refer approvingly" to Webb's conduct at Rio in his message to Congress; it might "aid *the great measure* through the House, besides being to me [Webb] most gratifying." After the passage of the bill Webb expected in the first mail "a furlough or leave of absence to visit the United States and inaugurate the enterprise." And, remarked Webb, it would not be more than he had "earned by vigilance and hard work," if he were "permitted to go home with" his "family in a good national war steamer." Following its inauguration at New York the minister hoped to return to Rio to look after the other end of the line. Shortly thereafter he hoped to be permitted to resign and return home, where he could be of service in returning Lincoln, Seward, and Chase to power in the elections of 1864.[34]

Unfortunately for the general and his friends, the scheme to floor England and to make the influence of the United States paramount forever did not work out as planned. For some reason or other Seward felt compelled to submit the confidential correspondence to the president's consideration, though at the time of submission he expressed the hope that it would be overlooked and forgotten for his friend's sake. The result proved to be almost disastrous. The president, who up until this time had been favorably disposed toward

[34] Webb to Seward, Oct. 15 and Nov. 16, 1863, bound in Despatches, XXIX.

the establishment of a line of steamers between the United States and Brazil, refused to submit Webb's proposal to Congress. The expectation of the minister to make himself the beneficiary of the project was entirely indefensible. The realization of this expectation would have been a violation of the statute which said "that no agent of the United States shall, in any case or by any evasion, receive for his official service any pecuniary reward beyond the compensation expressly provided for by law."[35]

Upon receipt of the news—through the famous instruction ninety—that the president would not submit his proposal to Congress, the general was so disappointed he thought at first of resigning his position. After an overnight's reflection, however, he changed his mind. Thinking that the adverse decision was due to a misapprehension of facts and circumstances resulting from an *ex parte* hearing, he resolved to defend his course by further argument. In his long reply—marked confidential—he met the imputation of corrupt motives in part by detailing a history of his services to his country and party during the past half century. In this account he reminded Seward how he had wrecked a private annual income of twenty to thirty thousand dollars by advocating in his paper *(Courier and Enquirer)* principles which had contributed to his personal success and to the triumph of the Republican party. He told the "Dear Governor" that the members of the crew of this triumph had been provided for, while the veteran commander (J. Watson Webb) was left to struggle with his poverty. He said he could not penetrate the mystery, "for never in thought, word or deed had I failed to be loyal to our personal friendship and devoted to your political success, beyond what has ever before been witnessed

[35] Seward to Webb, Dec. 7, 1863, in Instructions to Brazilian Ministers, XVI, 49-54.

in the history of politics in the United States." His "only political crime" had been adherence to the interests of his "friends at all times and under all circumstances."

But the veteran commander had not only been loyal to friend and party in the past; he promised to remain so in the future. At least he informed the "Dear Governor" that he intended for his son "Willie" to have one of the two agencies of the proposed steamship line with a five thousand dollar salary. All the general expected for himself was the remuneration to come from the presidency of the company.

Believing, or professing to believe, that his explanations and appeals would cause a change of heart at Washington, Webb asked Seward to reopen the case with the president with the view of bringing about a reversal of judgment. This was asking no more than Seward had demanded of Webb and his other friends on similar occasions. But in case the president refused to recommend the measure to Congress without change, the minister suggested certain modifications which he was willing to accept. Though reluctantly, he promised in good faith to decline the presidency of the company for himself and to permit the name of Cornelius Vanderbilt to stand in the bill beside that of Robert as joint concessionaire. He suggested that if time would not admit of the passage of the bill otherwise it might be attached as a rider to the general appropriation bill. Hundreds of measures possessing not one tithe of the merit of the steamship bill had been passed in that way. Furthermore, he argued that the bill must be passed by the Congress then in session or it would be too late.

Although he promised to respect the injunction not to prosecute the matter further in the form it then assumed, the general said he would do nothing to prevent the passage of the bill which was already before the Brazilian legislature.

To offer any opposition at that stage would be proclaiming that his government had repudiated him.[36]

This ominous document failed of its purpose. Although the Lincoln government had been inclined to overlook the previous communication of a similar nature, it replied that the explanation of the views which had governed the minister were insufficient to justify a departure from the policy already announced.[37] Partly as a result of President Lincoln's failure to recommend Webb's proposed bill to the American Congress, and partly because of the American minister's inability to look after his pet measure owing to an illness of several weeks, the Brazilian legislature refused the appropriation for subsidizing the steamship line.[38]

In the meantime, the American Congress, responding to the lobbying of rival steamship line promoters, passed the Alley Law, "an act authorizing the establishment of ocean mail steamship service between the United States and Brazil." Despite the fact that the Brazilian minister at Washington and an agent of an interested corporation went to Rio de Janeiro to use their influence for the measure, it met defeat in the Brazilian Senate. Provoked because his government had given encouragement to the rival project, Webb used his influence to bring about the defeat. But he did more than oppose the rival measure; he set about the task of perfecting a proposal whose terms would be more attractive to the governments concerned and which, therefore, would have greater chance of acceptance. It is not necessary to say that the new project named son Robert as the agent.[39]

Unfortunately for the Webb family, the second proposal

[36] This notorious dispatch, dated Mar. 9, 1864, is in Despatches, XXX.

[37] Instructions of Apr. 9 and 22, 1864, in Instructions to Brazilian Ministers, XVI, 63-66, 68.

[38] Webb to Seward, June 6 and 25, 1864, in Despatches, XXX.

[39] Dispatches of July 8, Sept. 20, Oct. 3 and 23, 1864, in *ibid.*, XXX, XXXI.

met no more favorable reception from Washington than the first. The promoter was told to forego all support of any project which came into conflict or competition with the plan sanctioned by Congress.[40]   At last the persistent general yielded—with the greatest reluctance!   He felt that his government was indeed ungrateful for a great service.[41]

In June, 1865, the Brazilian legislature finally passed an act authorizing the government to contract with the agent designated under the Alley Law for the establishment of a steamship line between the United States and Brazil. The subsidy of the Brazilian government was not to exceed two hundred thousand milreis annually for a monthly service. The contract was awarded to the United States and Brazil Mail Steamship Company of New York and service was begun at the end of 1865. Shortly after the inauguration complaint was made that exorbitant prices were charged both for freight and passenger service.[42]

Thus the year in which our Civil War closed witnessed the first direct steamship communication between North and South America. That the accomplishment eventually facilitated intercourse between the two continents and lessened the dependence of both upon Europe there can be no doubt. By way of comparison it is interesting to note that at the time of the inauguration of the line the nations of Western Europe, chiefly England, had no fewer than a dozen lines extending from the West Indies to all parts of Latin America and feeding a few main lines connecting the former with

[40] Seward to Webb, Sept. 22 and Dec. 26, 1864, in Instructions to Brazilian Ministers, XVI, 78-79, 94.

[41] See a communication to Seward, Nov. 19, 1864, in Despatches, XXXI.

[42] The American minister to Seward, June 23, Dec. 1, 1865, and Jan. 2, 1866, in Despatches, XXXI; Brazilian minister to Seward, Jan. 19 and May 9, 1866, in Notes from the Brazilian Legation, IV; American consul to Seward, Oct. 23, 1866, in Consular Letters (Pernambuco), VIII.

Europe. The American-Brazilian project was but the first feeble step toward the break in the European communication monopoly which continued until after the World War. Regard for fairness demands that General Webb be accorded considerable credit for making possible the initial venture, though this does not stamp with approval the methods which he often employed.

Brazilian neutrality and projects for Negro colonization and the steamship line did not occupy all the time at the command of the American minister. Among the other numerous topics with which he concerned himself was that of the French menace in Mexico. He said he ventured to call attention to this subject because of the bare possibility of its having received insufficient consideration at Washington owing to the mammoth rebellion in the Southern states. He was convinced that Napoleon III, whose army was then advancing toward the center of Mexico, would restore the Mexican capital after it had been conquered

on condition that Sonora and a strip of country extending from the Pacific to the Atlantic be transferred to France. To the United States such an acquisition by France, or any other European power, would be more dangerous and more offensive than converting Mexico into a monarchy. In the latter case, the people would ultimately rebel and reconquer their lost liberties; but cede Sonora and a strip along our line to France, and it would at once be peopled by Frenchmen; every soldier now in Mexico or shortly to be sent there would remain in this new Algeria, and we should be compelled to put down another rebellion in the southern states backed by the whole power of France.[43]

Webb thought the time for meeting the menace would arrive as soon as we had crushed out rebellion in the South,

[43] Webb to Seward, Jan. 17, 1863, in Despatches, XXVIII.

while our army was powerful and efficient, and the war spirit of our people was in full vigor. He said,

We can do it now; but omit to do it when we should, and we may find it impossible when we would. His [Napoleon's] occupation of Rome would be nothing to compare with it; because there, all Europe stands ready to prevent his appropriating the much coveted prize; while in Mexico, we should have to deal with him single handed, backed as he will be by a rebellious population within ourselves, occupying the country between him and us. We may as well, therefore, look the danger full in the face, for it is imminent; and the necessity for action is rapidly approaching.[44]

General Webb suggested two possible ways to meet this threatening situation. One was through an approach to the European powers that were nursing grievances against France and her "upstart Emperor." He claimed that the representatives of Russia, Austria, and Prussia at Rio de Janeiro had assured him their governments would coöperate in a plan to get Napoleon out of Mexico, especially if it contained a provision for punishing him for going there. He advised the immediate initiation of negotiations looking toward the consummation of such a program. He believed the preliminary step should be an offer to guarantee to Napoleon not only the payment of French claims against Mexico but the expense which France had incurred as a result of her intervention. As soon as the proffer was rejected—and he was willing to wager ten to one it would be promptly rejected—he advocated turning to Napoleon's enemies.

But the second proposal for meeting the French menace lay much nearer the general's heart. It was for an alliance between France and the United States in a war on England. Such alignment, Webb argued, would accomplish the imme-

[44] *Ibid.*

diate object of the United States, namely, getting France out
of Mexico, and would rejoice the heart of every American.
But how was it to be brought about?   The minister suggested
saying to Napoleon frankly,

You must leave Mexico, but we will make it your interest to do so.
England has dishonored and insulted us.   The hour has arrived for
France to wipe out the recollection of Waterloo on the soil of England, while the United States will balance with her the accounts of
the Trent and the Alabama.   Join us in a war with England, and
our joint fleets will sweep the commerce from the ocean.   We will
humble her arrogance; and when we grant her peace her North
American continental possessions shall belong to us, while Newfound-
land, Prince Edward's and the adjoining islands, and the West Indian and South Pacific possessions shall belong to France.[45]

Webb felt that a war against England would be popular
also with the people of continental Europe other than the
French, with the possible exception of the Prussians.   At
least they hated her arrogant, bullying policies and might
welcome an opportunity to "carve up the 'sick man' at Con-
stantinople, as best suited their convenience."   In view of the
Italian question, the grievances of Austria, and the jealousy
of Prussia one may wonder whether the American minister
reckoned well.   His hatred for England was so pronounced
that he was willing to recommend any measure that appeared
to have a chance at success.   The minister's hatred for England and Englishmen was in part—perhaps in large part—
the direct result of an acrimonious controversy between the
British minister and himself growing out of the former's refusal to permit one of his staff to attend a diplomatic function
given by Mrs. Webb and other disagreements of a purely
personal nature.   This controversy was carried so far that the
New Yorker threatened personal chastisement upon his ad-

[45] *Ibid.*

versary and prepared himself to accept, if not even to give, a challenge for a duel. As soon as the news reached his ears, President Lincoln disapproved of the agent's conduct as "absolutely indefensible and inexcusable," though a break in Anglo-Brazilian relations and the recall of the British minister from Rio had already brought the matter to a fortunate conclusion.[46]

Memory of the ideas which Seward had on foreign affairs in 1861 may have influenced Webb's recommendation for getting the French out of Mexico quite as much as his dislike for Englishmen. The minister may have been unaware that the man who wrote "Thoughts" in 1861 was not the man who was secretary of state in 1863. It would be interesting to know whether the transformation wrought by those memorable two years permitted the secretary to give serious consideration to Webb's proposal. We know he continued to impose considerable confidence in the general's judgment. At any rate, a year later he granted him a leave from his post and permitted him to return home via Paris in order to talk over the Mexican situation with the "upstart Emperor." Webb later claimed that at a breakfast conference to which Napoleon invited him an agreement was reached on the terms by which French troops were to be withdrawn from Mexican soil. The fact that notes on this conference, held November 10, 1865, were submitted to the president, and that there was never any official denial, gives Webb's claim to credit for adjustment some justification.[47]

But at the breakfast conference, according to Webb, Napoleon did more than agree to leave Mexico. In order to make amends for having meddled in Mexican affairs quite as much as for the purpose of annoying England, he proposed to sell to the United States French Guiana for the sum of

---

[46] Seward to Webb, Feb. 6, 1863, in Instructions to Brazilian Ministers, XVI, 6-8.
[47] Webb to Seward, Aug. 10, 1867, in Despatches, XXXIII.

ten million dollars.   Unfortunately, when the proposal was submitted to Secretary Seward, he refused even to consider the subject.   Webb thought this was because Napoleon, though intending no offense, had ignored the American secretary and ministers in Paris along with his own foreign minister in conducting negotiations on the Mexican question.   In any event the general, who had tried hard to convince Seward of the incalculable value of the possession to the United States, was greatly disappointed with the "Dear Governor's" attitude and sought an opportunity to reopen the matter. Thus on March 1, 1869, he wrote from St. Thomas, while en route from New York to Rio de Janeiro, a personal note to President-elect U. S. Grant with the hope of interesting him in the subject.   With the note he enclosed a sketch on the value and significance of Guiana to the United States which he had induced a companion traveller named Colonel J. W. Fabens to write.   Colonel Fabens, who was at the time an agent of the State Department in the Santo Domingan negotiations, had been a resident of French Guiana for nine years, during five of which he held the American consulship at Cayenne, and was well prepared to speak on the subject. Congratulating Webb "upon having had the privilege of presenting to our government a measure of such magnitude and prospective advantage," he proceeded to speak in the following terms:

France, as you are aware, claims the territory of Guiana to the mouth of the Amazon, and several hundred miles of the north coastline of that Father of Rivers.   The advantages to commerce and civilization to be derived from the navigation of the Amazon, and the development of the resources of the rich and fertile country along its banks, under the protecting sovereignty of the United States, are patent to all.

The geographical position of Cayenne, lying to windward of the great chain of West India islands, and at a commanding point on the continent of South America, clear of the parallel of hurricanes and earthquakes, combined with its secure and spacious harbor and the salubrity of its climate, in which the malignant types of tropical diseases are unknown, render it a most desirable station for our South American squadron and place of call for our African and East India ships seeking repairs, supplies, or a change of air for sanitary purposes.

The territorial area of French Guiana comprises, according to the French estimate, about 60,000 square miles, being considerably larger than Louisiana, for which the United States paid France the sum of $15,000,000. A large portion of this tract is covered with forests of valuable woods suitable for cabinet work or ship-building. The mountains of the windward coast from Cape Orange to Cayenne are reputed to contain gold and silver mines of great promise, and the soil is fertile to wonderful degree. All the productions of the West Indies and the tropical portions of South America, such as coffee, sugar, rice, cotton, cacao,—tobacco, etc. are here cultivated with success, and also the most valued spices of the East, such as the cloves, nutmeg, cinnamon, pepper, etc. Until within a few years—since in fact the introduction of the clove culture into the island of Zanzibar —the entire consumption of that spice in the United States was furnished from Cayenne.

Pointing out the fact that French Guiana would gratify the desire of his country for coaling stations in the West Indies and South America, Webb enclosed Colonel Faben's letter with the remark that he had no doubt he could induce Napoleon to make a renewal of the offer to sell. He said, however, that the negotiations to be successful must be quite unofficial until all the preliminaries had been arranged. Whatever the effect on the mind of the new president, this recommendation, like most of the others made by the proponent, failed to yield positive results. It seems to have gone the way of the proposals to purchase the island of Fernando de Noronha from Brazil, to rid Mexico of the French, and to colonize American Negroes on the Amazon.[48]

[48] Webb to Grant, Mar. 1, 1869, with Colonel Faben's enclosure, in *ibid.*, XXXIV.

Chapter VII

THE PARAGUAYAN WAR

D URING the latter half of Webb's mission at Rio de Janeiro Brazil was engaged in the Paraguayan War. Although allied with Argentina and the Colorado faction of Uruguay, Brazil was forced to carry a major part of the burden. More than once during the nearly five years of fighting she was on the verge of exhaustion. The American government became involved in this terrific conflict at several points.

At the outset it seems necessary to consider the causes of the war. In discussing causes, however, we shall not go further back than 1850 to pick up the threads. In that year, when Paraguay and Brazil were on most friendly terms, a treaty was entered into granting to Brazil transit by the Paraguay River to the imperial province of Matto Grosso. In the following year, however, while Brazil was at war with Dictator Rosas of the Argentine Confederation, the elder López, who was then president of Paraguay, seized the opportunity to occupy a strategic point on the Paraguay River which he had been wanting for some time and to which Paraguay had some claim. He also, after vainly urging the imperial government to recognize a certain boundary line in dispute between the two countries, imposed numerous vexatious restrictions upon Brazilian vessels destined for Matto Grosso. After the conclusion of the war with Rosas, Brazil protested in vain against the restrictive regulations on the use of the Paraguay. Finally, in 1856, the two governments concluded another treaty which restored to Brazil the right to navigate the Paraguay to Matto Grosso, though there was failure to reach agreement on the question of boundary. The six-year period following, at the end of which there was supposed to be a renewal of limitary negotiations, was one of disturbed relations. It witnessed several frontier conflicts between the armed forces of the two nations, and at the close found both better prepared for war. The fact that Brazil was urging Paraguay to grant fluvial concessions which Brazil would not grant to Bolivia and Peru in the use of the Amazon did not strengthen her position.

From this brief survey of the relations of Brazil and Paraguay over boundaries and fluvial rights it is clear that war was not improbable by 1862. In this memorable year Francisco Solano López succeeded his father as president of Paraguay. That the new dictator was not pacifically inclined is indicated by the fact that at the beginning of 1864 he had at his command a finely drilled army of sixty thousand men, the largest in South America.

The pretext López needed for commencing hostilities was afforded by the interference of Brazil in the affairs of Uruguay. In 1863 the latter republic was in her normal condition of civil war. The two great parties, the Colorados and the Blancos, which had been at enmity for many years, were fighting for the privilege of occupying governmental positions. During this conflict Brazilian subjects in Uruguay, as well as in the imperial province of Rio Grande do Sul, suffered numerous property losses and personal injuries. And notwithstanding the fact that these subjects had given frequent support to the Colorado cause in the internal conflict, the Brazilian government persistently demanded from the Blanco party, which happened to be in control, redress for the outrages. To the Blanco government the demands seemed not only extreme but designed to favor the enemy. Consequently they were rejected. Thereupon the imperial government delivered an ultimatum, non-compliance with which meant invasion for the purpose of reprisals. From this moment peaceful relations were interrupted, and in September, 1864, without a formal declaration of war, a Brazilian army crossed into Uruguay. Acting in concert with General Flores, the leader of the Colorado faction, it won several important engagements and finally marched upon the capital city of Montevideo. The Blanco government saw the futility of further resistance, entered into negotiations with the enemy, and concluded a treaty which placed Flores in charge of the republic. The new dictator continued to coöperate with the Brazilian government and the Uruguayan war came to an end.

The facts supporting this sketch uphold the Brazilian allegation that her subjects had suffered serious injuries in Uruguay—often with the connivance of Oriental authorities—for which reparations could not be obtained through diplomatic channels. Under the circumstances it was clearly within the right of the imperial government to use stronger measures to protect the just claims of its constituents. On the other hand, it is evident that it took undue advantage by pressing the claims during the existence of a factional quarrel in Uruguay and that it violated international law by making an invasion without a formal declaration of war. Moreover, a definite alliance with one party in the domestic wrangle was wholly unjustifiable.

President López of Paraguay observed the events in Uruguay with a keen interest. One of his first moves was to offer mediation between the contending parties. When this was refused, he sent an energetic protest against the reprisals which Brazil was threatening to make in Uruguay. An announcement from the imperial government that this protest had made it all the more determined to protect the lives and interests of its subjects brought the ultimatum that Paraguay would use force to make her protest effective. After this ultimatum no further diplomatic steps were taken by López, though Brazil proceeded to carry out her announced intention of interference in Uruguayan affairs. But his opportunity for retaliation was not long coming. On November 10, 1864, the Brazilian steamer *Marquis de Olinda* arrived at Asunción en route to Matto Grosso with a newly appointed provincial governor on board. After being refused communication with the shore, without any assigned reason, the vessel soon continued her journey up the Paraguay toward Corumbá. Before nightfall of the same day López ordered his speediest gunboat, the *Tacuari*, to overtake and capture the Brazilian vessel. On the following day the capture was made about two hundred miles above Asunción, the *Marquis de Olinda* was brought back to the Paraguayan capital and placed under guard, and the passengers were detained as prisoners. Within a few hours of the capture, López addressed a note to Vianna de Lima, Brazilian resident minister at Asunción, informing him that Paraguay was dissolving diplomatic relations with his government in consequence of the Brazilian invasion of Uruguay in defiance of a protest from Paraguay. In reply, Lima protested against the seizure of the Brazilian vessel without a previous declaration of war and asked for his passports, with the privilege of descending the river in the captured steamer. The passports were granted, but the steamer was not allowed to leave Asunción. It was only through the energetic intervention of the American minister that the imperial minister and his family were enabled to get out of the country safely.

Seizing the opportune moment, López sent his brother-in-law, Colonel Barrios, with an army into the Brazilian province of Matto Grosso. After taking possession of the

fort which commanded the entrance to the province, the in-
vading army ravaged the country in all directions, inflicting
horrible cruelties upon all who fell captive. When news of
the ravages reached Rio de Janeiro a month later, the imperial government announced that it would repel the aggressor by force, though the aggressor was the López *government*
and not the Paraguayan *nation.*

But this war was to have another participant. Before it
had progressed far, the Argentine Republic entered on the
side of Brazil and the Colorado faction of Uruguay. Although Paraguay and Argentina had had some unpleasant
relations over boundary questions almost from the time of
independence, the train of events resulting in the rupture of
1865 did not begin until Argentine interference in the domestic quarrel of Uruguay about two years previously. López
accused the Mitre government of Buenos Aires of aiding
General Flores in his war on the Blanco government of
Banda Oriental, the name still applied to Uruguay. While
the charge was denied by Mitre and his supporters, it cannot
be doubted that the Colorado leader received supplies from
the public men of the Argentine capital and that armed expeditions were organized on and left Argentine soil to make
war upon the neighboring state, with which the country was
at peace. President López called upon President Mitre to
put an end to these irregularities. When the latter failed to
do so, his country was placed in the class with Brazil.

Evidence of a different sort can be produced to substantiate López' charge that Mitre's professed neutrality in the
controversy between Brazil and Paraguay was not sincere.
The Argentine president fortified the island of Martín
García, lying in La Plata near the junction of the Paraná
and Uruguay. This must have been with the connivance of
the Brazilian government, for it was in violation of the neu-

tralization treaty entered into by the two countries in 1856. Protests from the Paraguayan president were ignored at Buenos Aires and Rio de Janeiro. Furthermore, after the rupture between Brazil and Paraguay the official press of Buenos Aires poured its invective on López and his country. Little wonder that the Paraguayan dictator thought Brazil and Argentina were in perfect accord! And there may have been grounds for the charge that the larger powers were planning to dismember the small republics of Paraguay and Uruguay and divide the spoils between them after the fashion of the partition of Poland in the Old World. The interference of the larger powers in Uruguay and the fortification of Martín García constituted only the prelude to the real tragedy. To López, Uruguay's cause was also the cause of Paraguay.

But, as in the case of Brazil, responsibility for the rupture of relations with Argentina rested upon Paraguay. On February 5, 1865, López asked Mitre's permission to send troops through Argentine territory in order to strike Brazil in her province of Rio Grande do Sul. Upon refusal of the request, a Paraguayan congress was convened at Asunción. This body authorized its president to send troops through Argentine territory and finally declared war on the Argentine government. A month later, apparently before official notification of the declaration had reached Buenos Aires, Paraguayans seized two Argentine vessels at Corrientes and soon thereafter captured the city. News of the invasion caused intense excitement in Buenos Aires and Mitre declared war immediately. The alliance which Brazil had been urging for some time was entered into on May 1, two days before official receipt of the Paraguayan declaration of war. When, to the indignation of the contracting parties, the terms of the secret alliance were made known the following year, it was discovered that the war was to be waged against the López government, not against the Paraguayan people, that the territorial integrity of the enemy country was guaranteed, though with contracted boundaries, that there should be free navigation of the Paraná and Paraguay rivers, and that Paraguay should pay all war expenses and in the future be denied the right to keep arms or munitions of war. These terms suggest that the allies may have been influenced by stronger motives than mere vindication of outraged national dignity; they suggest that López' fear of Paraguayan and Uruguayan dismemberment may not have been wholly unfounded.

On the surface it would appear as though López were insane to rush into war with two of the most powerful nations of South America. Whereas the population of Paraguay was scarcely a million, the combined population of Brazil and Argentina was no less than ten or twelve million. On the other hand, Paraguay possessed a well-trained army of sixty thousand men, which was two or three times the strength of the allied armies. Furthermore, Argentina was in the throes of a domestic quarrel between the Unitarians and the Federalists. And the Federalists were particularly strong in the provinces of Corrientes and Entre Rios, both of which were favorably situated to render aid, and both of whose populations were basically the same as the population of Paraguay-Guaraní. Still more assuring was the fact that the most powerful leader of the Argentine Federalists, General Urquiza, was impregnable in Entre Rios and, it was believed, could be counted on for support. Thus, as López viewed matters, Paraguay's chief opposition was to come from Brazil. And Brazil, with a small fighting force scattered through several far-flung provinces that were none too loyal to the central government, seemed by no means formidable to the great militarist. As eventually proved, López' reasoning was faulty at only two points: the great Urquiza preferred to remain neutral and thus to accumulate a fortune by selling supplies to both groups of belligerents, and the Brazilian government was able to hold on year after year with bulldog tenacity. But at the beginning it seemed that Paraguay, the Federalists of Argentina, and the Blancos of Uruguay would be pitted against Brazil, the Unitarians of Argentina, and the Colorados of Uruguay—not an unequal lineup.

From this summary it should be clear that the Paraguayan War was not caused entirely by the "overweening vanity and insane ambition of the Paraguayan dictator, Francisco Solano López."[1] Indeed, it was not caused by any individual or by any single circumstance. It was the result of a series of events set in motion by many hands. Underneath the events was the fear on the part of both Brazil and Argentina that the vain and ambitious López, with his key position, would become the arbiter of the Plate system of natural highways. Within Paraguayan boundaries the dictator had the support of the fanatical Guaraní, who derived their sense of exaggerated loyalty to superiors from the Jesuit rulers of colonial times. He might secure support from the portions of the same race which political fortune had placed under Brazilian and Argentinian boundaries. The dictator of this embryonic Guaraní state had to be eliminated before it was too late. He was getting obnoxious when he dared defy the larger powers in their programs of interference in Uruguay. If the allies were not permitted to partition Paraguay and

---

[1] H. G. James and P. A. Martin, *The Republics of Latin America*, p. 121.

Uruguay in the end, at least they could eliminate López and reduce the size of his patrimony.[2]

The military phase of the war can be disposed of in brief space. The prediction by Brazil and Argentina that the campaign would end within three months proved to be as erroneous as that made by the North at the outbreak of our own Civil War; the three months period was stretched until it finally reached far into the fifth year. After the first months, during which Paraguayan troops invaded the Brazilian provinces of Matto Grosso and Rio Grande do Sul and the Argentine territory of Corrientes and Missions, López kept his army within Paraguayan boundaries and fought a defensive war. It is doubtful whether any group of people ever displayed more bravery and heroism for any cause than the Paraguayans displayed for López and Paraguay. The allies, at first under the command of President Mitre, began the invasion of Paraguay in the spring of 1866. They suffered a terrible defeat in September of the same year when they attacked the strongly defended Curupaití, which guarded the Paraguay River just above its junction with the Paraná. Nevertheless, this fortress was later taken, and in February, 1868, the allied fleet passed Humiatá. Situated

[2] This summary is based on several volumes of material. The secondary accounts are: the three anonymous works, *General McMahon's Opinions in Regard to the Paraguayan War*; *Revelations on the Paraguayan War*; and *The Paraguayan Question*. Porter C. Bliss is probably the author of these three works. See also: G. Benites, *Anales Diplomática y Militar de la Guerra del Paraguay*, 2 vols.; J. P. Benitez, *La Causa Nacional*; P. H. Box, *The Origins of the Paraguayan War*; M. García, *Paraguay and the Alliance Against the Tyrant Francisco Solano López*; Commander A. J. Kennedy, *La Plata, Brazil, and Paraguay During the Present War*; G. F. Masterman, *Seven Eventful Years in Paraguay*; Dr. A. Rebandi, *Guerra del Paraguay*; *Sen. Ex. Doc.* 53, 41 Cong., 3 sess. (serial 1440); C. A. Washburn, *History of Paraguay*, 2 vols. For primary materials see: Washburn (American minister to Paraguay) to his government, particularly the first forty dispatches, in Despatches from Paraguay, I; the American government to Washburn, in Instructions to Paraguayan Ministers, I.

a league or so further up the river, this second redoubtable fortress was captured the following August. Early in 1869 allied flags were unfurled from the turrets of Asunción, though López was not overtaken on the banks of the Aquidaban until March 1, 1870.

As in any other catastrophe of such magnitude, the consequences of the Paraguayan War are difficult even to approximate. But surely one consequence was the enormous cost in human life and material wealth. Paraguay lost more than one-half of her population, either by the sword or from disease and privation; the allies lost about two hundred thousand men. Although no figures are available for Paraguay, the allied governments claim to have spent no less than one-third of a billion dollars. Most of the allied cost, in both men and treasure, was borne by Brazil. As in other wars, many individuals grew rich from war contracts. Most of the fortunes in the Paraguayan conflict were made by Argentine subjects. On the other hand, the subjects of Brazil and Paraguay were burdened for a generation to pay increased taxes resulting from loans or to rebuild industries destroyed by the fighting.

A beneficent consequence attributable at least in part to the conflict was the opening of the Plata river system to world commerce. The numerous restrictions which one nation or another had sought to impose were practically all removed. Equally important was the reduction of the rivalry between Brazil and Argentina, existing since colonial times, for the control of the intervening countries. Both seem to have learned the lesson that the independent existence of the small countries was necessary to a maintenance of the equilibrium of the whole.[3]

---

[3] These facts and opinions are based on dispatches of American agents in Brazil, Argentina, and Paraguay, and the enclosures which they contained. The *Anglo-Brazilian Times* and the Buenos Ayres *Standard* were especially important enclosures.

We must now direct attention to American connections with this far-distant conflict, particularly to such of these connections as seem to have influenced American-Brazilian relations. Although the American government refused to accept Webb's advice and offer mediation in the Brazilian-Uruguayan difficulty which led to the rupture of relations between Brazil and Paraguay, it was not long before another opportunity presented itself. Charles A. Washburn, American minister to Paraguay, felt constrained when appealed to as senior diplomatic representative at Asunción to use his influence in getting the Brazilian minister Lima and family safely out of the country following the seizure of the *Marquis de Olinda* in November, 1864. The intervention was successful, but President López let Washburn know that neither his attitude nor the language by which he made it known was pleasing to him. Strangely enough, the American reported a more favorable reaction from the dictator as the result of a later intercession in the interest of the safety of the prisoners captured with the Brazilian merchant vessel. López not only promised to observe the rules of war in the treatment of the prisoners, but he expressed regret that Washburn was taking leave from his post at such an important time.[4]

Early in 1865 the American minister engaged the Uruguayan representative at Asunción to transmit American dispatches to Washington, turned his archives over to the French consul, and set out home on a four months' leave. While at home, he did the customary thing of securing an extension of his furlough, which delayed his return until autumn. On arrival at Buenos Aires in November, he learned that he could not reach his post because of the blockade of the Paraguay

[4] Washburn to his government, Nov. 28 and Dec. 14, 1864, and Jan. 10, 1865, in Despatches from Paraguay, I; Webb to his government, Sept. 19 and Dec. 23, 1864, in Despatches from Brazil, XXX, XXXI.

River.   After spending more than two months in the Argentine capital and failing to induce Admiral Godon, commander of the South Atlantic fleet of the United States, to send him in a public ship, he proceeded up the Paraná in a merchant vessel.   When he reached Corrientes, a town of fourteen thousand people situated a few miles below the junction of the Paraná and Paraguay rivers, at the close of January (1866), he could go no further.   The allied fleet of sixteen vessels under the command of a Brazilian officer named Tamandaré, blockaded the Paraná at this point, though no formal blockade had been declared, while at the junction of the rivers above, two large armies faced each other—forty thousand Paraguayans in southern Paraguay commanding the batteries guarding both streams and sixty thousand allied troops making preparations for an attack.[5]

From Corrientes Washburn went to the headquarters of the allied army for the purpose of holding an interview with Mitre, the commander-in-chief, on the subject of proceeding to his post.   In the interview the commander seemed to admit that the minister had the right to pass through allied lines, but he was not convinced that he ought to avail himself of that right.   He felt that Washburn's presence in Paraguay would give encouragement to López, who was believed to be discouraged; and, knowing something of the American record in other instances, he was afraid that at the critical moment López might find refuge in the American embassy.   In case Washburn insisted on going to Asunción in a war vessel of his country, he might be denied the privilege, for the United States had recently set a precedent in refusing to permit foreign men-of-war to enter Confederate ports blockaded by the Lincoln government.   To be

[5] Washburn's communications of Jan. 16 and Nov. 9, 1865, and Feb. 1, 1866, in Despatches, I.

sure the situation in South America was not identical with that in North America. For one thing the allies had issued no formal blockade of Paraguayan ports; but Washburn was not anxious to discuss this question of international law. It would be an easy matter for the allied governments to convert an actual into a formal blockade.[6]

On the whole the Yankee minister was encouraged by the conference. Not only did the commander admit that he had a right to pass through allied lines, but he intimated that he thought permission would be granted. He desired, however, to communicate with his ministers on the matter. If consultation with them led to a favorable decision—and Washburn got the impression that it would—a conference would be held with the allies in order to reach a final answer. Thinking he might exert a salutary influence and speed up the procedure, Washburn hastened to Buenos Aires. Whatever his influence on the conferences at the Argentine capital, Elizaldi, the foreign minister, prepared a favorable reply to the question submitted and dispatched it by the same steamer which took Washburn back to Corrientes. This reply was submitted to General Mitre with high hope. But high hope was soon turned into disappointment. As a result of the allied conferences, the minister was refused permission to proceed to his post. Washburn believed the adverse decision was due to the opposition of Tamandaré, the Brazilian who commanded the allied fleet; he thought Mitre had yielded in order to preserve harmony of allied policy. Whether or not this version was accurate, the result was the same.[7]

But the American minister was not the sort to yield without still further effort. He renewed his request to the allied general, who promised to submit it again to the consideration

---

[6] Washburn's dispatch of Feb. 8, 1866, and its enclosures, in *ibid*.
[7] Dispatches of Mar. 16 and Apr. 27, 1866, with enclosures, in *ibid*.

of his government.   In addition he entered into negotiations with Brazil's special agent at Buenos Aires, Octaviano, whom he reminded of the aid rendered Brazil in getting Lima and family out of Asunción following López' capture of the *Marquis de Olinda*.   Washburn told the Brazilian that except for the delay in taking his leave caused by his solicitations in behalf of Lima, he would have been back at his post before the blockade of the Paraguay River by the allied forces. Octaviano gave these arguments courteous attention.

Early in July (1866) the Yankee minister took boat from Buenos Aires to Corrientes, where he went into conference with General Mitre.   Discouraged and exasperated, Washburn pressed for an answer—long overdue—from the allied chief.   When it finally came, about six months after the request had been made, it was adverse.   This time General Mitre denied Washburn's right to proceed to his post, that is, by the route he was insisting on taking, and justified in part his position by reference to the view of the American Admiral Godon.[8]

Meanwhile, the American government had entered the arena.   Soon after learning of the hindrance to Washburn's proceeding to his post, the secretary of state dispatched instructions to our ministers at Rio de Janeiro and Buenos Aires, as well as to Washburn, directing them to request of the allied authorities explanations for their attitudes.   Enclosed with the instruction to Washburn was a second instruction which the Department of the Navy had issued to Admiral Godon.   The latter document, which was to be delivered only in case the hindrance to the minister's proceeding continued after the delivery of his instructions to the

[8] Washburn's dispatches of June 8 and 15, July 9, 23, 26, and 27, 1866, in *ibid.*, II.

allied commander, ordered the admiral to send Washburn to his post in a public vessel under convoy.[9]

Instead of presenting these instructions to General Mitre, as he was told, Washburn left Corrientes for Buenos Aires. He saw no necessity for repeating a request which had just been rejected. Furthermore, General Mitre had just told him that future representations should be directed to the Argentine government and not to a busy commander. Perhaps he failed to give sufficient weight to a request accompanied by an order from his superiors. On August 8 (1866), the day following his arrival at the Argentine metropolis, the exasperated minister addressed a letter to Admiral Godon in which he enclosed copies of the instructions from Washington. But, as the admiral was on a cruise up the Brazilian coast, he did not get the message for several weeks. In the meantime, Washburn and the United States minister at Buenos Aires had ample time to present the American case to the Argentine government.

When Admiral Godon finally replied (September 16), he declined to furnish a vessel to convey Washburn to his post until the latter had complied with his instructions and presented another request to the allied commander and the Argentine government, and until presentation of proof that the request had been denied by the proper authorities. Thus continued the disagreement between the two American agents which had begun the preceding January, when the admiral, after offering many excuses, refused to send the minister to Asunción in a vessel under his command.[10]

At this point it is well to note the nature of negotiations

[9] Copies of the instructions to Washburn and Admiral Godon are in Instructions to Paraguayan Ministers, I, 79-81.

[10] See especially Washburn's dispatches of Aug. 10, and Oct. 3 and 8, 1866, in *ibid.*

at the Brazilian capital. It will be remembered that the imperial government seemed to offer strongest opposition to Washburn's passing allied lines, and that the Washington government directed its agent at Rio de Janeiro to request an explanation for the opposition. Since Webb was on a furlough in the United States, negotiations were for a time handled by Chargé Lidgerwood, who presented the views of his government during the first days of July (1866). In the conferences with the Brazilian foreign minister, which were attended by Admiral Godon, there was a manifestation of cordiality on both sides. Still it was made clear that the Brazilian cabinet was opposed to granting the request that was being pressed. While there had been no opposition to Washburn's going to his post a month before, at the particular time he wanted to go the allies had their forces drawn up ready for an attack. In addition to the military inconvenience was the moral effect of his passing; it would strengthen the peace party in Argentina and greatly hearten the followers of López. To be sure, the American chargé had to marshal arguments to sustain the position of his government, absurd though it might be. Among other things he said it would be unneutral for the United States to send representatives to one group of belligerents and at the same time withhold them from the other.

The arguments between the two American agents and the Brazilian minister finally narrowed down until they centered on the question whether it was preferable to permit Washburn to slip quietly through the military lines of the allies or to have him go through in a war vessel of the United States. Although the Americans hoped the latter method might be avoided, largely because of the advantage Europeans would take of the break in the fluvial blockade, they said there was no alternative unless Brazil yielded. Finally, at a private and confidential interview, of which no records were kept, there was agreement on the milder of the two methods. Even so, Washburn was to pass to his post under Brazil's *protest*, which meant that there would be further discussion at some future date.[11]

The time for reopening the discussion was not long deferred. But it was reopened by Minister Webb, not by Brazil. As soon after his return from the United States as his physical condition permitted, he delved into the matter. The investigation revealed that Lidgerwood had made the error of not showing his instructions to the Brazilian foreign minister. If he had done so, he could have secured more, for they were peremptory. From the conferences which he held Webb got the *inference* that the order had been given to permit Washburn to pass through allied lines; but he was not satisfied with this. He must have something more than *inference* to send to his government. Just at the strategic moment he received Seward's instruction of June 27 which directed him to demand an explanation peremptorily. In case it were denied, Webb was to ask for his passports. This was all that Webb desired. He rushed to the foreign minister and placed the instructions in his hand, pretending, however, that they should have been submitted after he had asked for his passports. The result was that the decision reached in the private and confidential interview between Admiral Godon and Lidgerwood and the foreign minister before his return was made known to him—at least officially. To this confidential agreement Webb now secured open sanction. It goes without saying that the New Yorker

[11] Chargé Lidgerwood to the secretary of state, July 2 and 8, and Aug. 9, 1866, with their many enclosures, in Brazilian Despatches, XXXII.

scored his own column of the credit sheet for the accomplishment.[12]

Returning to the stranded minister, we may note that he was finally granted the privilege he so much desired—going through allied lines in a war vessel of his beloved country. Admiral Godon finally yielded, probably because of fear of removal from his command rather than because of a change of judgment, and complied with the order which had been sent from Washington some time before. On October 24 the U. S. S. *Shamokin,* Crosby commanding, took the minister and family aboard and set out up the Paraná. When she reached Tres Bocas, the commander communicated with Tamandaré of the allied fleet, from whom was secured permission to pass, and proceeded up the Paraguay. But on account of low water and danger from floating torpedoes the *Shamokin* ascended the Paraguay only a short distance when Washburn and family disembarked and took a coach to Humiatá. Later they boarded a small Paraguayan vessel which landed them at Asunción. At last the American minister was back at his post, after an absence of twenty-two months, half of which time had been spent in an attempt to secure permission to pass through the military lines of Paraguay's enemies. Obviously, he had incurred an enormous personal expense, for which he laid much blame on the commander of the American fleet in the South Atlantic. He accused the commander of being under the influence of the officials of the Brazilian government. A glance at Washburn's conduct after his return may help one to believe that Admiral Godon rendered

[12] Webb's dispatch of Aug. 24, 1866, with enclosures, in *ibid.;* instructions of the State Department, Apr. 21 and June 27, 1866, in Instructions to Brazilian Ministers, XVI, 143-146.

his country a great service. In a way it seems unfortunate that he saw fit to obey orders at all![13]

The summer before Washburn returned to Asunción, after his long absence, our minister at Rio de Janeiro again urged his government to offer mediation in the Paraguayan conflict. He thought the terrible suffering in allied ranks, both from disease and the obstinate resistance offered by the enemy, and from the difficulty of recruiting armies would probably make interposition acceptable. If the United States did not intervene, he argued, England and France were certain to do so; and under the circumstances his country could not object. By all means the United States should follow up the action which had led to the recent agreement for the withdrawal of French troops from Mexico and assume her right to interpose in all the international conflicts of the Western world. She should, thought Webb, impress on all American governments that it is their duty, as well as their interest, to look to the great republic for protection and advice—protection from European interference and friendly advice and counsel in their difficulties with one another. The minister hoped his government would give him instructions to carry out his suggestions; but if a crisis arose before he heard from the Potomac, he thought it would be his duty to act uninstructed.[14]

The Washington government declined to act on Webb's suggestions and offer unsolicited mediation in the conflict, though it did indicate a disposition to tender its services in case one or more of the belligerents signified a willingness

[13] Washburn to Seward, Nov. 6, 1866, and Jan. 9, 1867, in Despatches from Paraguay, II; Seward to Washburn, June 27 and Oct. 23, 1866, in Instructions to Paraguayan Ministers, I, 83-84, 90-92.
[14] Webb to Seward, Aug. 7, 1866, in Brazilian Despatches, XXXII.

to accept them. Whether or not it received from any source any intimation of the attitude of any belligerent, a circular offering mediation was soon dispatched to each of the warring nations. It proposed a cessation of fighting and a congress to be held in Washington—so the United States could be the umpire—for the discussion of terms of peace. When Washburn presented the proposal to Paraguay early in March (1867), it was accepted. But a few days later when he passed through the military lines and presented the identic proposal to the Marquis of Caxias, now commander of allied forces, it was declined. The Brazilian said the allies would never treat with López; the elimination of the dictator was a *sine qua non* for discussing peace. In May Webb received a similar reply from the Brazilian government. Following the answers from imperial officials, came statements from the governments of both Brazil and Paraguay setting forth the causes which precipitated the conflict. Interestingly enough, the events detailed in justification of the procedure of each country were for the most part accurate, though of course the respective interpretations and emphases differed.

The staunchest opponent of mediation had spoken for the allies. Washburn was at the time, as he had ever been, very suspicious of Brazil's motives in the war. The large army and powerful fleet which she was assembling might foreshadow menacing intentions in the entire region of La Plata. Had she not boasted that if she wanted territory in Paraguay and Uruguay the United States had already set her an example in taking California? Webb's version of her opposition to mediation, however, was that peace on any other basis than victory meant an end to Emperor Pedro II and to monarchy, which incidentally was a true one. In both Brazil and Argentina opponents of the cessation of war were to be found among those who were making fortunes by selling war supplies.[15]

Not long after the close of negotiations on the mediation proposal of the United States, and within less than sixteen months after Washburn's return from his prolonged furlough, events came to pass in Paraguay which enlivened the dull routine of diplomacy. On February 21, 1868, it was announced in Asunción that several Brazilian iron-clads had passed the fort of Humiatá and were on their way up the river. Two days later came the presidential order for the complete and immediate evacuation of the capital, which was to be turned into a military post. López announced that he expected to move his seat of government to Luque, a small village ten miles inland, and requested all foreigners to take themselves thither also. The American minister refused to obey the order to leave the capital, claiming the right to choose the seat of his official residence. Furthermore, he said the Paraguayan government had no right by mere proclamation to compel foreigners of non-official status to move their residences, for to do so involved the loss of business and property and imposed many personal hardships. Of course, López refused to accept these contentions. Then followed a diplomatic encounter which served only to embitter feelings on both sides and with the details of which we need not concern ourselves. There was never again cordiality between the American minister and López.

As soon as the evacuation order was made known, many foreign residents of Asunción sought Washburn, the only diplomatic agent in the country with the rank of minister,

[15] These statements are based on Washburn's communications of Dec. 25, 1866, Jan. 5 and 9, Mar. 11, 12, 25, and 26, and Aug. 6, 1867, in Despatches from Paraguay, II; Webb's communications of Jan. 24 and May 3, 1867, in Despatches from Brazil, XXXII; Seward's instruction of Oct. 10, 1866, in Instructions to Brazilian Ministers, XVI, 158-159.

to learn what course he would pursue. Upon being informed that he would remain at his post, most of the enquirers took themselves and their valuables to the American legation for safety. Among the persons received were a score of English subjects, the Portuguese consul, and two former officials of Uruguay; the rest of the half hundred were Americans.[16]

The Brazilian gun-boats arrived before Asunción as expected; and on February 24 they bombarded the single fort that guarded the town. But after the bombardment they returned down the river to allied lines. It was not until a month later, after the fall of the strong fort of Humiatá, that López and followers sought safety in the interior and that the capital was evacuated by Paraguayans. After evacuation the colony of foreigners shut up in the American legation found it difficult to secure food and supplies to maintain existence. Still the American minister insisted on remaining rather than to become a camp-follower; he insisted on remaining even though it incurred the ill-will of López and placed in jeopardy the very lives of himself and those who sought his official protection.

The five months' period between the evacuation of Asunción and Washburn's departure from Paraguay was indeed one of suspense and trepidation for those shut up in the American legation, including the American agent himself. During much of the time the occupants were afraid to venture from the building over which fluttered the Stars and Stripes. Only the servants entered and left the premises to assemble food and other necessities for the restless shut-ins; even these lowly ones went about the execution of their orders with much inconvenience, for a dozen, twenty, or forty

---

[16] Washburn's dispatch of Apr. 7, 1868, in Despatches, II.

policemen were stationed to halt, to query, and otherwise to
molest. But why the close confinement and the many policemen? With details omitted, it was because López and Washburn had fallen into a violent controversy. The controversy,
like most altercations, had begun with a disagreement—the
removal of the American legation from Asunción—and had
gathered force with the passing of time and the exchange of
communications.

Following the disagreement over removal of the legation,
was López' request for the surrender of the Portuguese consul, who for some not obvious reason had sought cover of the
United States flag instead of that of his own country. And
for some reason not obvious to all, the request was denied
until evidence was produced showing a specific charge. Next
came the request for dismissal from the legation of all who
were without official connections, including specifically two
citizens of the republic of Uruguay, an American named Porter C. Bliss, and an Englishman named George F. Masterman. Again refusal was Washburn's reply. But López'
persistence finally caused so much fear among the non-Amer-
icans that most of them left voluntarily, preferring to throw
themselves upon the mercy of the dictator rather than further incur his wrath by remaining. Still López was not satisfied. He insisted on the surrender of Bliss and Masterman.
As a last resort, Washburn attempted to give the men protection by claiming that they were members of his official
family. He announced that Bliss was his translator and that
Masterman was his family physician. When this device
failed of its purpose, the Yankee minister had no recourse
left except that of asking for his passports, of which he soon
availed himself.

At this point—about the middle of July—López made it
known that a conspiracy against his government had been

discovered. Many were implicated: several officials of the Paraguayan government, including the minister of foreign affairs; at least two refugee Uruguayans who had held high office under the Colorados; high officials of the allied army; Bliss, Masterman, the American minister and others. With the exception of the Paraguayans, the conspirators were sheltered at the American legation; indeed, the arch-conspirator was no other than the American minister himself. Three of the conspirators who had fallen victims to López deposed that Washburn had made frequent use of his office to facilitate communication between their group and the group of colleagues in allied ranks. It was alleged that the fourteen months which the minister consumed ostensibly in getting permission to pass through allied lines were in reality spent in working out the plan of the conspiracy. It was said that even J. Watson Webb at Rio de Janeiro was an accomplice in the plot. According to the charge, the conspirators aimed to overthrow López and place the Paraguayan government in the hands of a spineless group which would favor bringing the war to a close on terms entirely favorable to the allies and a conciliatory policy toward all foreigners.

Needless to say that Washburn denied all the allegations which in any way implicated him or brought disrepute upon his office. He even questioned the existence of any plot or conspiracy against López; he thought such was impossible under the system of espionage prevailing in Paraguay at the time. To the reviewer of the evidence the arguments of the defendant seem indeed weak. For the extreme solicitations in behalf of those taken under the protection of the American flag and for the minister's frequent sojourns in the allied lines the explanations were inadequate.

Notwithstanding López' displeasure at Washburn's conduct, he decided, except in two cases, to issue the passports for which request had been made almost two months before. On September 10, after receipt of news that the American war vessel *Wasp* was at Villeta, a small village a few miles below Asunción, to which it had been agreed the ship might come, the Yankee minister and his official family boarded the Paraguayan *Rio Apa* and bade farewell to Asunción. En route to the dock Bliss and Masterman, to whom passports had not been granted, were taken into custody by López' policemen. Although it availed nothing, Washburn sent a warm note of protest to López before crossing Paraguayan boundaries. Going via Buenos Aires, where he found the papers filled with obloquy for him, and Rio de Janeiro, where he reminisced with Webb, he reported to his superiors at Washington during the first days of 1869. Soon he was to assume the rôle of historian as a means of self-defense.[17]

Once more we must turn back in order to get some conception of negotiations at the Brazilian capital. As soon as Watson Webb learned that the *Wasp,* which Commander Davis of the South Atlantic squadron had ordered to Asunción to convey Washburn and family out of Paraguay, had not been permitted to pass the allied blockade after waiting forty-seven days, he prepared to use his cudgel. In a note of July 1 (1868) he told the Brazilian government that the refusal of Marshal Caxias to open his lines to the American vessel was a repetition of the insult of 1866 and was, there-

---

[17] Dispatches of Sept. 26, Oct. 5 and 13, 1868, with their voluminous enclosures, in *ibid.*; the Buenos Aires *Standard* for Sept. 26, 1868; the three works of Bliss and the one of Masterman already cited. Washburn's *History of Paraguay*, 2 vols., written upon his return to the United States, the writer considers wholly unreliable for the Paraguayan War. Written largely for self-defense, it presents an account almost entirely at variance with that found in the minister's dispatches sent before he fell into controversy with López. Interestingly enough, the biased history became the Bible of all American, most English, and many Latin-American writers who have touched upon the history of Paraguay during the period of the war. In such manner is our history often written.

fore, doubly offensive. Although he assumed that the
commander had acted without orders, he requested an explanation and an apology. A week later, the day before he
had a reply, he wrote Seward that he expected to follow the
instructions sent him two years before on the occasion of a
similar episode and ask for his passports in case of failure of
the imperial government to comply with his request.

The imperial government replied (July 9) that the conduct of Marshal Caxias met its approbation rather than its
censure. While the government had acquiesced in the passage of the *Shamokin* in 1866, it had never admitted the
principle; the acquiescence had been accompanied by a protest. At the same time Webb was reminded that the recent
request to pass the blockade had been vitiated because of its
having been presented by a subordinate who was incompetent
to make such request and that two alternative methods of
leaving Paraguay had been offered Washburn, namely, by
land or by a Brazilian vessel under a flag of truce.

Four days later came Webb's long and angry reply. It
stated that the commander of the *Wasp* had not approached
Marshal Caxias to make a direct request, but rather to inform him courteously of his definitive intentions. As to the
right of the American vessel to pass to her destination, the
hot-headed minister said he had no mandate. Hadn't Seward declared Brazil's policy—in a different case two years
before—"disrespectful in itself, and entirely inconsistent
with the law of nations?" The alternatives proposed for
Washburn's exit he denounced as absolutely unfriendly and
offensive. The epistle closed with a threat of a break in
diplomatic relations, though it urged Brazil to reconsider in
order to prevent it.

At this point a change in the Brazilian ministry, necessitated by the opposition of the Assembly to the continuance

of the war, caused a brief delay in negotiations. When they were resumed, the government of Emperor Pedro II tried to shift a part of the responsibility for its policy to its allies in the war. The American minister would not countenance the evasion. Moreover, he took advantage of the ministerial crisis at Rio de Janeiro to press his program all the harder. He made known, in his matchless way, the contents of a cablegram which he had sent to Washington urging preparedness on the part of his government to enforce its demands. In his opinion Brazil would be compelled to pay the cost, amounting to two million dollars, of the American iron-clads to be dispatched to force the passage to Asunción! Finally, the Brazilian government yielded to bullying and agreed to permit an American vessel to pass the allied blockade. Thereupon the *Wasp*, under command of Captain Kirkland, proceeded to Villeta, Paraguay, where it met the *Rio Apa* bearing Washburn from Asunción. Webb, yet unaware that his conduct had not met complete approval at Washington, reported to his government that he had won a complete victory.[18]

Although he thought he had won a complete victory in securing Brazil's acquiescence in the right of American public vessels to pass the allied blockade, Webb contended that his own country had done only half her duty in sending the *Wasp* to Villeta. In a private and unofficial letter to Seward on August 25, 1868, he implored the secretary to send a large naval force to Paraguay to make a demonstration of American power. But before receiving Seward's private reply to his private communication the minister's usual impatience had once more exerted itself. Feeling that his

[18] For this acrimonious controversy see Webb's dispatches of July 7 and 22, and Aug. 7, 1868, and numerous enclosures, in Despatches, XXXIII; Seward's instructions of Aug. 17 and Sept. 22, 1868, in Instructions to Brazilian Ministers, XVI, 207-210, 213.

country's honor was at stake, he attempted to convince Rear Admiral Charles H. Davis that it was his duty to send a force—every vessel under his command if necessary—to Paraguay to secure the release of Bliss and Masterman. Such action would vindicate our national honor and prove to England that she was not the only nation capable of giving protection to the lives, property, and diplomatic rights of her subjects. Notwithstanding the fact that Webb offered to assume responsibility for the venture, the admiral was not disposed to make the expedition without instructions from his superiors. Webb persisted in his view to such extent that the commander got the impression he was interfering with his business. The disagreement developed until it became an acrimonious dispute which involved an exchange of bitter epithets.

At this point a third party entered the arena. General M. T. McMahon, who had been appointed minister resident to Paraguay in July (1868), had just stopped off at Rio de Janeiro to confer with Webb, as instructed. In the conferences on conditions in Paraguay Webb told the new minister he should proceed to his post and demand the release of Bliss and Masterman; but under no circumstances should he present his credentials to López, who had put himself and country beyond the pale of civilization. The second suggestion was supported by the fact that McMahon's instructions were out of date, since they had been issued before it had become known in Washington that two members of the American legation were being detained by López' orders. Suffice it to say that once more the Webbonian arguments accomplished no good result. Quite to the contrary, they produced ruffled feelings, as they had in the case of the rear admiral. General McMahon soon departed for Buenos Aires, where he made further inquiries concerning the Paraguayan situation before proceeding to his destination in the *Wasp*, commanded by Rear Admiral Davis himself.

After arrival at the army headquarters of López, General McMahon and Admiral Davis gave first attention to Bliss and Masterman, for whose security there had been a great deal of anxiety. The captives were found in comparative safety and following a few preliminaries the dictator took them from the custody of a Paraguayan court and turned them over to the American representatives. The chief condition of the release was that the men be placed aboard an American vessel as prisoners and taken to Washington and tried for the serious crimes with which they were charged. Agreement to this anomalous condition of release caused Webb to denounce the conduct of both Minister McMahon and Admiral Davis. The prestige and honor of the United States had been dragged in the mire; what was worse, the conduct of Washburn and Webb had been repudiated! But the conduct of McMahon and Davis had secured the results; the conduct of Washburn and Webb could not have done so under any circumstances.

This part of the story may be concluded with a few observations of General McMahon, who resided near López' army headquarters for several months. While he made no attempt to deny that the Paraguayan dictator had practiced barbarities, he considered the abuses on the allied side not one whit less barbarous. The charges of inhuman practices by the dictator had geen grossly exaggerated by the allied press, the only medium by which news reached the outside world. López had not murdered his mother and sisters; McMahon saw them living in comfort near the dictator. But the minister was impressed with the barbarous conduct of the allied armies, whose officers and privates pillaged and plundered at will. And others than Paraguayans were often the victims. The American legation abandoned by Washburn in September (1868) was soon robbed of its contents valued at a quarter of a million dollars—not by Paraguayans, but by Brazilians. The furniture used by the former American minister had been removed to fit out the residence of the allied commander, Marshal Caxias; the archives of the legation were found strewn in the streets of the capital. Moreover, the Paraguayan flag and the flag of truce were used and abused in a fashion befitting the society of the remotest jungles. Read two sentences from the pen of General McMahon:

Of the atrocities real or reputed committed on the Paraguayan side it is needless to say a word as the allied governments and press have spared no means, honorable or otherwise, to defame their enemy and having the ear of the world they have succeeded in causing President López to be accepted as a monster of atrocity. On the other hand the infamies authorized or permitted by the allied armies now operating in Paraguay surpass if possible the atrocities they charge upon their enemy.

But a change of administrations in the United States resulted in McMahon's recall in the spring of 1869. In a few weeks after receiving the notice he set out for home via Buenos Aires. The few days spent in the Argentine capital were indeed unhappy ones for the ex-minister. The press attacked him in a manner unusually violent—even for a Latin-American press. Before the appointment of a successor to McMahon in May, 1870, the allied army had run down López and he had committed suicide on the banks of the Aquidaban. The United States contributed her part in preventing even the consideration of the dismemberment of Paraguay by the allied powers.[19]

[19] These statements are based on Brazilian dispatches of Oct. 8 and 24, Dec. 20 and 26, 1868, Jan. 25, Feb. 9, Mar. 25, and Apr. 7, 1869, in Despatches from Brazil,

During the critical period of the Civil War in the United States the American minister to Brazil, following instructions from the Potomac, had desisted from pressing the claims of his countrymen against the Rio government. During such a crisis it seemed unwise to take the chance of offending a friend. Yet while this friend was engaged in a deathlike grapple with Paraguay the same minister—again in pursuance of instructions—pressed assiduously for the settlement of these claims. Such were the ethics of American diplomacy under management of the two New Yorkers.

The outstanding cases which Webb pressed for settlement during the Paraguayan War were those of the *Nebo*, the *Edna*, the *Caroline*, and the *Canada*, vessels which suffered injuries in the eighteen-fifties. Briefly, the case of the *Nebo* arose when a portion of her goods was seized by imperial customs officers and the vessel fined because her captain "clearly violated the revenue laws of Brazil." Notwithstanding the fact that Webb's immediate predecessor, under whose administration the case arose, and Webb himself admitted the claim had no legal basis and that the final claimant had purchased his interests from an insane agent of an insolvent insurance company at a very low figure, the case was pressed until the Brazilian government finally allowed the sum of nine thousand milreis in settlement. This sum, which represented the sale price of the forfeited goods plus six per cent interest, was paid, however, as an act of *grace*, not as a duty.[20]

XXXIV; Paraguayan dispatches of Dec. 11, 1868, Jan. 23 and 31, Apr. 21, May 27, June 1, July 13, 19, and 29, Nov. 18, 1869, May 5 and 9, and July 11, 1870, in Despatches from Paraguay, III; instructions to Webb, Sept. 22, 1868, in Instructions to Brazilian Ministers, XVI, 213; instructions to McMahon, Mar. 15, 1869, in Instructions to Paraguayan Ministers, I, 141-142. The dispatches contain countless enclosures.

[20] See Webb's dispatches of Oct. 7, 1862, Oct. 24, 1866, and Mar. 31, 1867, in Despatches, XXVIII and XXXII; Seward's instructions of Sept. 27, 1862, and Aug. 3, 1866, in Instructions to Brazilian Ministers, XVI.

In the case of the *Edna* the vessel was wrecked on the coast of Rio Grande do Sul in the summer of 1855. According to the laws of Brazil the portion of the cargo saved should have been sold on the scene of the disaster under the supervision of a board of survey. Instead of proceeding legally, the board transported the salvaged cargo, chiefly flour, at considerable cost to the customs house at São José do Norte. Later, the owner was paid the amount for which the goods sold, minus the cost of transportation from the place of the wreck to the place of sale. Dissatisfied with the amount received, the owner placed an exorbitant claim with the Brazilian government for the losses which he had incurred. In the course of the litigation, the claim had been sold by marine insurance companies to a third party, one Mr. Peck by name, for a nominal sum. As a result of the pressure brought under General Webb, the third-party claimant secured fourteen thousand milreis as a compromise settlement, half of which was interest charges accumulated during the twelve years of litigation.[21]

The facts in the third case, that of the *Caroline*, need not detain us. It is sufficient to say that the case had less basis in justice than either of the preceding cases. As in the case of the *Edna*, this claim had been purchased from insurance companies which had given up hope of an adjustment. The purchaser, who had been let out of the consular service of the United States because of irregularities, had offered to take many times less for his claim than the amount finally wrested from the Brazilian government. Of greater interest is the method through which the claim was adjusted. Although Brazil had rejected it peremptorily several times, it was finally presented during the critical period of the Par-

---

[21] Webb's communications of Oct. 7, 1862, and Apr. 22, 1867, with enclosures, contain sufficient data for this case (Despatches, XXXII, XXXIII).

aguayan War. After another refusal of the Rio government
to discuss the question of validity, the impetuous American
minister threatened to break off diplomatic relations and resort to reprisals. When this bluff seemed unlikely to succeed of itself, he interviewed an influential member of the
opposition party and secured his support. Finally, largely
because of embarrassments consequent upon the war, the imperial government reluctantly decided to allow the claim.
The settlement brought strong criticism upon the American
government and violent attacks upon the ministry responsible
for it.[22]

But the sequel of the *Caroline* settlement is more interesting than the settlement proper. Shortly after the adjustment was made Webb sent to Washington a bill on the
Brazilian financial agent in London for five thousand pounds.
In the State Department the question of to whom the money
should be delivered arose and was referred to the office of
the attorney general for decision. When the reply from the
latter office finally came, more than four years later, strangely
enough there was no applicant for the money. Under the
circumstances the only honorable thing to do was to return
the twenty-five thousand dollars to the Brazilian government. Accordingly, the secretary of state, Hamilton Fish,
arranged a conference with the Brazilian minister at Washington to make arrangements for the return. At this conference Fish learned that Watson Webb had received from
the Brazilian government not one bill of exchange on London for five thousand pounds but three bills of exchange for
a total of fourteen thousand one hundred and fifty-two
pounds. As a result of this startling revelation, Fish ordered an investigation at Rio de Janeiro with the hope of

[22] Dispatches of Oct. 1, 1867, Feb. 10 and July 8, 1868, *ibid.*, XXXIII.

getting further information on the *Caroline* settlement. Since some of the pertinent documents were not to be found in the archives of the American embassy at Rio, the only information gained through the investigation was that Webb had receipted for the full amount asked for in the case, that he had received the money paid by Brazil's financial agent in London, and that he secured the settlement from Brazil by a threat to break off diplomatic relations. But this was sufficient, and on May 16, 1874, while the Consular and Diplomatic Appropriation Bill was under consideration, Hamilton Fish and E. R. Hoar appeared before the House of Representatives with enough evidence supporting the allegations against Webb to convince the legislative body that it should pass appropriations to make possible the return to Brazil of the seventy thousand dollars with interest. Later in the same year the attorney general brought suit against the ex-minister in the United States court for the southern district of New York to recover the difference between the amount turned over to the government (twenty-five thousand dollars) and the amount received from Brazil (about seventy thousand dollars). It seems that the suit never came to trial.[23] If this be true, the explanation may lie in the fact that the powerful trio, Evarts, Southmayd, and Choate, were the defendant's attorneys.

General Webb returned from a lengthy sojourn on the Rhine, where he had gone for recuperation following the termination of his strenuous mission to Brazil, and undertook to defend himself against the allegations connected with the *Caroline* settlement. In a pamphlet which he wrote for the

[23] The writer has a letter, dated Nov. 21, 1927, from the office of the clerk for the United States court for the southern district of New York stating that the records fail to show that any cause was instituted against Webb and suggesting that the case never came to trial.

purpose, he asserted that Seward knew the claim would be paid through Brazilian influences and that "the money would go to reward partisans"; yet the secretary had approved of his conduct, energy, and sagacity in the settlement—probably a true statement. The remainder of the defense lay in the fact that Webb's ancestors had been good patriots from Bunker Hill down, and that he himself had been as good a party man as any "hundred percenter" could possibly be— no doubt a true statement.[24]

A fourth claim pushed by Webb arose from the wreck of an American whaling vessel, the *Canada*, on Garças Reef in 1856. Althbugh the claim had a strong basis in fact, like most other American claims the amount requested by the claimant was absurd. But again we are not so much concerned with the basis upon which the claim rested or with the amount demanded as with the tactics employed in the negotiations and their consequences. Not long after the American minister had reopened the case, in the autumn of 1869, the Brazilian foreign minister, probably because of his dislike for Webb, sent the papers relating to the case to the imperial minister at Washington and requested him to confer with Secretary Seward with the view to getting a settlement more favorable to Brazil. When Webb, who at the time did not know of the intention to transfer negotiations to the Potomac, learned of the move, he was furious. There had been a gentleman's agreement not to submit to superiors the details of the negotiations in this case. Strange the secrecy of these negotiations! It is reminiscent of the *Caroline* settlement.

[24] *General J. Watson Webb vs. Hamilton Fish and E. R. Hoar;* Minister Partridge to Fish, May 14, 1872, in Brazilian Despatches, XXXIX; Secretary Fish to Partridge, Mar. 14, 1872, in Instructions to Brazilian Ministers, XVI, 355-359; Brazil, *Relatorio*, 1868 and 1875.

For some reason or other, ostensibly for health and on account of business, General Webb spent the winter of 1868-1869 in the United States. While at home, he learned that the Brazilian foreign minister had over-reached him; yet he gave of his time and information in straightening out the *Canada* claim. Indeed, he claimed a large share of the credit for a more generous attitude on the part of the American government toward the claim; he practically wrote the more considerate instruction sent out from Washington in the early part of 1869 for guidance in a changed policy. When, after his return to Rio de Janeiro, the time came to carry the new instruction into execution, he abandoned his conciliatory rôle and resumed his older and more natural one. The excuse for the change was the refusal of the Brazilian foreign minister to reopen negotiations on the *Canada* claim until notification should be received from the imperial minister at Washington that the case had been transferred back to Rio de Janeiro for settlement; without doubt the reason was the fact that the case had been transferred to Washington in the first place without Webb's consent.

As a consequence of the refusal of the foreign minister to reopen negotiations, Webb flew into a rage. Stating that such refusal was a denial of Seward's right to issue an instruction and an insult to his government, he directed a blazing communication to the foreign minister in which he asked for his passports. When the reply came, it was accompanied by the passports. After both parties had made public such documents and explanations as gave support to their respective courses, the British envoy at Rio de Janeiro, George Buckley Mathew, offered mediation. As a result, the offensive communications on both sides were recalled and official relations were restored. Two hours after the reconciliation Webb's boat sailed for New York and a mission of almost eight years was brought to a close. Before learning of the final outcome the new administration at Washington set about the task of repairing a breach which it felt certain existed but which did not meet the approval, either of the new secretary of state or of the American press.[25]

It is with relief that one turns from the diplomacy of Seward and Webb. While it is possible to credit the two New Yorkers with several temporary victories, in the end the prestige of the United States suffered. For a quarter of a century Brazilians remembered the methods and tactics of these two men, especially of the minister.

[25] Instructions of Webb and Chargé Lidgerwood, Jan. 23 and June 18, 1869, in Instructions to Brazilian Ministers, XVI, 217-221, 231-232; dispatches of May 8 and 27, June 8 and 26, 1869, in Despatches, XXXIII and XXXIV; Secretary Fish to Brazilian Minister Magalhães, June 18 and 21, in Notes to the Brazilian Legation, VI; *Anglo-Brazilian Times*, May 22, 1869.

CHAPTER VIII

OPENING BRAZILIAN RIVERS TO WORLD COMMERCE

FOR FOUR hundred years after the Spanish and Portuguese explorers first sighted the eastern coast of South America in the later fifteenth and early sixteenth century, communication with the interior of the region was entirely dependent upon the Plata and the Amazon river systems. Indeed, the statement would need little modification if the time were extended up to the present hour. Yet it was not until the latter half of the last century that the systems were made free to the use of nations other than those which owned the territory at their mouths. In the negotiations which culminated in opening them to the world the United States played an important rôle.

The scope of this study precludes anything more than a summary of the negotiations on the opening of the Plata. During the internecine struggles which followed the attainment of independence the government at Buenos Aires, basing its action on a treaty with Great Britain in 1825, claimed the right to open or close the river at pleasure. Since inclination always dictated closing, the interior provinces of Argentina, all of Paraguay, whose independence Buenos Aires refused to recognize, the eastern portions of Bolivia, and the southern provinces of Brazil were denied access to the sea. For more than a decade England and France vainly strove to induce General Rosas to adopt more liberal views regarding fluvial navigation. Finally, in 1849, both signed separate treaties with the dictator which recognized the navigation of the Paraná as purely a domestic matter.[1]

A change of policy with reference to the use of La Plata was not to be brought about directly by Europeans, but by Latin Americans themselves, who were more vitally concerned. Aroused because of the closing of their water communications, the inhabitants of the up-river provinces united under the leadership of General Urquiza, governor of Entre Rios, joined Brazil and the Rivera faction of Uruguay, and shattered the magic power of Rosas at Caseros on February 3, 1852. In the process of the formation of the coalition Urquiza entered into several treaties with Brazil, one of which declared for the common navigation of the Uruguay and urged the other riparian states of La Plata to agree to similar arrangements for the Paraná and Paraguay. After the defeat of Rosas and Urquiza's elevation to the office of provisional director of the Argentine Confederation, one of his first measures was the decree of October 3, 1852, declaring free to the merchant vessels of all nations the navigation of the Paraná and Uruguay rivers.[2]

The United States was one of the first nations to take advantage of the changed political situation at La Plata. Our minister at Rio de Janeiro (Robert C. Schenck), who had just witnessed the overthrow of Rosas at Caseros, wrote his government on February 14 (1852) that it was a favorable time to begin negotiations for opening the Plata River. Brazil was even willing to coöperate in the undertaking. Acting immediately, the Fillmore administration instructed Schenck to return to Buenos Aires and in conjunction with American Chargé Pendleton to conclude all treaties neces-

[1] John F. Cady, *Foreign Intervention in the Rio de la Plata, 1838-1859*, pp. 22 et seq.

[2] Secretary Webster to Miller, June 11, 1852, in Instructions to Bolivian Ministers, I, 11; *British and Foreign State Papers*, XLII, 1313.

sary for the security of our commerce and the opening of the rivers. On receipt of instructions the minister set out upon his new mission. Unfortunately, because of civil strife between the province of Buenos Aires and the confederation, his initial endeavors to negotiate with Urquiza ended in failure. Before returning to his post at Rio, however, he and Pendleton secured the ratification of a treaty at Montevideo which, among other things, opened the Uruguay River to American commerce. The following year (1853) Schenck returned to Buenos Aires and joined the British and French representatives in negotiations with the contestants for power in Argentina. After vain attempts to mediate between the contending factions, the three foreign ministers followed General Urquiza to his camp at San José de Flores, where they overcame what at first appeared to be insuperable difficulties and on July 10 signed separate but identical treaties providing for perpetual free navigation of the Paraná and Uruguay. The treaty to which the United States was a party—and presumably those made with the other powers—was ratified over vigorous protests from both the province of Buenos Aires and Brazil.[3]

On March 4, 1853, four months before the negotiation of the treaties with the Argentine Confederation, John S. Pendleton, who had gone from Buenos Aires to Asunción, concluded a commercial treaty with Paraguay, some of the terms of which provided for the free navigation of the Paraguay and the right side of the Paraná up to the Brazilian borders. But a series of unfortunate incidents occurred which brought the United States into hostile relations with Paraguay and prevented the ratification of the treaty. In

[3] Schenck to his government, Feb. 14, Sept. 4 and 17, 1852, May 12, Aug. 16 and 22, 1853, in Brazilian Despatches, XIX, XX; secretary of state to Schenck, Apr. 29, 1852, in Instructions to Brazilian Ministers, XV, 199-205.

brief, the incidents resulted from the asinine conduct of United States Consul Edward A. Hopkins, who undertook to use his official position to further his own private interests. As frequently happens, the selfish ambitions of one individual caused a whole national policy to suffer.

The acrimonious quarrel which Hopkins raised was continued when Lieutenant Thomas Jefferson Page of the United States Navy sought to induce President López of Paraguay to exchange ratifications of the Pendelton treaty. Page had gone to Paraguay in command of the steamer *Water Witch* to explore and survey all the tributaries of the Rio de la Plata so that Yankee goods might find their way into the heart of the South American continent. After experiencing considerable difficulty in securing from suspicious Brazilian officials permission for his venture, he had coöperated loyally with American diplomatic agents in the negotiation of the treaties. But the lieutenant was not unlike Consul Hopkins; his hot head soon brought him into conflict with President López over trivial formalities. Then, in October, 1854, came the decree of the Paraguayan executive prohibiting foreign vessels of war from navigating the rivers of his country. Thereafter it was necessary to limit exploration to the confines of the Argentine Confederation. Unluckily, early in the following year one of Page's officers, Lieutenant William N. Jeffers, fell into an altercation with Paraguayan officers while navigating the *Water Witch* in the Paraná. Subsequently, on February 1, as she was passing under the guns of a Paraguayan fort, the vessel was fired on and the helmsman killed.

Partly because of conditions at home, our government took no immediate action in regard to the episode on the upper Paraná. It did, however, send Richard Fitzpatrick as special commissioner in a further attempt to secure an exchange of ratifications of the treaty. But López refused to ratify until the settlement of the pending questions, and the matter was dropped until President Buchanan brought it before Congress in his message of June 2, 1858. Congress authorized the executive to take such action as he deemed necessary. Consequently, a new commissioner was sent, accompanied by a naval force of nineteen vessels. Whatever the effect of the show of force, two treaties were signed on February 4, 1859—one providing for the settlement of claims, and the other for commerce and navigation. Ratification of the latter treaty finally settled the most important questions connected with the use of the Paraná and Paraguay for world commerce. The opening of the Plata system was used as a wedge in the opening of the Amazon.[4]

In the opening of the Amazon the United States played an even more important rôle. Although the question seems to have been broached a quarter of a century before, it did not assume importance until the middle of the nineteenth century. Inasmuch as our government's interest was an outgrowth of the expansionist fever, it is not surprising that the negotiations did not get under way earlier.

The interest of the American public and government officials in the opening of the "King of Rivers" was largely the result of the untiring energy of Lieutenant Matthew Fontaine Maury, an officer of the United States Navy, superintendent of the hydrographical office, and astronomer of the naval observatory at Washington. Honored by scien-

---

[4] T. J. Page, *La Plata, the Argentine Confederation, and Paraguay; British and Foreign State Papers*, LXII, 3, 718, LXIV, 1071; J. B. Moore, *History and Digest of International Arbitration*, II, 1487 *et seq.*; E. A. Hopkins, "The Plata and the Paraná-Paraguay," in *DeBow's Review*, XIV, 238-251; E. Schuyler, *American Diplomacy*, pp. 319-328; Schenck to his government, Apr. 30, May 12, and Oct. 4, 1853, in Brazilian Despatches, XX; Trousdale to the Washington government, July 28, 1854, in *ibid.*, XXI; Secretary Cass to Minister Lamar, Oct. 23, 1857, in Instructions to Argentine Ministers, XV, 113.

tific bodies throughout the world for his work in hydrography, Lieutenant Maury brought his great learning and imagination to the promotion of industrial and commercial progress in the South. Between 1849 and 1855 he set forth his ideas in numerous articles which appeared in the *Southern Literary Messenger*, the *National Intelligencer*, the *Washington Union*, and *DeBow's Review*. Several of the items appeared under the pseudonym of "Inca"; most of them reached a larger reading public through republication, either in *DeBow's Review* or in pamphlet form under the title *Letters on the Amazon and Atlantic Slopes of South America*.[5]

Lieutenant Maury's ideas and hopes were extended and popularized still further through the Southern conventions which were held during the time. Toward the close of 1851 he wrote a committee of the Southwestern Railroad Convention, which was to convene at New Orleans in January of the following year for the purpose of considering questions of an economic nature then confronting the section, and under the title "On Extending the Commerce of the South and West by Sea," submitted certain suggestions about which he had been thinking for some time. His last, and to him the most important, suggestion for improving the industrial status of New Orleans and the entire South was the opening of the Amazon River. In expatiating upon the suggestion he said, "the free navigation of the Amazon is the greatest commercial boon that the people of the South and West—indeed that the people of the United States can crave." Following this statement was a long argument to show that the basin of the Amazon "is but a continuation of the Mississippi Valley." Between the head of the "Father of Waters" and the sources of the southern tributaries of the "King of

[5] Pereira Pinto, *Apontamentos*, II, 420.

Rivers" grew every product on the face of the earth, except tea. Finally, he asserted that the opening of the South American river in its effects upon the prosperity of the country would be equivalent to the acquisition of Louisiana, the reason for which was the fact that the direction of the winds and ocean currents would send all vessels passing out of the mouth of the Amazon through our own southern ports.[6]

Eighteen months later the lieutenant-scientist presented his ideas to the convention which assembled (June 7, 1853) at Memphis, Tennessee. Although the representatives from a large number of the southern and southwestern states met to consider questions which concerned their sections more immediately,[7] Maury took advantage of the occasion to further his own peculiar interest. The result fulfilled all hope. The convention adopted a memorial prepared by the hydrographer and authorized its author to present it to the Congress of the United States. More than thirty printed pages in length, the document described the marvelous fertility of "the Garden of the Hesperides," as the Amazon valley was called, enumerated the species of flora, fauna, and minerals which it produced, and pointed out its importance to the people of the United States. In depicting the future, the author saw the valley, whose area was more than twice that of the valley of the Mississippi, supporting a population of more than six hundred million, a prediction which to date has been fulfilled to less than a six hundredth part.

Lieutenant Maury faithfully performed the task which the convention placed upon him and in due time presented

[6] Maury's communications to the committee were printed in *DeBow's Review*, XII, 381-399, and later in the documents of the convention.

[7] P. A. Martin, in his article in *The Hispanic American Historical Review*, I, 148-162, entitled "The Influence of the United States on the Opening of the Amazon to the World's Commerce" is mistaken in assuming that Maury called the convention for the consideration of the question in which he was especially interested, or that he called the convention at all.

the memorial to the Washington legislators. On March 3, 1854, the House of Representatives referred the document to its committee on foreign affairs and ordered it printed.[8]

Meantime, the executive branch of our government, reacting from the stimulus furnished by the distinguished naval officer and other American citizens, had become concerned about the opening of the Amazon. On May 8, 1850, Secretary of State Clayton addressed to Secretary Preston of the Navy Department a letter in which he stated that his department had "for some time past had in contemplation certain measures for procuring for the citizens of the United States the navigation of the river Amazon and some of its tributaries." Alluding to "the advantages to be anticipated from a free transit on that mighty river" (reminiscent of Maury's language), Clayton requested his colleague to send a ship of war to explore the stream and its branches. In case a special permit from the Brazilian government were deemed necessary, the foreign minister felt that a copy of his letter placed in the hands of the American minister at Rio de Janeiro by the commander of the ship would serve as an instruction in securing such document or any other facilities.[9]

Whatever the reason, nine months elapsed before the Navy Department was ready to proceed with the suggested exploration, and before it did proceed, the original plan had been somewhat changed. When instructions were sent out by the secretary of the navy on February 15, 1851, instead of stipulating that exploration should begin at the mouth of the Amazon and extend upward, they provided that it should start at the sources of the tributaries and extend downward. The instructions directed Lieutenants William L. Herndon

[8] *House Misc. Doc.* 22, 33 Cong., 1 sess. (serial 741).
[9] Secretary Clayton to Secretary Preston, May 8, 1850, in Domestic Letters (MSS Dept. of State), XXXVIII, No. 21.

and Lardner Gibbon, both attached to the United States ship *Vandalia* then at Valparaiso, to set out by land from the Pacific side of the continent and explore the Amazon from its source to its mouth, together with its important tributaries. The explorers were to note the potential resources and the feasibility of water communications with the United States.

Furnished with adequate funds and scientific equipment, Herndon and Gibbon—the former in command—set out from Lima together in May, 1851. Soon, however, the company was divided into two groups, each under the command of one of the lieutenants. Taking the northernmost course, Herndon's party descended the Marañon—the name applied to the main branch of the Amazon in its upper course—and the Amazon proper to Pará, turning aside frequently to explore a tributary of the main stream. The task of this party required about eleven months. Consuming more time, Gibbon's group crossed Bolivia and descended the Madeira to its confluence with the Amazon.

Early in 1853 President Fillmore submitted Lieutenant Herndon's report to Congress and it was soon published in two volumes.[10] Circulated widely over the country, the report on the activities of these intrepid explorers exercised an indirect, though powerful, influence on the subsequent opening of the Brazilian river to world commerce.[11] It should not be forgotten, however, that Lieutenant Herndon's kinsman, Lieutenant Matthew Fontaine Maury, whose intriguing propaganda had been largely responsible for the exploring expedition, continued to wield the pen of a wizard in the interest of the opening of the "mighty river."[12]

[10] *House Ex. Doc.* 43, 32 Cong., 2 sess; *Sen. Ex. Doc.* 36, 32 Cong., 2 sess.

[11] It is perhaps significant that the commerce of the United States through the port of Pará made an immediate jump from $3,000,000 to $5,000,000 annually. See *House Report* 95, 33 Cong., 2 sess. (serial 808).

[12] See, for example, *DeBow's Review* for February, May, June, and July, 1853.

While the officer-scientist was stimulating his country-men to an interest in the Amazon, and his kinsman and fol-lowers were supplying him with first-hand information gained through exploration, the wheels of American diplo-macy began to turn. And just as the Navy Department had decided on a flank attack for making known the potentialities of the great valley, so the State Department decided on the same flank attack to secure the opening of the river. On July 26, 1851, a few weeks after Lieutenant Herndon set out from Lima on his expedition, J. Randolph Clay, United States minister to Peru, concluded a treaty of friendship, commerce, and navigation which guaranteed to the citizens of both signatories most-favored-nation treatment. In addi-tion to the general provision, a specific clause guaranteed that citizens of the United States who might establish lines of steam vessels between the different ports of entry within Peruvian territories should enjoy all the privileges and favors given to any other association or company whatsoever.

Unfortunately, this auspicious beginning could not be followed by more important results. Suspicious of American tactics and motives, the Brazilian government laid plans to block them. As soon as the Herndon expedition was known at Rio de Janeiro, Duarte da Ponte Ribeiro was sent to Peru and Bolivia as special envoy to negotiate treaties providing for the exclusion of United States citizens from the naviga-tion of the Amazon and from the trade of the South Amer-ican hinterland. Later, another envoy was dispatched to Ecuador, New Granada, and Venezuela for similar duty.

For some time Ribeiro and Clay carried on in Peru and Bolivia a lively, and not unevenly-matched, diplomatic bat-tle. The first tangible evidence of the Brazilian's endeavors at Lima was the treaty of October 23, 1851, article two of which provided that the navigation of the Amazon "should belong exclusively to the respective states owning its banks." Another provision of the agreement obligated Peru to subsidize to the extent of twenty thousand dollars annually a Brazilian steam navigation company, should one be organized for use on the Amazon and its tributaries. Despite the protests of the United States minister, the treaty was ratified. Moreover, under the treaty the Brazilian government the following year gave to one of its subjects, Irineo Evangelista de Souza, the exclusive right of steam navigation on the Amazon for thirty years. When Clay heard of the Souza contract, he approached the Peruvian minister of foreign affairs, calling attention to the most-favored-nation provisions of the treaty he had negotiated in July, 1851. Nevertheless, the agreement between Peru and the Souza company was approved by the Peruvian president, though with the omission of certain articles which the Yankee minister considered especially objectionable.

Shortly thereafter, however, (April 15, 1853) the Peruvian executive issued a decree by which the towns of Loreto and Nauto were made ports of entry, and the privileges given to Brazil were extended to all the most-favored nations. Knowledge of this decree, together with the knowledge that the Peruvian government had entered into an agreement with an American for the delivery of two steamers at Loreto, caused the Brazilian minister at Lima, now Cavalcanti, to register a strong protest with Peru, and the Brazilian government to attempt other measures to close the Amazon to the United States. One result of the renewed solicitations was the decree of January 4, 1854, by which Peru modified the April decree of the preceding year sufficiently to restrict the use of the Amazon to Brazilians and Peruvians. The fluvial convention, signed by the two countries in 1858, and designed to supersede the treaty of 1851, contained the same exclusive provisions. Furthermore, Peru, in 1863, terminated her treaty which had been made twelve years before with the United States.[13]

Meanwhile, the policy of the United States found more favorable reception in Bolivia. By an executive decree of January 27, 1853, the Bolivian government, over the protests of Brazil, opened to the navigation of the world the rivers and navigable waters flowing through its territory and discharging into the Amazon or the Rio de la Plata, and offered a prize of ten thousand dollars to the first steamer that should arrive at any Bolivian port from the sea. Five years later the privileges granted by the decree were confirmed in a treaty with the United States.[14]

While Clay and Ribeiro were struggling to secure acceptance of their respective policies in Peru and Bolivia, a similar struggle between other agents of the American and Brazilian governments was going on in Ecuador, New Granada, and Venezuela. As soon as the Rio government got wind of the flank attack of the Americans, it dispatched Lisboa to the three republics in an attempt to neutralize it. As in the case of Peru and Bolivia, the outcome of the struggle was a partial victory for both contestants. With New Granada, the Brazilian envoy succeeded in concluding a treaty whose terms kept the tributaries closed to the outside world. On the other hand, with the little republic of Ecuador, the United States agents entered into a treaty on November 26, 1853, which declared the navigation of the Amazon and its branches within the confines of Ecuador free to the vessels of all nations. The negotiations in Venezuela appear to have been less decisive for either side.

[13] *House Misc. Doc.* 22, 33 Cong., 1 sess. (serial 741); "Inca," "Shall the Valleys of the Amazon and Mississippi Reciprocate Trade?" in *DeBow's Review*, XIV, 136-145.

[14] See Lieutenant Maury's introduction to the memorial of the Memphis convention in *House Misc. Doc.* 22, 33 Cong., 1 sess. (serial 741); *Foreign Relations*, 1871, p. 41.

From the foregoing discussion it must be obvious that the flank attack of the United States was not highly successful, even in the attainment of the immediate end. But if it had been entirely successful in the negotiations with the Andean republics, the effect on the attainment of the ultimate goal—the opening of the Amazon—could have been only indirect. The opening of the great river to the world's commerce depended in the end upon the success of direct negotiations with Brazil, who owned both banks for three thousand miles above the stream's mouth. The Washington government found little difficulty in opening direct negotiations, for, as noted already, the Brazilian government had become uneasy as a result of the chauvinistic outburst in the United States and its consequent expression in the Amazon region of South America.[15]

Direct negotiations may be said to have begun on April 4, 1853, when Carvalho Moreira, Brazilian minister at Washington, made inquiry of the American government concerning rumored expeditions of merchant or naval vessels to the Amazon. Evidently based on newspaper accounts, clippings of which were enclosed, the inquiry ended with an assertion of Brazilian sovereignty over the river.[16] Before replying, Secretary Marcy directed Moreira's communication to the Navy Department and learned that no public ship was then on the Amazon under instructions from that department. Thereupon (April 20) he informed the Brazilian minister of the result of his interdepartmental investigation, telling him that he suspected his apprehensions had arisen from accounts of the recent scientific expedition to the Amazon under

[15] In addition to the references just cited, see Secretary Marcy to Green, minister to New Granada, Aug. 15, 1853, in Instructions to Colombian Ministers, XV, 163; Secretary Marcy to White, charge d' affaires to Ecuador, Aug. 20, 1853, in Instructions to Ecuadorean Ministers, I, 36.

[16] Moreira to Marcy, Apr. 4, 1854, in Communications from Brazilian Agents, III.

the direction of Lieutenants Herndon and Gibbon, the latter of whom had not returned to the United States. But in regard to this expedition Moreira was reminded that it was not only made for the purpose of "gratifying a liberal curiosity, and extending the limits of geographical knowledge in which Brazil and all other civilized states have a common interest," but was made with the explicit approval of the Brazilian government. The American secretary was cognizant of the fact it was impossible to know the whereabouts of all the ships belonging to the United States merchant marine. But the customs officials of the country would not knowingly violate the laws of Brazil by giving permission for the departure of such vessels. In the unlikely event that a merchantman had violated her country's regulations and the laws of Brazil, the offender would have no interference from the United States government. Under no circumstances, would there be any infringement of Brazilian rights.[17]

The fears of the Brazilian minister were not allayed by Marcy's reply. Aroused again by newspaper rumors, in August he became so apprehensive for the safety of his country that he directed a further inquiry to the American foreign office. The particular disturbance on this occasion was the report that certain adventurers were fitting out steam vessels in New York for the purpose of forcing an entrance into the Amazon and ascending the stream to Bolivian and Peruvian ports. Lieutenant Porter of the United States Navy, according to rumor, had received a two years' leave of absence in order to take command of the expedition.[18]

With his reply of September 22, Marcy enclosed a note from the secretary of the navy which denied that Lieutenant Porter had been granted a furlough to make the alleged ex-

[17] Marcy to Moreira, Apr. 20, 1853, in Notes to Brazilian Legations, VI, 95-98.
[18] Moreira to Marcy, Aug. 15, 1853, in Communications from Brazilian Agents, III.

pedition. The reply stated that the government of the United States had never countenanced any enterprise which would involve it in hostility with a foreign power and that in any event its laws were sufficient to take care of such matters as that for which complaint was being made. Nevertheless, the American secretary promised to order the district attorney and the collector of customs at New York to exercise unusual vigilance in the performance of their duties. After the application of the ointment, however, a little salt was added. The New Yorker admitted that the people of the United States saw the great advantages which the opening of the Amazon would bring them and remarked that he

permitted himself to entertain the hope that the Brazilian government, actuated by an enlightened regard for the interests of the empire, will strive by all proper means to develop its vast resources. It appears to the undersigned that no means would be more certain to lead to this result than the removal of unnecessary restrictions upon the navigation of the Amazon, and especially to the passage of vessels of the United States to and from the territories of Bolivia and Peru, by the way of that river and its tributaries. It is hoped that by means of treaty stipulations those advantages may be obtained for citizens of the United States.[19]

Moreira's suspicions were still rampant on occasions. Nettled by having just read in a Baltimore paper an account of a proposed expedition to the upper Amazon, and aware of a change in the office of the collector of customs in New York, at the end of November he directed another note to the State Department urging vigilance.[20] Marcy's reply was reassuring, though at the same time it reminded the Brazil-

[19] Marcy to Moreira, Sept. 22, 1853, in Notes to the Brazilian Legation, VI, 102-106.

[20] Communications from Brazilian Agents, III.

ian that conviction of United States citizens must result from an overt act and not from newspaper rumor.[21]

Properly to appreciate the apparently exaggerated suspicions of Moreira and other Brazilians—indeed of all Latin Americans—one should transplant one's self to the United States of the early eighteen-fifties and inspect the atmosphere of that time. Immediately following the advance of American arms to the heart of the Mexican republic and the despoilment of one-half of its fair land, there came the period when the very atmosphere of the United States was resounding with the shouts of the "Young Americans" for further conquests. It was the period when the American filibusters were taking the initial steps in the fulfillment of the dreams of the disciples of chauvinism. As the expressions of American orators and writers and accounts of the exploits of their advance agents appeared in translation in foreign countries, it is not surprising that fear of conquest seized the public and their representatives.[22]

The instructions to Trousdale, August 8, 1853, mark not only a transfer of negotiations to Rio de Janeiro but a change in emphasis and tactics at Washington as well. The new minister was told that

The most important object of your mission—an object to which you will devote your early and earnest efforts—is to secure the citizens of the United States the free use of the Amazon. There are several republics with which our countrymen have commercial intercourse situated on the upper waters and tributaries of that great river. With these states they would carry on an extensive trade were not our vessels excluded from approaching their internal ports by the selfish and unjustifiable policy of the Brazilian government, which claims and has hitherto exercised the right to obstruct the trade of the countries bordering upon and contiguous to the Amazon with

[21] Notes to the Brazilian Legation, VI, 106-108.
[22] For the effect on Brazil see Schenck to Marcy, Oct. 7, 1853, in Despatches, XX.

foreign nations through this great natural highway. The assumption and exercise of this right is not only injurious to the interests of the states on the navigable waters of the Amazon, but to all other nations wishing to use these waters for the purpose of commercial intercourse.

After stating that the restrictive policy of Brazil was "the relic of an age less enlightened than the present," the instructions set forth the basis upon which the American demands were to be made. The basis was found in Wheaton's *Elements of International Law:*

Things of which use is inexhaustible, such as the sea and running water (including, of course, navigable streams) cannot be so appropriated as to exclude others from using these elements in any manner which does not occasion a loss or inconvenience to the proprietor. This is what is called an *innocent* use. Thus we have seen that the jurisdiction possessed by one nation over sounds, straits, and other arms of the sea leading through its own territory to that of another, or to other seas common to all nations, does not exclude others from the right of innocent passage through these communications.

With his argument firmly grounded in international law, Trousdale was to claim for United States citizens the *natural* right to use "the Amazon to carry on commercial intercourse with Ecuador, Peru, and Bolivia, New Granada and Venezuela." While the right was recognized as being subject to some restrictions imposed by Brazil, the restrictions were not to be such as would approximate exclusion. The claims of the United States were based not only on international law but on the practice "adopted by the allied sovereigns at the Congress of Vienna in 1815."[23]

Impressed with the portion of his instructions which stated that the most important object of his mission was to

[23] Marcy to Trousdale, Aug. 8, 1853, in Instructions to Brazilian Ministers, XV, 215-220.

secure the opening of the Amazon, Trousdale lost no time in broaching the subject to the Brazilian officials. In an interview with the foreign minister on October 28 (1853), he claimed that both international law and the practice of nations since the Congress of Vienna gave his countrymen the right to use the stream. The imperial official denied the right asserted in behalf of the Yankees and made the application general, excepting only the citizens of the republics situated on the headwaters of the river whose interests were taken care of by special treaties. At the same time, however, he admitted that the question was a grave one, and asked for a written statement of the views held by the United States.[24]

Although the request for a formal statement of the views of the United States was complied with immediately, the answer of the Rio government was delayed almost a year. Various excuses were offered for the delay, but the genuine reason seems to have been the difficulty of getting a decision from the council of state, whose very influential president was strongly opposed to opening the Amazon. When given, the belated answer was adverse, though it contained a promise that an affirmative decision would be made when conditions rendered it necessary. The arguments sustaining the reply refused to admit the placing of the Amazon in the category of the high seas for navigation purposes—unless the doctrine of force was to be substituted for right and justice—but suggested putting it in a class with the St. Lawrence, which Great Britain still kept closed to the world's commerce, even to that portion of it which concerned the several million inhabitants living near the northern border of the United States. They definitely refused to classify the Amazon with the Mississippi while the lower course of the latter was in the

<hr>

[24] Trousdale to Marcy, Nov. 18, 1853, in Despatches, XXI.

hands of Spain, for Spain owned very little of the right bank
of the "Father of Waters," whereas Brazil owned both mar-
gins of the "King of Rivers" for a distance of four hundred
and eighty leagues or through two-thirds of its navigable
course. The arguments pointed out further that the valley
of the Amazon was not only undeveloped but was inhabited
by merely a few savage-like people who needed little intercourse with the outside world, and that the nations directly
concerned in the navigation of the upper courses of the river
had the privilege of following in the footsteps of Peru and
entering into treaties with Brazil to take care of their specific
needs.[25]

That there was genuine fear, whether founded or unfounded, back of Brazil's opposition to the opening of her
great river, no one who examines the documents can doubt.
Copy upon copy of Brazilian newspapers carried accounts of
the imperialistic designs of the Yankees. At times, all the
Brazilian journalist had to do was to quote what had appeared in the newspapers of the United States only a few
weeks before, for Lieutenant Maury and his cohorts were
receiving ample publicity in the press. One of the many
evidences that fear penetrated official circles is the executive
decree of October 2, 1854, altering the original contract between the imperial government and the Amazon Company
of Navigation and Commerce. The altered contract provided, among other things, that the company should establish
upon the borders of the Amazon and its tributaries twelve
colonies of six hundred persons each, to be made up of immigrants from countries selected by the imperial government.
Composed of people loyal to the principles of monarchy,
these colonies would enable Brazil to carry out police reg-

[25] Trousdale to Marcy, Mar. 16, Apr. 21, July 10 and 28, and Sept. 7 and 15,
1854, with enclosures, in Despatches, XXI.

ulations along the river after it had been opened to foreigners; they might prevent the northern part of the empire from falling prey to political heretics who were certain to resort thither.[26]

After a change of ministry at Rio de Janeiro in the summer of 1855, Trousdale reopened the Amazon question. On this occasion, albeit he based his supporting arguments on the doctrine of natural right, the American minister attempted to reach his goal through a treaty, which proposed that Brazilian coffee should enter the United States duty free in return for the privilege of Yankee traders to navigate the Amazon. Fortunately, a recent treaty with Great Britain opening the St. Lawrence strengthened the American position; unfortunately, however, a statement accompanying the new proposal to the effect that the United States was *determined* to have the right for which she was asking more than offset this advantage, for imperial officials did not relish the implied threat of coercion. The compensatory plan was rejected by the imperial government; but American persistence continued, and fifteen months later Trousdale repeated the offer of a treaty with similar reciprocal terms. Again Brazil refused, giving as an excuse her unwillingness to depart from the policy of entering into treaties only with the small nations adjacent to her. More specifically, she refused because she feared the sudden opening of the great natural highway might encourage adventurers of every class and country to resort thither, endangering her sovereignty, and because she was confronted at the time with complicated boundary questions with New Granada, Venezuela, England, and France involving territory situated on the river. With this adverse

---

[26] The executive decree appeared in the Rio *Journal do Commercio*, Oct. 27, 1854, a copy of which was enclosed in Trousdale's dispatch of Nov. 4, in *ibid.*, XXI. See also Trousdale's communication of Mar. 12, 1855, in *ibid.*, XXII.

reply Trousdale gave up hope. A few days later he sent a dispatch to Washington in which he said,

> I am convinced that no treaty can be made with this [the Brazilian] government for the present, and that the Amazon is yet to be closed for a long time, unless our government adopts some measure to hasten that period, when it shall be opened to general commerce.[27]

Trousdale's successor, Richard K. Meade, was instructed to defer specific discussion on the opening of the river until he became acquainted with the general views of the Brazilian government on the subject. After these had been obtained and communicated to Washington, special instructions were to be dispatched to Rio de Janeiro. These were never sent, for soon after assuming his duties (December, 1857), Meade wrote his government:

> It may be sometime before I broach the subject of the free navigation of the Amazon. The government is exceedingly sensitive on that subject, and our threats official and otherwise have produced a prejudice against us in the community. It is sufficient for the present that we have entered our claim to the right under the law of nations, of navigating that river, and have declared our determination of enforcing it, whenever our relations with the people residing on its headwaters, shall make it our interest to do so. If it be desirable to precipitate the question, I can do it by a treaty with Peru or Ecuador giving us the free navigation of the upper waters of the Amazon, to some port of entry to be established by them. But the entire valley is yet a wilderness, and will remain so, until the African race in Brazil has subdued it. The white men never will and a quarter of a century will pass away before the slave labor of Brazil will be directed to the Amazon.[28]

---

[27] Trousdale's communications of July 30, 1855, and Oct. 24, 1856, with enclosures, in Despatches, XXII and XXIII.

[28] Instructions of Meade, Sept. 15, 1857, in Instructions to Brazilian Ministers, XV, 269-274; Meade's dispatch of Jan. 15, 1858, in Despatches, XXV.

Not only was the question deferred during the remainder of Meade's incumbency (until 1861), but the rise of several other more pressing matters consequent upon the Civil War in the United States caused a still further postponement. After all, perhaps the delay was more fortunate than otherwise, for it gave time for a change of sentiment in Brazil, without which the stream never could have been opened. Although the details fall beyond the scope of the present work, the history of the change of sentiment from almost unanimous opposition to hearty approval is indeed interesting. Briefly, it may be attributed largely to the powerful influence of the distinguished Brazilian statesman and publicist, Tavares Bastos. As far back as 1853, when Lieutenant Maury's violent and ill-timed diatribes appeared in Portuguese translation in the *Correio Mercantil,* Bastos dared to differ with his fellow-countrymen on the Amazon question. He thought it would be a policy of enlightened self-interest for Brazil to throw open to the world the valley of the great river; in this way only could its marvelous natural resources ever be developed. His countrymen, on the other hand, both in official and unofficial circles, expressed much apprehension of the peril enveloped in the propaganda of the American hydrographer. They believed that Maury carried on his campaign with the knowledge and protection of his government.

After several years' persistence, Tavares Bastos' efforts began to bear fruit. Interestingly enough, among his very first converts was Gonçalves Dias, one of Brazil's most noted lyric poets, who used his talents to popularize his teacher's cause. By 1860, a few imperial statesmen, the majority of them from the provinces most vitally concerned, had adhered to the liberal view and had begun to score the policy of Chinese exclusion. The following year Bastos himself proposed a law opening the river to world navigation and championed it with an eloquent speech—so eloquent and so important that it was later translated and printed *in extenso* in the New York *Journal of Commerce*. But he did more. In order to educate public opinion and thus gain support for his important project, he composed a series of letters and had it inserted, under the heading *Cartas do Solitario* (Letters from the Hermit), in the *Correio Mercantil*. Although Bastos' efforts bore fruit all along, the yield was not prolific for a considerable period. Powerful opposition from certain conservative members of the council of state, especially from Pimento Bueno, was the blighting curse for several years. Finally, an incident occurred in 1866 which served to silence much of this opposition, enough of it at any rate to enable the Vasconcelos ministry to announce a change of policy on the Amazon question.[29]

The fortunate incident was the scientific expedition to Brazil led by Professor Louis F. Agassiz of Harvard University. After arrival in Brazil, the expedition was divided into several small groups in order that the investigation might be made in as many parts of the country as possible. The group under the direct guidance of Agassiz explored the great Amazonian region and parts of the provinces of Ceará and Rio de Janeiro. From the time of arrival, the entire expedition was the recipient of gracious attention from the imperial government. Emperor Pedro II placed at the disposal of the distinguished naturalist a steamer in which to visit the Amazon and its affluents, while the governors of the various riparian provinces vied with each other in rendering personal aid to his labors. It was acknowledged at the time

[29] J. Nabuco, *Um Estadista do Imperio*, II, 382 *et seq.*, III, 12 *et seq.*; Brazil, *Relatorio*, 1866, 1867; *Correio Mercantil*, 1853, 1861; P. A. Martin, *op. cit.*, pp. 156-162.

that the hospitality bestowed by the Rio government enabled the expedition to accomplish more in a single year than it could have accomplished unaided in five years.

A fitting climax to the Agassiz achievement came on the evening of June 25 (1866), just before the departure of the explorers, when American Chargé Lidgerwood tendered a dinner to the party of the eminent naturalist. On this occasion, the high officials of the Brazilian government and many of the most influential non-official persons of Rio de Janeiro had an opportunity to see and hear the man who was the embodiment of American natural science; and they were not disappointed. The compliments paid the "Emperor-Scientist" and his counsellors and ministers for their enlightened policies, and the expressions of appreciation for their recent exhibitions of hospitality were applauded as a matter of course. But the Brazilians received with equal enthusiasm Agassiz's word picture depicting the wonders of the Amazon valley; they found no objection to his apparently incidental comment that the first means necessary to the development of the marvelous region was the opening of the river to navigation. The effect of the seven-hour session of sociability was clearly in evidence at the close, when the Marquis of Olinda, now minister of empire, expressed regret that Professor Agassiz could not remain long enough to be the bearer of the decree, which he felt would soon be passed, opening the Amazon to all nations. At the close, the Marquis escorted his guest to the navy yard, where an imperial barge was waiting to convey him to the mail steamer bound for New York.[30]

Five months after Agassiz's departure the Brazilian council of state came to agreement on the form the decree

[30] See Chargé Lidgerwood to Secretary Seward, July 5, 1866, in Despatches, XXXII; Professor and Mrs. Louis F. Agassiz, *A Journey in Brazil*.

should take. Signed December 7, 1866, the final order provided that after September 7, 1867, the Amazon should be free to the merchant vessels of all nations as far as the borders of the empire. It also provided for the partial opening of the main tributaries to the "King of Rivers"—the Tapajós to Santarém, the Madeira to Borbá, and the Rio Negro to Manâos. The same decree opened the Tocantins to Cametá and the São Francisco to Penedo. When Peru followed the example set by Brazil and opened her rivers to the world on December 17, 1868, the Amazon and its most important tributaries became free throughout their courses.[31]

The agitation started by Lieutenant Maury, the expeditions of the American naval officers Herndon and Gibbon, the diligence of American ministers at Rio de Janeiro, the perseverance of a few Brazilian liberals—especially Tavares Bastos—the tact of Louis Agassiz, and Time—that most potent of all factors—coöperated in the opening of the world's greatest river system.

[31] The Brazilian minister at Washington enclosed a copy of the imperial decree in his communication to Seward, Jan. 22, 1867, in Notes from the Brazilian Legation, IV; see also the consular letter from Pará, Oct. 8, 1867, in Consular Letters, IV.

CHAPTER IX

CONFEDERATE EXILES TO BRAZIL

THE THREE or four years following the close of the Civil War in the United States witnessed an exodus of some eight or ten thousand people from the Southern states to the various countries of Latin America. Between three and four thousand of these *emigrés* established homes in the Brazilian empire.[1]

Southern interest in Brazil dates back to the antebellum days when Lieutenant Matthew Fontaine Maury, perhaps the most ardent advocate of expansion into the tropics, was using his powerful influence to direct attention to the marvellous possibilities of the Amazon valley.[2] But this early interest had become dormant and eventually might have become extinct except for the new source of stimulation furnished by the conflict over slavery. The disappointments resulting from the outcome of the struggle and the dastardly crimes connected with Reconstruction brought the Southern people to a state of desperation. A government under the control of Brownlows, carpet-baggers, scalawags, and "niggers" offered no protection to "life, liberty, and property"; certainly it would do nothing to "conserve honor, chivalry, and purity," that inestimable trinity without which life was not worth living and without which no community could be termed Christian. Moreover, such crimes as those which

[1] These figures have been arrived at after a long and careful study of the whole question of expatriation following the Civil War. See an article by the writer entitled "Confederate Exiles to Brazil," in *The Hispanic American Historical Review*, May, 1927. But at the time this article was written the writer's investigations were in their preliminary stages.

[2] Consult the preceding chapter.

shocked Memphis, New Orleans, and other regions of the South were thought to be but the precursors of deeds that would invade Southern homes and hang rebel leaders.[3] A perusal of the literature of the Reconstruction era or of the present[4] concerning it would almost convince the skeptic that these fears were not unfounded. Whether founded or unfounded, some people were desperate enough to go to the extremity of taking their own lives; others pursued the milder course of turning their backs on friends and relatives and sought new homes in foreign climes.

As large numbers of Confederates talked of going into voluntary exile, the editors of their papers gave them frequent warning that a positive decision would prove perilous.[5] It was perhaps fortunate that notes of caution were sounded on every side, for this led those who could not be deterred from making the adventure to exercise greater precaution in formulating their plans. In this manner the exodus was robbed of some of its precipitateness, if not of some of its radicalness. As is usual in such movements, there were a few wiseacres who rushed off in headstrong fashion; but the vast majority who left the country acted after deliberation.

One of the results of this deliberation was the formation of companies or associations throughout all the Southern states by means of which emigration was to be facilitated. Through these organizations pertinent information was gathered and disseminated, and agents were dispatched to foreign lands to make all arrangements preliminary to settlement.

---

[3] Ballard S. Dunn, *Brazil, the Home for Southerners*, pp. 1-13; editorial in the *New Orleans Times*, October 1, 1865.

[4] Whitelaw Reid, *After the War, a Southern Tour;* Claude G. Bowers, *The Tragic Era.*

[5] Among the Southern papers which were adverse to emigration might be mentioned the *Times*, the *Daily True Delta*, and the *Crescent* of New Orleans, the *Alabama State Journal* and the *Daily Register* of Mobile, and the *Daily Courier* and the *Daily News* of Charleston.

To Brazil—the only land of exile with which this work is concerned—the companies sent prospecting agents by the score.[6] On arrival at Rio de Janeiro these agents were accorded a welcome that was not soon forgotten. From the highest ministers of state they received warm personal greetings and from the bands which accompanied the processions they heard their beloved "Dixie" once more. Yet the three or four days spent in the capital constituted hardly more than an introduction to the period of genuine cordiality which followed, for as the prospectors, accompanied by government engineers, interpreters, and guides, pursued their journeys through the various provinces, they found themselves continuously the honored guests of both town and countryside. They were truly convinced that all hospitality had not vanished from the earth with the surrender of General Lee.[7]

After four or five months spent at inspection, the agents chose the sites and returned to Rio de Janeiro to draw up the contracts providing the general terms of settlement. By the agreements the Brazilian government gave provisional titles to the colony sites, each of which usually aggregated over a half million acres, with the guarantee of permanent titles to the individual holders as soon as the purchase price had been paid. Including the cost of surveying, the settlers paid from twenty-two to forty-two cents an acre for the farms which the associations marked out for them. In order to satisfy Anglo-Saxon thirst for self-government, each colony was to be permitted to elect its own association officials, consisting of a director and seven other functionaries. As isolation seemed likely to present the greatest difficulty in the

---

[6] *New York Herald*, Sept. 3, 1865.

[7] Excellent examples of the cordiality accorded the prospecting agents are exhibited in the itineraries of Reverend Ballard S. Dunn and General William Wallace Wood. For accounts of the two tours see Dunn's *Brazil, the Home for Southerners*, pp. 26ff., and the *Daily True Delta*, Feb. 15, 1866.

establishment of the settlements, the government pledged itself to connect each community with the railways by means of substantial wagon roads. In addition to these aids, Brazil agreed to help the immigrants reach their new homes by long-time loans for passage, by exempting their belongings from import duties, by furnishing board and lodging for twenty days on arrival at Rio de Janeiro, and by providing free transportation from the capital to their destinations. Finally, when established in the country, citizenship was to be conferred by the mere taking of an oath and eternal exemption from military service was promised for the asking.[8]

At the same time the Brazilian government was entertaining in regal fashion the representatives of the emigration associations and entering into liberal contracts for the introduction of colonists, it was also maintaining its own agents at various points in the United States for the purpose of acquainting discontented people with all the advantages which Brazil had to offer. Although there were several of these promoters active in the centers of large population, the two best known were Bocayuva, stationed at New York, and Goicuiria, stationed at New Orleans. These two propagandists appear to have been as vigorous in their activities as twentieth century real estate agents. Amidst his routine duties, the former found time to call the editor of the *New York Herald* to task for alleging that the Brazilian government was not fulfilling its agreements with the emigrants; while the latter seemed no less devoted to the carrying out of his particular program.[9]

Through these American and Brazilian agents, who operated in each other's country, most of the arrangements were

[8] The colonization contracts naturally varied in their details. See Dunn, *op. cit.*, pp. 44ff.; the *New York Herald*, Jan. 27, 1868; and the *Daily True Delta*, Feb. 15, 1866.

[9] *New York Herald*, Feb. 7 and July 21, 1867.

made for the emigration from the United States. After the
signing of the contracts, which could take place in either
Brazil or in the United States, the next problem was that of
finding desirable people to make the venture. While there
were always those who were willing to enlist in the enterprise, it was more difficult, in the face of the adverse attitude
of the newspapers as well as of a few of the returning agents,
to secure those whose experiences and possessions fitted them
for the tasks to be confronted in the new country. Nevertheless, by advertisements in Southern papers and other means,[10]
considerable numbers were induced to try home-building in
Brazil. Included among the self-imposed exiles, were people of almost every social and economic class then existing in
the United States. There were generals, colonels, doctors,
lawyers, merchants, planters, ministers, teachers, barroom
loafers, bounty jumpers, and vagabonds.[11] As it was later
discovered, not all who went were American citizens, for
some of the *emigrés* were of English and Irish lineage and
had never become naturalized.[12]

Although all available figures on the number of Southerners who left the United States to establish homes in
Brazil during the four or five years subsequent to the close
of the war represent hardly more than approximations, it is
certain that the exodus never attained the proportions fixed
in the imaginations of many people. A reporter of a New
York paper estimated that about eighteen hundred left for
the South American country during the first six months of
1867, but he fails to inform us as to the source of his in-

[10] For an example of a newspaper advertisement see the *New Orleans Times*, Apr.
2, 1868. Without a doubt Reverend Dunn wrote his book, *Brazil, the Home for
Southerners,* largely for the purpose of inducing Southerners to emigrate to his colony.
[11] *New York Herald*, May 14, 1868.
[12] Minister Blow to the secretary of state, Jan. 15, 1870, in Despatches, XXXV.

formation.[13] Some of the emigrants themselves wrote that they lodged with five hundred fellow countrymen at the "Emigrant House" in Rio de Janeiro en route to the settlements, though their statements also furnish a very insecure basis for estimates as to numbers.[14] As late as September, 1871, at which time a steady stream of disillusioned colonists had been flowing northward for many months, the United States minister to Brazil wrote his government that there remained in the province of São Paulo alone between three and four hundred American families.[15] This estimate is likely to be misleading, however, unless we are reminded that the success of the exiles in this province caused them to remain longer than at most places.

Whatever may have been their number, the American exiles to Brazil established themselves from the province of Rio Grande in the south to the Amazonian province of Pará in the north, or over a distance greater than that from Cape Cod to the Golden Gate. Instead of being uniformly distributed over this vast area, of course, most of them settled in a few colonies, chief of which were in Pará, Espirito Santo, and São Paulo. The hardships endured by the emigrants on the long and perilous voyages to South America seem comparable to the sufferings of those who came to the eastern shores of North America in the early seventeenth century. Unfortunately, the difficulties encountered on the voyage usually continued after landing. But perhaps a little particularization will better reveal the nature of the novel experiences.

Among the interesting colonies in Brazil was that established on the middle Amazon, in the province of Pará. The

[13] *New York Herald*, July 7, 1867.

[14] *Ibid.*, June 21, 1867.

[15] Partridge to Fish, Sept. 8, 1871, in *Foreign Relations of the United States*, 1871, p. 64.

site, selected by the Confederate Major Lansford Warren Hastings, was at the mouth of the Tapajós River, a distance of six or seven hundred miles from the coast city of Pará. Not many months after the surrender at Appomattox a company of Tennessee and Alabama planters, "disgusted with free niggers, the United States government, the defeat, and everything connected with the country," assembled farming implements and provisions for six months at Montgomery preparatory to a journey to Brazil as soon as their agent, the above named major, should return with the announcement of a site.[16] Hastings returned with the expected report, but before the completion of all arrangements for the departure several months had passed. Notwithstanding the delay, the preparations seem to have been inadequate, for the expedition came to grief and was compelled to return to Mobile. After another period of waiting, a second start was made toward the south. All went well for a while, but the repaired vessel was able to go no further than the island of St. Thomas where the passengers were obliged to plead for space on a regular packet which took them to Pará. From the provincial capital the last lap of the long journey to Santarém was made in a river steamer.[17] Thus, in September, 1867, after two years of hope and anxiety, the first of the Hastings followers, numbering about one hundred and fifteen weary and downcast souls reached the scene of their El Dorado—if such it remained.

Although severe, the experiences before arrival were not more bitter than those yet to come. Only six miles of the road which was to be constructed in order to make the little town of Santarém accessible to the colonists after settlement had been completed, and it became necessary to carry bag-

[16] W. Reid, *After the War, a Southern Tour*, p. 374.
[17] *New Orleans Times*, Apr. 8, 1868.

gage and food on foot, over steep hills and through torrents of
rain, for distances of ten and fifteen miles. Hardly less oner-
ous was the necessity of waging constant and costly warfare
against fevers and dysentery, as well as against beasts, birds,
reptiles, and insects which infested the land. The establishment of homes under such conditions would have challenged
the mettle of hardy frontiersmen; the task was too great for
the followers of Hastings, some of whom were old men,
many others of whom had never done a full day's work, and
all of whom knew nothing of the language they found it
necessary to use. To complete the story we must add that the
newcomers, most of whom were almost destitute on arrival,
had to purchase their provisions in a market regulated by
monopoly.[18]

Under the circumstances it is not surprising that before
the expiration of six months many of the exiles were appealing to the American consul at Pará for relief. In the communications they alleged that the Brazilian government had
failed to carry out the terms of the contract entered into with
Major Hastings in November, 1866, and that to this fact
was attributable much of the impending suffering. The consul gave the memorials early replies, placed them before the
president of the province, by whom the contract had been
negotiated and through whom relief was expected, and began
an investigation. As a result of the examination into the
charges, he induced the government to continue to supply
the colonists with small sums of money for the purchase of
provisions and to rescind the order of the local police which
prohibited removal from the site on the Tapajós, though he
at the same time insisted that the colonists reimburse the gov-

---

[18] *New Orleans Times,* Nov. 9, 1867. See also a communication of Consul Bond
(Pará) to the secretary of state, June 4, 1868, with its enclosures, in Consular Letters,
IV.

ernment for passage and for consumed provisions in case they contemplated leaving the country.

Notwithstanding the relief measures provided through the provincial president, large numbers of the settlers found passage to Pará. Unfortunately, they failed to receive a hearty welcome there, for the consul's instructions prevented him furnishing provisions or transportation to the United States to any except those who fell in the class of distressed seamen. Nevertheless, through one means or another most of the refugees managed to keep alive and eventually to return to their native land.[19]

Originating with the refugees, and broadcast through their acquaintances and relatives, the report appeared in many of the newspapers of the United States that the Santarém colony was a complete failure.[20] If the accounts of those who remained on the Amazon can be trusted, the report has another version. Writing from Valley Home on May 24, 1868, to a friend in Tennessee that he "had better pick up bag and baggage and come out, and so get rid of Brownlow, Negroes, Yankees, and taxation," a Mr. Pitts remarked that "the colony is in fine condition and doing well" and that "there is no truth in the reports that the enterprise is a failure." To substantiate the general statement he said further:

I planted Brazilian corn in January and raised a fine crop, and have planted three times since—will have an abundance to do me. I have sugar cane, cotton, pumpkins, squash, five kinds of sweet potatoes, Irish potatoes, cornfield peas, snap beans, butter beans, ochre, tomatoes and a fine chance of tobacco. I have made enough to live well on and am better pleased than ever. I have a great variety of fruits on my place.[21]

[19] For the memorials, Bond's replies, and other communications see Consular Letters, IV.

[20] For an example see *Flake's Semi-weekly Bulletin* (Galveston), Jan. 9, 1869.

[21] The letter of this writer may be found in the *Charleston Daily Courier*, July 9, 1868.

Sixteen months later another resident of Santarém, Mrs. N. F. White, sounded the same note in a letter to an Alabama friend. The writer's husband appeared to be prospering in the manufacture of rum and molasses from cocoa and sugar cane, and the only bar to supreme contentment was the want of some of the ordinary institutions of society. Fortunately, prospects were bright for the future, for good families were arriving slowly and setting up their establishments.[22]

These apparently contradictory reports on the success of the Amazon venture can be explained by the fact that those emigrants who went without means and without a willingness to "kiss the rod" were soon disillusioned and ready to return home, while those who emigrated reasonably well supplied with money and endowed with energy settled down and became happy and contented.[23]

Three hundred miles north of Rio de Janeiro, in the province of Espirito Santo, was a much larger and more prosperous colony of Southern exiles. Given to Colonel Charles G. Gunter of Alabama, and consisting of several thousand acres, the grant was situated thirty miles above the mouth of the Rio Doce. In the heart of the tract, and embracing some eighty square miles, was the beautiful fresh water lake of Juparanão, about which twenty settlements were planted. Eastward from the lake the level land extended back for several miles, while westward small arms of water reached a low range of distant mountains, through whose gaps could be seen towering peaks of still more remote ranges.

To the spot thus endowed by the Creator the Confederate colonel conducted exiles until there were upwards of fifty families, many of whom had left the Crescent City in the spring

[22] For the letter see the *Mobile Daily Register*, Nov. 17, 1869.

[23] A short paragraph on the establishment of the Hastings colony may be found in A. Carvalho, *O. Brazil: colonisação e emigração*, p. 244.

of 1867 with the expectation of settling in Reverend Dunn's colony in São Paulo. The families claimed Alabama, Florida, Louisiana, Mississippi, Texas, and Virginia as their former homes and included many persons of education and refinement. But on arrival at their new homes army officers, doctors, and lawyers laid aside their professions and entered the forests with the determination to succeed at the occupation of farming or perish in the attempt. Acting perhaps from a sense of duty rather than of pleasure, the women, too, caught the new spirit and performed manifold household tasks hitherto left to servants. In spite of the numerous handicaps and inconveniences incident to pioneering, such as monthly steamship service, canoe transportation, dwelling in single room huts, covered with palm in Mexican style and without door or window shutters, at the end of the first year the settlers contrasted their own happy situation with that of friends and relatives in the homeland, for whom they offered "many sincere prayers." This boasted contentment was no doubt sincere, for in its early history this was reputed to be the most successful of all the exile colonies. In addition to possessing a wise director, Lake Juparanão appears to have been peculiarly fortunate in the selection of its settlers.[24] Since many of the Rio Doce settlers moved into the interior of São Paulo after a few years, it seems quite probable that the early prosperity did not have a long continuance.

If Espirito Santo could claim for a time the most successful of the Confederate settlements, São Paulo could claim the largest number, and ultimately the most prosperous. Although experiments were made in many parts of the southern

[24] This account is based very largely on a long letter which Miss Josephine Foster, a resident who formerly lived at Chatawa, Pike County, Mississippi, sent to the *New Orleans Times*. See the Crescent City paper for Apr. 26, 1868. See also the *New York Herald*, May 14, 1868.

province, the two chief centers of colonizing activity were on the Ribeira River, a few miles toward the interior from Iguape, and at Santa Barbara, some eighty miles northwest of the city of São Paulo. Among the grants on the Ribeira was that made to Ballard S. Dunn, formerly rector of St. Phillip's Church in New Orleans, and later a member of the Confederate army. Soon after the close of the war the fighting parson went to Brazil and, after four months of diligent searching, selected a tract on the Juquiá River, a tributary of the Ribeira, embracing nearly two-thirds of a million acres, where

the war worn soldier, the bereaved parent, the oppressed patriot, the homeless and despoiled, can find a refuge from the trials which beset them, and a home not haunted by the eternal remembrance of harrowing scenes of sorrow and death.

Following the choosing of the tract, called Lizzieland, Dunn made two voyages to Rio de Janeiro in order to perfect the title and to complete other arrangements. With these matters disposed of, he departed for the United States to arouse an interest in his Utopian enterprise with a view to enlisting settlers. A facile pen[25] and a magnetic personality aided him in the accomplishment of his object and soon he had several persons ready to launch upon the venture.

The vanguard of the Lizzieland colonists left New Orleans aboard the *Talisman*, Dom Pedro II line, January 30, 1867, and about ten weeks later a much larger group followed in the *Marmion*. After voyages of approximately a month's duration, the vessels docked in the harbor of Rio and the passengers took lodging at government expense in the emigrant hotel. At the end of a few days of recuperation

---

[25] The fascinating little book of the minister, *Brazil, the Home for Southerners*, has been referred to above.

the journey was continued by coast steamer to Iguape, though the numbers had been greatly diminished by the decision of many to desert Lizzieland for Rio Doce.[26]

While Dunn and his followers were making preparations to settle in Lizzieland, other plans were in progress looking toward the occupation of an adjoining survey. Early in 1866, following an inspection tour of five months, Frank McMullen and William Bowen of Texas secured title to several thousand acres situated on another of the tributaries of the Ribeira and then hastened home to complete arrangements for taking out settlers.[27] In the advertisements sent out for the purpose of soliciting colonists the promoters sounded the warning that no persons would be considered unless they could qualify morally and politically—that is be Southerners and hold proslavery sentiments.[28] Whatever may have been the effect of the announcement, a shipload of emigrants assembled at Galveston very shortly and put out for Brazil. But, notwithstanding his warning to emigrants against contracting with unreliable transportation companies, the chief promoter himself set out with the first colonists without taking due precautions. As a consequence, the vessel was wrecked on the Cuban coast and the passengers lost all their possessions except a few clothes. Nevertheless, the dauntless courage of the stalwart band prevented the possibility of turning back, and at the end of six hectic months the destination was finally reached.[29]

[26] *New Orleans Times,* Apr. 8 and 26, 1868.

[27] A chapter in Dunn, *op. cit.,* contains the report of McMullen and Bowen on the selection of lands.

[28] Frank McMullen, writing from Galveston, Texas, in the *New Orleans Times,* Jan. 24, 1867.

[29] The disastrous voyages of the emigrant ships were attributable to the unseaworthiness of the vessels, which were usually the hastily constructed blockade runners worked over so as to be equipped with two or three decks. When loaded, the new vessels were topheavy, for the passenger's equipment was not sufficient ballast. See

Unfortunately, the story of attempts at home-building on the Ribeira, whether on the Dunn or the McMullen-Bowen survey, is a dismal one. Depleted funds, a lack of means of communication, and sickness conspired to play havoc with all plans and to render futile all efforts. A few seasons of unrewarded endeavor, during which death took a heavy toll from among those of both high and low rank, were sufficient to cause most of the exiles to seek other regions. While most of the Iguape settlers returned to their old homes in the United States, others joined relatives and friends who had established themselves in the interior of the same province.[30]

Simultaneous with the endeavors on the Ribeira, the Rio Doce, and the Amazon, was the attempt to plant a Dixieland in the vicinity of Santa Barbara, in the heart of historic São Paulo. As in the former cases, this adventure into the interior of Brazil's most important province smacks of the dramatic. For Confederates, interest in this hidden hinterland dates back to the early months following the close of the Civil War, when General William Wallace W. Wood of New Orleans, who visited this and many other regions as prospecting agent for some two dozen emigration associations of the Southern states, returned home and made his report.[31]

Dunn's long advertisement in the *New Orleans Times*, Apr. 8, 1868. See also the Apr. 26 issue of the same paper.

[30] A few years ago a Mr. Johnson, a son of one of the original colonists of the McMullen-Bowen survey, went from Texas to Brazil to make an effort to prove title to a tract of land which had been granted to his father in the middle sixties. Unfortunately, he was not successful in his mission. The writer acquired this information through Mr. Robert L. Keiser, formerly American consul at São Paulo who is now residing in Washington. On the success of the Ribeira settlements see the *Mobile Daily Register*, Feb. 23, 1870, and the *New York Herald*, May 14, 1868. The latter paper was always particularly anxious to magnify the failures and to minimize the successes of the exile experiments.

[31] Although the writer has not found General Wood's report—to his keen disappointment—a companion of the general, writing from Rio de Janeiro, Jan. 2, 1866, gives an account of the tour. See the *Daily True Delta*, Feb. 15, 1866.

Probably influenced by this report, Colonel William H. and Robert C. Norris, father and son, laid down their arms in Alabama and went to Brazil for the purpose of selecting homes which would be safe from the ravages of the despised Yankee. Passing from Rio to the overgrown village of São Paulo, where property could have been purchased almost for a song, the Norris pair loaded their few chattels into an ox-cart and walked eighty miles to the northwest where they purchased lands for a settlement. With this accomplished, the family was notified. Following the completion of a few arrangements, the Norris family left the Crescent City in a small sailing vessel. Again the precautions had not been sufficient, and adverse winds wafted the light craft through a seventy-nine day journey over the middle Atlantic. But, after an unexpected visit to the Cape Verdes, the vessel finally reached Rio and the trip was continued to Santa Barbara.

During the subsequent six months some fifty families, mostly from Alabama, Tennessee, and Texas, arrived and settled in and around the little village. Nor did immigration cease then, for within the course of a few years it is reputed that approximately five hundred American families found their way into the community. Part of the accretion was the result of new arrivals from the terror-stricken Southern states and part resulted from the removal thither of those who had met disaster in other portions of Brazil.

Although the colonists endured many privations and hardships, their efforts were generally rewarded by a fair degree of success. They cultivated beans, corn, cotton, and sugar cane on the extensive plantations which they laid out for themselves, and became successful cattle breeders. Among the industries introduced into the country by the newcomers was that of watermelon raising, credit for which fell to a Mr.

Whittaker, fondly called "Uncle Joe," an original settler who happened to bring out the first seeds. Unfortunately, cotton growing, to the development of which the colonists pinned great faith, never became very important, not so much because the soil was unsuited to the development of the plant as because of the high cost of transportation over long distances by mule or oxcart.[32]

So successful was the colony at Santa Barbara that there remain to-day several traces of its existence. One of these is exhibited in the name of "Villa Americana," an appellation attached before the close of the century because of its establishment by American exiles. At present Villa Americana is a bustling little railway town of four or five thousand people with its churches, schools, shops, and paved streets. But the character of the present population belies its name and origin, for nearly all persons of North American—unpardonable to say Yankee—birth or lineage have moved to the cities or purchased plantations in the rural districts and their immediate places have been taken by the sons and daughters of Italy. Even Uncle Joe Whittaker's Alabama and Georgia watermelons are now grown by Italians.[33]

Meantime the descendants of the founders of Villa Americana have not been lost in the bustle of the world. Many of them have entered the fields of commerce and the professions, where they have achieved distinction. For ex-

[32] In some quarters of the United States apprehension was felt lest the cotton industry in Brazil, stimulated by exiles from the South, might offer keen competition to the same industry in the northern republic. Accordingly, the United States minister was instructed to report on possibilities. Apparently there was little ground for fear. See Minister Blow to Secretary Fish, July 22, 1870, in Despatches, XXXVII.

[33] Yet in 1914 the inhabitants of the town extended an invitation to the American consul at São Paulo, Maddin Summers, to deliver an address at a Fourth of July celebration. Although unable to go at that time, Consul Summers, accompanied by his most estimable wife, visited Villa Americana later. Mrs. Summers is now in the Division of Publications of the Department of State.

ample, one of the most distinguished surgeons of Brazil to-day is Dr. Franklin P. Pyles, the son of E. B. Pyles of Morgan raid fame. Furthermore, residing in the national capital of the United States and occupying important stations in government service, are two young women who not only have the distinction of being the daughters of the self-exiled Confederates who were the principal founders of Villa Americana but who are themselves natives of that Dixieland town.[34] It must be admitted, however, that in this, as in the other colonies, many of the Americans have intermarried with the Brazilians, and are fast losing their identity.

Although many of the several thousand voluntary exiles achieved success and established permanent homes in Brazil, many others found only disappointment and sought early opportunities to get back to the United States. Only a few months after arrival, as already noted, disillusioned colonists began to petition the American consuls and minister to provide them with return passages. But for some time the appeals went almost unheeded, not so much because of a lack of sympathy for the distressed on the part of these officials as because of the desire on the part of the Washington government to inflict upon those who were the victims of their own folly a bit of retributive punishment. Then, too, the administration in charge of the American government was

[34] One of these natives of Villa Americana is Mrs. Maurice H. Bletz of the Department of Commerce of the United States government. Her father was the Mr. Robert C. Norris referred to above and her mother, who is now living in Washington at the advanced age of more than three score years and ten, was formerly a Miss Steagall who accompanied her family from Gonzalez, Texas, to Brazil when eighteen years of age. The writer and his wife recently have had the peculiarly good fortune of passing a number of very pleasant and profitable evenings with Mr. and Mrs. Bletz, from whom most of the information on Villa Americana was acquired. In the *Saturday Evening Post* for Oct. 17, 1925, occurred a few paragraphs, under the name of Isaac F. Marcosson, on the history of Villa Americana. Although the source is unacknowledged, the account was either written by Mrs. Bletz or based upon information secured from her.

not disposed to lay itself liable to public criticism by rendering aid to traitors. Finally, however, there was a little relenting and toward the close of 1869 the minister at Rio was informed that the secretary of the Navy had instructed the commander of the South Atlantic squadron to order his returning vessels to stop at Brazilian ports when possible and take in United States emigrants who at that time found themselves in distress.[35] In compliance with this order considerable numbers of unfortunates found passage home on the *Guerrière*, the *Kansas*, the *Portsmouth*, the *Quinnebaug*, and other public vessels.[36] Although the American government steadfastly refused to consider other measures,[37] many more returned to their former allegiance through the generosity of more fortunate Americans residing in Brazil or of friends in the United States.

The Brazilian government, notwithstanding discouraging results from the expenditure of vast sums of money with a view to stimulating a large immigration, continued to exhibit a very liberal attitude toward the emigrants from the United States. While the complaints from the distressed colonists were frequent and loud, they were usually not justified, for the government in most cases faithfully carried out its pledges. Indeed, on more than one occasion it went beyond the contractual period in furnishing provisions to the destitute. Furthermore, on other occasions it rendered gratuitous service by returning to their homeland women and children who had become broken in spirit and fortune and by transporting other unfortunates to the Alto da Serra to pre-

[35] Instructions to Brazilian Ministers, XVI, 260.

[36] See Monroe to the secretary of state, June 22, 1869, and Blow to the same, Aug. 6, 1869, and June 10, 1870, in Despatches, XXXV and XXXVI. See also the *New York Herald*, July 25, 1865.

[37] Secretary of state to Blow, February 17, 1870, in Instructions to Brazilian Ministers, XVI, 271.

vent death from a yellow fever peril then raging in the capital. Fortunately, the distressed also found a friend in the American minister, who always lent a sympathetic ear if not a helping hand.[38]

A number of interesting questions arose as a result of the emigration from the United States to Brazil. Not the least interesting of these was that of the inconsistency between the theory which impelled expatriation and the choice of Brazil as a future home. It will be remembered that those who abandoned their native country did so partly because of equality of rights between the two races. Yet these same people in selecting a home chose to cast their lots in a country where the black man born free had equal rights with the native white man, and even more rights than the white foreigner. And it should not have required a statesman to see that a movement was fast gathering momentum which would soon make free men of all slaves.

A subject which eventually assumed more importance was that of citizenship. Although in Brazil naturalization was a relatively easy matter, most of the immigrants from the United States had no desire to become subjects of the imperial government. This position was taken by the majority in order to avoid military service, for only recently they had seen too much war in the native land. To be forced to fight the "Huns" of López in the jungles of Paraguay would be unbearable! But they did not stop at refusing to become Brazilian subjects; the Confederates and their sons for thirty years sought positive protection from the United States government. During times when domestic or international affairs seemed threatening, such for example as the period 1893-1895, and drafting into service loomed as a possibility,

[38] Consult Blow's communications of Jan. 19 and Sept. 3, 1870, in Despatches, XXXV.

applications were made for passports to the northern republic. Unfortunately, the frequency of the requests and the long and indefinite periods for which the papers were sought revealed the fact that they were desired for security in Brazil rather than for travel in the United States. Naturally this discovery eventually led to adverse decisions on the applications and to the discontinuance of this method of protection, though it was resorted to with effectiveness for a time. Other expedients were likewise called into use for similar purposes. So again it may appear that the self-imposed exiles were somewhat inconsistent in seeking protection from a country upon which they had turned their backs.[39]

[39] On the question of passports consult communications of Minister Thompson to his government, May 3, 1894, and June 24, 1895, in Despatches, LVII, LVIII. Also consult Instructions to Brazilian Ministers, XVIII, 58-59, 137-141.

CHAPTER X

FROM EMPIRE TO REPUBLIC IN BRAZIL

GENERAL Webb's departure from Rio de Janeiro late in May, 1869, marked a turning point in Brazilian-American relations. The unpleasant incidents which frequently marred the intercourse at an earlier date are practically absent from the more recent period. The spirit of cordiality which some writers have erroneously ascribed to the entire century does in reality accurately characterize the later period. Perhaps one reason for the improvement was the fact that the foreign office at Washington, partly because of improvement in means of communication and partly because of an increased interest in Latin American affairs generally, kept in more intimate touch with its diplomatic agents in Brazil. But the motives which impelled the policy underwent little change. The United States government continued to advocate for the entire hemisphere the set of political principles which it cherished and professed to follow in shaping its own conduct. These principles or ideals were generally opposed to those practiced by the nations of the Old World. The United States government likewise continued the attempt to secure for its people a due share of the commerce which Brazilians had to offer.

Soon after taking office Webb's successor, Henry T. Blow of St. Louis, realized that many obstacles had to be removed before the United States and Brazil could fully understand and appreciate each other; in his own words he could "see nothing in our recent intercourse which would warrant me in relying on any very great sympathy, either of the government or people in favor of our country or countrymen."[1] When he sought from Brazilian officials an explanation of the change in sentiment toward his country and countrymen from profound admiration to coolness, he got the frank answer that J. Watson Webb had been responsible for the modification. As a result of the negotiations during the Paraguayan War, the old suspicion that the United States sympathized more readily with republics than with monarchies was revived. The imperial officials apparently placed the wrong interpretation on the high-pressure methods of the American minister.[2]

Nevertheless, the restoration of cordiality, which awaited only a judicious policy on the part of the new American minister, was not long in abeyance. The proposal of the United States to submit the *Canada* claim to the arbitration of Edward Thornton, British envoy to Washington, was promptly accepted by Brazil, the award of a little more than $102,000 was made in favor of the claimant, and the last difference between the two countries was brought to a happy termination.[3] It was in the same spirit that the United States secured the inclusion of a Brazilian on the tribunal of arbitration in conformity with the Treaty of Washington signed in May, 1871; and in appreciation of the honor Brazil appointed to the position Baron de Itajubá, one of her most learned and renowned statesmen.[4]

The visit of Dom Pedro and the empress to the United States on the occasion of the Centennial Exposition may be taken as evidence of the growing cordiality between the two

---

[1] Blow to his government, Nov. 19, 1869, in Despatches, XXXV.

[2] Blow's dispatch of Feb. 8, 1870, in *ibid.*, XXXVI.

[3] The United States government to Blow, Jan. 21, 1870, in Instructions to Brazilian Ministers, XVI, 270-272; Blow to his government, Mar. 19 and Sept. 19, 1870, in Despatches, XXXVI and XXXVII.

[4] Dispatches of Aug. 26 and Sept. 23, 1871, in Despatches, XXXIX.

countries. And the warm reception which the royal pair received everywhere served as a stimulus to the increasing esteem. The nature of the reception and the popularity of the visit are indicated by the emperor's election to membership in the National Geographical Society and by the inclusion of his biographical sketch in the annual report of the Smithsonian Institution. An author was so impressed with Dom Pedro that he later dedicated a book to his memory. But the emperor's many-sided interests were capitalized not alone by representatives of the academic world: the promoters of Bell's telephone took advantage of them to give wide publicity to their product.[5]

Many evidences of the continued friendship between the northern republic and the southern empire are not wanting. Space, however, will permit mention of only a few of these, among which were the imperial decree conceding to the American firm of Bright and Company favorable terms for the construction of submarine telegraph lines connecting Rio de Janeiro with the cities both of northern Brazil and Argentina; the $23,000 monthly subsidy granted by the Brazilian government to the W. R. Garrison Company of New York for the establishment of a steam passenger and mail line from Rio de Janeiro to Pará; the contract and subsidy from the same source for the establishment of the Roach Line of packets between the Brazilian capital and New York; the trade-mark convention between the two countries (1878); the permission given by the Rio government for the scientific expedition to the Amazon led by Professor Starr of the University of Michigan and for the expedition to the same river by a public vessel of the United States; the designation by

[5] For the visit see Partridge's dispatches of Apr. 12 and May 25, 1876, in *ibid.*, LXII; the Smithsonian Institution, *Annual Report*, 1876, pp. 173 *et seq.*; Frank Vincent, *Around and About South America*, p. 253; F. H. Sweet, *Power Plant Engineering*.

the American government, later approved by the emperor, of a Brazilian to the Franco-American claims convention of 1880; and the amicable settlement of the most important claims of American citizens against Brazil.[6]

It was in the same spirit that Brazil accepted James G. Blaine's invitation (1881) to send delegates to the first Pan-American Conference to be convened in Washington. Before Brazil received official notice that the meeting had been indefinitely postponed, however, considerable criticism of the proposal arose. To certain influential members of the conservative Senate it was absurd to consider methods of preventing war between nations; they averred that the nations of Europe had futilely considered the question just prior to the Crimean War. The criticisms seem to have been in part repercussions of the meddling and unsuccessful rôle which the United States had just attempted in the controversy between Chile and Peru. They represent opposition to and fear of the growing power and influence of the young giant of the north.[7]

Yet, despite the criticism from this and other sources, when the invitation was repeated seven years later, the reply was again favorable. Indeed, Brazil sent an eminent commission to represent her at the great gathering of American states held at Washington in the autumn of 1889. That the members of the commission played a prominent part in the deliberations of the conference, the published proceedings bear convincing testimony. Furthermore, the Brazilian government gave loyal support to the various projects which issued from the initial conference at Washington, such as the

---

[6] The most pertinent dispatches on these topics were those of Apr. 20 and June 10, 1870, May 31, 1877, May 14 and Oct. 1, 1878, Jan. 11, May 2, and June 6, 1879, and Oct. 1, 1880, in Despatches, XXXVI, LXII, LXIII, and LXIV.

[7] See Osborn's communication of Mar. 23, 1882, in *ibid.*, LXV.

creation of the Bureau of American Republics. In supporting these projects the Rio and Washington governments
usually found a basis of coöperation.[8]

While the delegates of the first Pan-American Congress
were discussing means of coöperation in the solution of the
common problems confronting their countries news came of
the overthrow of the Brazilian empire and the establishment
of the republic. To the casual observer the revolution came
as a bolt out of the blue; to the high officials of the American government it should have occasioned little surprise, for
American ministers at Rio de Janeiro for almost twenty years
had written of the profound changes that were undermining
the imperial frame. They had written how the powerful,
landed aristocracy was alienated by the abolition of slavery
without compensation;[9] they had written of the birth of the
new Republican party in 1870, of the launching of its official organ *(A Republica)*, and of many demonstrations in
support of its program;[10] they had written voluminously of
the enervating influences on the empire of the conflict between civil and ecclesiastical authorities;[11] and finally, two
months before the change, one of them, after describing fully
the ominous political situation in Brazil, wrote Washington
of his confidential information that the Republicans had sent
secret emissaries "to the United States to inquire if that government would give moral and material support to them in
an attempt by revolution to overthrow the Imperial Government."[12]

[8] Dispatches to the United States government, Feb. 20 and July 6, 1889, May 3
and Sept. 20, 1890, Jan. 6 and 21, 1891, and June 17, 1892, in *ibid.*, XLVIII, XLIX,
L, LII.

[9] For example see dispatches of Apr. 23, May 24, and June 18, 1870, Mar. 7, May
18, Aug. 25, and Sept. 9, 1871, in *ibid.*, XXXVI-XXXIX.

[10] Dispatches of July 24, 1875, Feb. 27 and June 4, 1879, in *ibid.*, XL-XLII.

[11] Dispatches of July 23, 1873, Mar. 23, Apr. 22, July 25, and Dec. 14, 1874,
Sept. 25 and 30, 1875, and July 10 and 28, and Oct. 14, 1876, in *ibid.*, XL-XLVII.

[12] Adams's dispatch of Sept. 9, 1889, in *ibid.*, XLVIII.

On November 17, 1889, two days after the overthrow of the imperial régime and the deposition of the aged emperor, and on the very day of the departure of the royal family for the Old World, Robert Adams, Jr., American minister to Brazil, cabled his government that it was important for it to be the first to acknowledge the Brazilian republic. Two days later he sent a dispatch describing the revolution in which he said: "In my opinion the Republican form of government is securely established even though the present ministry should fall. Our constitution and flag have been copied and looking to future relations I desire our country to be first to acknowledge the Republic."[13]   These pleas failed to bring the result hoped for by their author; several of the Spanish-American neighbors accorded formal recognition to the new government almost as soon as receipt of the news of its birth. The American government went part of the way, however, by immediately instructing its minister to "maintain diplomatic relations with the provisional Government of Brazil."[14]   It might have gone the whole way and extended formal recognition immediately but for the fact that its minister changed his position on the question. In about a month after the establishment of the new régime, in contrast to his early fervor, he confessed "serious doubts as to the outcome of the acts of the present military Dictatorship." The very wording of the decrees "by the authority of the Army and Navy in the name of the Nation" showed that little regard was paid to the voice of the people, he declared.[15]   Unwilling to take the chance of strengthening a military despotism, when its design was to advance the cause of popular government in the New World, the Harrison administration deemed it wise not to hasten formal recognition.

[13] Dispatch of Nov. 19, 1889, with cablegram of 17 enclosed, in *ibid.*, XLIX.
[14] Adams's dispatch of Nov. 27, 1889, with enclosures, in *ibid.*
[15] Dispatch of Dec. 17, 1889, in *ibid.*

Upon its announcement to Congress Harrison's fabian policy received considerable criticism, particularly from the aggressive members of the opposition party, who argued that immediate recognition would strengthen the republicans in Brazil in their contest with the monarchists and spoil any possible designs of interference from Europe. It is sufficient to say that the friends of the administration were numerous enough to prevent great embarrassment or a change of policy.[16]

In the American press opinion was also divided on the question of recognition. Among the newspapers which advocated immediate recognition were the Omaha *Bee*, the Atlanta *Constitution*, the Indianapolis *Sentinel*, the Savannah *News*, the New Orleans *Picayune*, and the New York *World*. Of the six, the Omaha *Bee* was the only Republican paper. Among the papers which counseled delay in recognition were the Boston *Advertiser*, the Chicago *Herald*, the Macon *Telegraph*, the New York *Sun*, the Philadelphia *Ledger*, and the Washington *Star*. Of these, three were Democratic, two were independent, and one was Republican. Which of the two groups of papers played the greater part in influencing governmental policy, or whether either group greatly affected that policy, is a matter of speculation.[17]

Wherever the truth may lie, the interests and sympathies of James G. Blaine, who was then secretary of state, would hardly admit of an indefinite delay. Accordingly, on January 29, 1890, formal recognition was extended to Brazilian agents at Washington; three weeks later Minister Adams, following instructions, made known the attitude of his gov-

[16] *Congressional Record*, 51 Cong., 1 sess., pp. 216, 313 *et seq.*, 323, 871.

[17] For an analysis of press opinion in the United States, see J. F. Rippy, "The United States and the Establishment of the Republic of Brazil," in *The Southwestern Political Science Quarterly*, III, No. 1, pp. 1-15.

ernment; and on April 1, Adams's successor, Chargé James F. Lee, presented to the government of the new republic the joint resolution of the United States Congress congratulating the people of Brazil on the assumption of the duties, powers, and responsibilities of self-government. In the following summer, upon learning that the draft of the constitution to be submitted to—and probably adopted by—the forthcoming constituent assembly provided for the American system of executive responsibility rather than the European system of parliamentarism, Lee again presented the congratulations of his government on the particular form the new republic was about to assume.[18]

Expression of appreciation on the part of Brazil for the kindly interest and profound sympathy of the United States took many forms. One of the first acts of the Brazilian republican congress was the passage of resolutions expressing thanks to the friendly neighbor; the American squadron which made a "friendly visit" to Rio de Janeiro in the summer of 1890 to salute the sister republic was accorded "unprecedented Courtesies—official & Social"; the Brazilian government reciprocated immediately by sending a naval force to the United States; and one of the first international agreements of the new government granted to the United States favorable commercial concessions.[19]

The topic of commercial concessions needs further comment. For the past twenty years, or since the opening of the friendly era between the two countries, American ministers had been solicitous about the status of the trade of

[18] Dispatches of Feb. 24, Apr. 2, May 28, and June 27, 1890, in *ibid.;* John Bassett Moore, *A Digest of International Law,* I, 160-161.

[19] American dispatches, July 7, 1890, and Feb. 6, 1891, in *ibid.,* LXIX and L; President Deodora to President Harrison, Oct. 30, 1890, in Notes from the Brazilian Legation, VII.

their countrymen in Brazil. In 1870, Blow reported that
the United States was purchasing Brazilian goods to the extent of twenty-five million dollars annually, while Brazil
was buying from the United States slightly less than one-
fourth as much, and suggested that the remedy for the
unfavorable balance was the improvement in the means of
communication between the countries. He thought that his
government should follow the practice of European nations
of granting large subsidies to encourage the building of fast
steamers in order to provide the needed communication facilities. Two years later a successor of Blow, James R. Partridge, after a careful study of the consular reports, called
attention to a matter he considered equally as serious: sev-
enty-five per cent of Brazilian-American trade was carried
in European vessels. Stating that the five steamship lines
under the British flag—operating seventy-one vessels carrying eighty thousand tons—and the two each under the
French and the Italian flags were the results of governmental subsidies, he proposed the same remedy for meeting
the competition.[20]

These proposals availed nothing in improving the status
of American commerce in Brazil. Indeed, at the time of the
overthrow of the empire Brazil took less than five and one-
half per cent of her imports from the United States, notwithstanding the fact that the latter country purchased sixty-one
per cent of what Brazil had to sell. England, France and
Germany—chiefly England—were the recipients of a favorable balance in trade at the expense of the United States.[21]
Fortunately, the change of government in Brazil, and the
friendliness that soon developed between the new régime

[20] Dispatches of Dec. 18, 1889, Oct. 30, 1870, Jan. 6 and 8, 1872, in Despatches,
XXXV, XXXVIII, XXXIX.
[21] Adams's dispatch of Aug. 16, 1889, in *ibid.*, XLVIII.

and the United States as a consequence, paved the way for a change in commercial policy favorable to the northern republic. And the northern republic did not delay long in taking advantage of her opportunity; the McKinley tariff act of 1890 carried provisions placing certain articles commonly imported from Latin-American countries, such as coffee, sugar, tea, and hides, on the free list, with the proviso that the president could impose duties on them in the event any country levied "unjust or unreasonable" duties on American products. Largely responsible for the reciprocity feature of the act, Secretary of State Blaine hastened negotiations to give practical application to it in Brazil. As a result, the Brazilian government issued a decree on February 5, 1891, inaugurating the new principle. The agreement provided for admission into the United States of a list of Brazilian articles, including coffee, sugar, hides, and rubber, at a reduction of twenty-five per cent from the normal rate, which in most cases meant duty free, in return for similar favors to American products entering Brazil. Also it prevented any increase in export duty by Brazil on enumerated articles or on any article on the free list of the United States.[22]

The reciprocity arrangement was a strong bid to regain for Yankee traders the enviable position in Brazil which they had held a half century earlier. But the difficulties to be overcome were great. In the course of time the Brazilian habit of purchasing from Europeans had become fixed. Old World merchants had catered to the tastes and whims of their New World customers in packing and labeling; they even took American goods and by repacking and relabeling sold them to Brazilians at good profits. Moreover, the

---

[22] The decree setting forth the reciprocity arrangement was enclosed with American Minister Conger's dispatch of Feb. 6, 1891, in *ibid.*, L.

transportation and banking facilities gave them a strong advantage over their American competitors.[23]

As might have been expected, the reciprocity experiment had a rocky road to travel in Brazil. No sooner had the arrangement been made public than the American minister cabled Secretary Blaine that the Brazilian press, evidently as a result of pressure from foreign influences, was adverse in sentiment.[24] At the end of a month he wrote his chief that the press generally was opposed and that the Brazilian assembly before adjournment had alleged the agreement was entered into without due consideration. Again he thought the opposition was attributable to the large body of European merchants and importers which had been organized for furious attacks and which spread the rumor that Brazilian finances would be ruined through cutting off European credit.[25] At the close of another four weeks the Yankee minister reported regretfully: "the general expression, here in the city [Rio de Janeiro] both by the Press and by individuals is still adverse to the Reciprocity arrangement, and it seems quite apparent, that when Congress convenes in June, a strenuous effort will be made, to repeal or alter the decree of the Provisional Government on this subject, unless prohibited by the terms of the agreement."[26]

Blaine was sorely disappointed that his pet project was meeting such strenuous opposition at the beginning. He instructed Minister Conger to let the Brazilian government know that the president of the United States would regard abrogation of the agreement by the Brazilian Congress as unfortunate for the friendly relations of the two countries,

[23] See Conger to Blaine, Feb. 27, 1891, in *ibid.*
[24] Telegram of Feb. 11, enclosed in dispatch of Feb. 26, 1891, in *ibid.*
[25] Dispatch of Mar. 6, in *ibid.*
[26] Conger to Blaine, Apr. 2, 1891, in *ibid.*

especially if it came before an opportunity had been given to test its merits.[27] Conger carried out the instruction; but it availed little so far as the Brazilian congress was concerned, for when the chambers met, opposition to the reciprocity arrangement showed itself strongly. The points of attack were many. The arrangement had been entered into with the hope that it would help the sugar industry at Bahia, Pernambuco, and Pará, which had been languishing for some years. But the hope went glimmering when the United States effected an agreement with Spain whereby Cuban sugar might enter the United States under the same privileges as Brazilian sugar; Cuba's soil, climate, and position gave her planters the American market. In the next place, it was obvious that the arrangement would reduce the income of the Brazilian states as well as limit their rights of self-control. On these vulnerable points the critics, who usually got their queues from European merchants and diplomats, centered their attacks. They were joined by those who for any reason desired to obstruct and weaken the national executive.[28]

In order to stem the tide of opposition, the president of Brazil called home Mendonça, the minister to the United States, who had conducted the negotiations with Blaine for the reciprocity agreement. Soon after arrival at Rio de Janeiro, Mendonça spoke behind closed doors to the Brazilian Congress on the agreement with the United States. Whatever the tactics of the influential minister, an accord was reached with the opposition leaders of congress. Perhaps it is significant that the reorganization of the cabinet

---

[27] Blaine's instructions of May 23, 1891, in Instructions to Brazilian Ministers, XVII, 517 *et seq.*

[28] See especially dispatches of June 18 and July 7, 1891 in *ibid.*, L, LI.

which followed shortly made room for two of the opposition leaders.[29]

But the announced accord reached with the congressional leaders in the summer of 1891 was only a truce. In the spring of the following year William H. Lawrence, who was acting as chargé during Conger's absence in the United States, reported the beginning of another vigorous campaign in Brazil against reciprocity. The *Jornal do Commercio,* perhaps the most influential paper in Brazil, led the renewed campaign; the editor, José Carlos Rodriguez, had become imbued with British ideas during a residence in England or else he had fallen under British influences after return to his native land. Other papers joined the attack. Soon the infection spread to Congress and to every other Brazilian organization. And from the time of the renewed attacks to the abrogation of the reciprocity treaty by the Wilson-Gorman tariff law of 1894 there was little surcease for the Brazilian administration.[30]

Notwithstanding the severity of the sustained attacks from the numerous critics, the Brazilian executive stood as a staunch defender of the reciprocity agreement throughout the four years of its operation. His attitude was shown clearly when various of the Brazilian states levied duties both on imports from the United States and exports destined for the same country. Although it was not possible to stop the action of the states, inasmuch as the federal constitution of 1891 upheld it, the president advocated and put through the national assembly appropriations to take care of the claims growing out of contraventions of the reciprocity arrangement. Perhaps more important in revealing the executive's attitude

[29] Conger's letters of Sept. 17 and 28, 1891, in *ibid.,* LI.

[30] Dispatches of Feb. 10 and May 23, 1892, and Sept. 12, 1894, in *ibid.,* LII, LVII.

was the fact that he supported the arrangement when the congressional opposition was using it as a fulcrum for their lever in prying him from his position. The following extract from the American minister's dispatch of November 13, 1891, bears on this point.

I must also say that one of the strong grounds of their congressional opposition to the President has grown out of his reciprocity negotiations with the United States.

He has all the time been a true friend of this policy, and has fought loyally for the arrangement, even against almost overwhelming odds.

There can be no doubt, that combined systematic, and stubborn efforts of European officials, merchants, and capital, have been continually made to bring about its repeal.

Especially has this been done by the English banks in this city and London, who [sic.] have been able to practically control the credit of this country by actually fixing the value of Brazilian money, in their arbitrarily established daily rates of exchange and having forced the price down to the lowest point, attempted to make the Brazilians believe it is but one of the logical results of the reciprocity arrangement.

Yet the President has never wavered, and I am informed through his Minister of Foreign Affairs that he still proposes that the Government shall stand by the arrangement.[31]

This unwavering support of reciprocity by President Deodora was continued by his successor Floriano Peixoto.[32]

Both executives may have considered themselves partially repaid for their support, for the Washington government showed a solicitous attitude toward their administrations. When on November 3, 1891, Deodora illegally dissolved the Brazilian Congress and assumed dictatorial powers, Sec-

---

[31] Despatches, LI.

[32] See dispatches of Mar. 13, 1893, Sept. 25, 1894, and Jan. 15, 1895, in *ibid.*, LIV, LVII, LVIII, respectively.

retary Blaine instructed the American minister at Rio de Janeiro to:

Convey to the President of Brazil the friendly solicitude of the United States, in behalf of the Republic of Brazil, and the fervent hope of our people, that nothing may happen to destroy or impair the free political institutions so recently and so happily established in that great country. Our counsel would favor a wise moderation; for bloodshed too certainly brings retaliation; while a firm yet merciful defense of the just prerogatives of a free government will make enemies to be friends.[33]

This solicitude and advice did not save President De-odora, for on November 23 he abandoned the struggle with the opposition and turned over the government to the vice-president, General Floriano Peixoto. Like Deodora, like most militarists who essay to play the rôle of statesmen, Floriano soon began to resort to the only methods he knew —praetorian methods. In defense of both Deodora and Floriano, however, it may be said that they had extraordinarily difficult positions to fill. Brazil was passing from a monarchical to a republican form of organization and confusion and disorder were almost inevitable in any event. At any rate, during 1892 outbreaks flared up in various states, the most serious of which was that in Rio Grande do Sul, where the famous gaucho chieftain Gumercindo Saraïva assumed the leadership. In the same year occurred the revolt of the garrison in command of one of the fortresses at the entrance of the Rio harbor; and in September of the following year Admiral José de Mello raised the emblem of revolt above the cruiser *Aquidaban* in the harbor itself. Shortly thereafter practically the entire navy, several members of Congress, and a number of private citizens joined the revolt.

[33] Blaine's cablegram to Minister Conger, Nov. 13, 1891, in *ibid.*, LI.

Since the admiral had control of the entire harbor and could bombard the capital at will and since he could communicate readily with the disaffected elements in Rio Grande do Sul and elsewhere, it seemed as though he would have little difficulty in rendering the position of Floriano untenable. But at this point an imponderable factor operated against the insurgents.[34]

Upon the outbreak of the naval revolt in the harbor of the Brazilian capital the American minister, Thomas S. Thompson, acting in conjunction with the representatives of the European nations, declined the invitation of President Peixoto to confer with him on measures which should be adopted in the event the insurgents resorted to bombardment of the city. The declination was made in order to observe strict neutrality. At the same time Thompson urged his government to dispatch a naval force to Brazil sufficient for the protection of American citizens and their commerce.[35]

Although the term neutrality was called into use several times to explain the attitude of the United States toward the Brazilian quarrel, strictly speaking it was quite inappropriate to define the actual status. Certainly there could have been no status of neutrality, inasmuch as one of the contestants to the quarrel was never accorded the position of belligerent; and the Mello faction throughout most of the six month's struggle sought to achieve from the outside nations recognition of the belligerent status.

On October 24 (1893) Admiral Mello announced that a provisional government had been established ten days before at Desterro, the capital of Santa Catharina, and re-

---

[34] Felisbello Freire, *Historia da Revolta de 6 de Setembre de 1893*, pp. 1-186.

[35] Thompson's cablegrams to his government, enclosed in dispatches of Sept. 18 and 19, 1893, in Despatches, LIV.

quested from the United States recognition as a belligerent. The reply of the Cleveland government to this request was that "thus far the insurgents do not appear to have put on footing and maintained a political organization which would justify the United States in recognizing them as belligerents and recognition would be a gratuitous demonstration of moral support to the rebellion, an unfriendly act toward Brazil." The communication containing the official reply told Minister Thompson he was expected to keep the State Department advised on events occurring at Rio de Janeiro and elsewhere in Brazil and espouse the cause of neither side.[36]

During the succeeding three or four months the insurgents repeated several times their request for recognition as belligerents. On one occasion they based their claims on the statements that the state governments of Santa Catharina and Rio Grande do Sul, the entire Brazilian navy, and a majority of the Brazilian people supported their cause. On another occasion they rested their case on the arguments that they had maintained a government for four months and that their opponents revealed their weakness by declaring martial law as many as seven times. So far as the United States was concerned the arguments fell on thorny soil. The insurgent manifesto proposing the reëstablishment of the imperial form of government, even though the change was to be subject to ratification by the Brazilian people, absolutely precluded the possibility of recognition at Washington. Although it was rumored from time to time that Germany or Great Britain was on the verge of extending recognition, the European na-

---

[36] Secretary Gresham to Thompson, Oct. 25, 1893, in Instructions to Brazilian Ministers, XVII, 695-696. See also Thompson to Gresham, Oct. 24, 1893, in Despatches, LV.

tions pursued the same general policy as that pursued from the Potomac.[37]

An incident closely connected with the question of American neutrality was that of the conduct of Commodore O. F. Stanton, commander of the South Atlantic naval forces of the United States, who in pursuance to orders arrived at Rio de Janeiro shortly after the outbreak of the revolt. While the commodore had shown every official courtesy to the Peixoto government on entering the harbor, subsequently he exchanged salutes with the insurgent squadron and made an official call upon Admiral Mello. The subsequent conduct brought a protest from Floriano Peixoto and an order of recall and a public disavowal from President Cleveland. In the opinion of the American executive the officer had violated "our fixed policy of impartial neutrality." After according him the opportunity to make an explanation—which in all probability had no bearing on the verdict—the Department of the Navy decreed that Stanton had committed "a grave error of judgment." To the "impartial observer" it would appear as though the commodore was impartial in fact rather than in law. The United States had not recognized the insurgent forces as entitled to belligerent rights. Although the American minister discouraged a public demonstration in Rio de Janeiro in approval of Stanton's recall, he was probably well pleased with his government's action; the commander had not been a faithful colleague at all times.[38]

The method employed by the American government to protect the commerce of its citizens with Rio de Janeiro is worthy of consideration at this point. Shortly after the out-

[37] Thompson's communications of Nov. 10, Dec. 13, 18, and 26, 1893, and Feb. 3, 1894, in Despatches, LV.

[38] Thompson's dispatch of Nov. 10, 1893, in *ibid.;* Secretary Gresham's instruction of Dec. 20, 1893, in Instructions to Brazilian Ministers, XVIII, 9-10; J. B. Moore, *Digest of International Law,* I, 240.

break of the revolt, before receipt of instructions from Washington on the matter, the American minister, Thomas S. Thompson, "advised" the commander of the U. S. S. *Charleston* to "protect by force, in case of necessity, American goods" which barges were conveying from anchored merchantmen to the shore.[39]   Three days later Thompson received from his government an instruction sanctioning a policy which he had already inaugurated.   The instruction said "every possible effort should be made to protect American persons and property and all the naval force of our Government should be exerted by protest and otherwise to prevent further destruction and bloodshed."   At the request of the secretary of the Navy a copy of the document was to be placed in the hands of the commander of the *Charleston*.[40]

For several weeks the American minister and the United States naval commander coöperated in enforcing the protective policy.   During this time the barges and launches engaged in lighterage service flew the Stars and Stripes and were not molested by the insurgent forces.   The American policy was so successful that the Argentine minister at Rio de Janeiro requested the protection of the commercial interests of his countrymen by the United States naval vessels. Thompson submitted the request to Washington; but before the Cleveland government had time to give a negative reply the Argentine government had repudiated its agent's effrontery.   Other nations having naval forces at the Brazilian capital pursued similar courses, though with not quite the same success.   At least upon one occasion the insurgents seized an English registered barge.[41]

[39] Dispatch of Sept. 28, 1893, in Despatches, LV.

[40] The instruction by cablegram of Sept. 29 was acknowledged in Thompson's dispatch of Oct. 1, 1893, in *ibid.*

[41] Dispatches of Oct. 13 and 30, Nov. 7, 1893, in *ibid.*; the State Department instructions of Nov. 8 and 18, 1893, in Instructions to Brazilian Ministers, XVII, 697-698, 701.

But if the American program was attended by greater success, it may have been because it was the more rigid. The American government continued to insist on the right of Yankee goods to be conveyed from the anchored vessels to the shore as long as the barges or lighters did "not cross or otherwise interfere with Mello's line of fire."[42] When the insurgent's fire became more or less desultory, it was natural that all commerce should be subjected to a serious impediment. This serious impediment was turned into almost complete prohibition when the foreign commanders, accusing the Peixoto government of violating its pledge not to fortify and equip with armament strategic positions within the city limits, withdrew intervention in behalf of foreign commerce. Before reporting the agreement of the foreign commanders concerning the attitude toward commerce, Captain Picking, who now commanded the American squadron, was inclined to give a very liberal interpretation to the "line of fire" maintained by the insurgents. The American minister thought this interpretation favored the insurgents, placed American commerce in jeopardy, and upset the whole American policy. As a result, an acrimonious controversy between him and the captain ensued over the meaning of their respective instructions. But before long the officials at Washington intervened with a change of naval commanders.[43]

Admiral Benham, the new commander, was sent to Rio de Janeiro with instructions to protect American commerce en route from designated places of anchorage to the Brazilian docks. He had his opportunity soon after arrival. When one of the discharging vessels was fired on by an insurgent

[42] Secretary of state to Thompson, Nov. 1, 1893, in Instructions to Brazilian Ministers, XVII, 696-697.

[43] Dispatches of Dec. 17, 21, 22, and 31, 1893, in Despatches, LV; State Department instruction of Jan. 9, 1894, in Instructions to Brazilian Ministers, XVIII.

cruiser, the U. S. S. *Detroit,* which had taken a strategic position, returned the fire with a six pounder, the shot striking
under the bows of the insurgent.   At the end of the harmless
exchange of lead came an exchange of words between Admiral Benham and Admiral Da Gama of the insurgent fleet.
Whatever the nature of the word battle, American vessels
were not again molested, though they were not allowed to
interfere with the "line of fire."   The commerce of other
nations was resumed as a result of Benham's action.[44]

The question of the attitude of the United States toward
bombardment of the city of Rio de Janeiro can be disposed of
very briefly.   Soon after the outbreak of the revolt the foreign diplomats and naval commanders effected an agreement
with the hostile parties that a bombardment of the capital
would be averted so long as the Peixoto government afforded
no pretext for an assault by fortifying the city or directing
active hostilities against the insurgents therefrom.   Later, it
was agreed that bombardment was permissible to either party
with forty-eight hours notice.   Notwithstanding the complaints of American merchants that frequent shots found
their way into the city, the insurgents, stimulated no doubt
by the presence of foreign war vessels, seem to have kept
faith reasonably well.   On the other hand, the insurgents
accused their opponents of bad faith, and the accusations
were sustained by the foreign commanders, who withdrew
in protest their engagement to prevent bombardment.   Nevertheless, the feature of the agreement for the forty-eight
hours notice continued in force to the end.   Finally, it was
invoked by the Peixoto government on March 11 (1894)

---

[44] Dispatches of Feb. 1 and 3, 1894, in Despatches, LV; instructions of Jan. 10
and Feb. 1, 1894, in Instructions, XVIII, 19-21, 27-28.

and two days later the insurgents surrendered without firing a shot.[45]

It is difficult for one who studies the correspondence to arrive at any other conclusion than that the American policy during the revolt very definitely strengthened the cause of the Peixoto faction. If the insurgents had been permitted to shell the capital city and to prevent supplies from reaching their opponents, victory would have been theirs. But notwithstanding the fact that they held out more than six months, they never succeeded in getting recognition as belligerents; and their failure to achieve this enviable status is attributable primarily to the aggressive opposition of the United States. Without doubt American opposition would have been less persistent had not the insurgents made the fatal mistake of declaring for monarchy; American agents envisaged Old World monarchies ever anxious to regain a foothold in the Western Hemisphere. One favorable comment can be made on Cleveland's Brazilian policy of 1893-1894: the stakes were placed on the winner. Not as much can be said of Hoover's policy during the disturbance of 1930.[46]

Three incidents which took place in the Brazilian capital evidenced appreciation for the attitude of the United States

[45] Dispatches of Oct. 2, 9, 21, 22, Dec. 5, 25, and 30, 1893, Jan. 12, Feb. 14, Mar. 11 and 16, 1894, in Despatches, LV, LVI; instruction of Jan. 10, 1894, in Instructions, XVIII, 19 et seq. Many of the communications cited for the naval revolt are printed in Foreign Relations, 1894, pp. 26-148; but inasmuch as many are not to be found in this publication the citations to the manuscripts have been continued. See also Felisbello Freire, Historia da Revolta de 6 de Septembro de 1893, I, 187-227, 295 et seq.; Brazil, Relatorio, 1894; Custodia José de Mello, Apontamentos para a Historia da Revolução de 23 de Novembro de 1891.

[46] During the Brazilian naval revolt most of the large newspapers in the United States criticised the American minister at Rio de Janeiro for favoritism toward the insurrectionists. This is an excellent example of how our papers often acquire and disseminate misinformation on foreign affairs. See Philadelphia Public Ledger, Dec. 28, 1893; Baltimore News, Dec. 29; Chicago Herald, Dec. 30; New York World, Jan. 3, 1894; San Francisco Call, Jan. 1; Baltimore Sun, Jan. 2; New York Tribune, Jan. 15; Philadelphia Press, Jan. 14.

during the insurrection.   In the early summer of 1894 the national Congress which bestowed a gold and platinum medal upon Floriano Peixoto voted a like reward to President Cleveland.   On July 4, the national holiday in recognition of the Declaration of Independence of the English colonists in North America, was observed as a Brazilian holiday. Closed business houses, unfurled flags, decorated ships and dwellings, and resounding salutes from the fortresses displayed the spirit of appreciation of the sister republic to the north.   On November 15, when the new Brazilian president, Dr. Prudento de Moraes Barros, was inaugurated as Floriano's successor, the cornerstone of a monument to the memory of James Monroe and in honor of the doctrine which bears the name of the illustrious American statesman was laid in Rio de Janeiro.   In the summer and autumn of 1894 the understanding between the two greatest republics of the New World hardly could have been more cordial.   By this time the Brazilian republic was secure.[47]

[47] Thompson's dispatches of June 17, July 13 and Nov. 21, with their many enclosures, in Despatches, LVII.

Chapter XI

RECENT TENDENCIES

O N THE whole the most satisfactory epoch in Brazilian-American relations has been the period since the advent of Moraes Barros, the first of Brazil's civilian presidents. It was natural that cordiality should improve after Brazil adopted the republican form of government. Often there is more efficacy in form than in spirit.

Early in the period came President Cleveland's award in the Misiones boundary controversy to stimulate the esteem between the great republics of North and South America. With its roots extending as far back as the Treaty of Tordesillas of 1494, the dispute between Brazil and Argentina had at time assumed acrimonious proportions. When the president of the United States accepted the rôle of arbiter in 1892, the point of contention was the identification of two small streams, tributaries of the Iguassú and Uruguay rivers mentioned in the eighteenth century negotiations of Spain and Portugal. In the nineteenth century it was discovered that two pairs of streams answered the descriptions of the earlier negotiators. Of the two pairs, Argentina claimed the easternmost and Brazil the westernmost. Several years of direct negotiations failed to bring an agreement; then came the treaty of 1889 making the president of the United States the arbiter.

After listening to arguments ably presented by both groups of distinguished counselors, and after a careful examination of volumes of material reviewing the controversy's history of four centuries, President Cleveland, February 6, 1895, rendered a decision in favor of the line formed by the

Pepiry and San Antonio rivers, or that claimed by Brazil. One of the important factors determining the decision was the presence of a considerable Brazilian population in the disputed region. Besides, the wedgeshaped territory was very important for the defense of two of Brazil's southern provinces. Argentina's claims were based more on sentiment than on practicality. Argentina accepted the disappointing award gracefully; Brazil held a rousing demonstration that found expression and reëxpression in all the publications of the country. In popularity Grover Cleveland was second only to the Baron of Rio Branco, the distinguished Brazilian counselor whose legal acumen and painstaking arguments had been so powerful a factor in the successful outcome.[1]

It is little wonder that Cleveland's Venezuelan message, which was delivered later in the same year, met with general favor in Brazil. Soon after it became known in Rio de Janeiro the Brazilian Senate passed a resolution congratulating the United States Senate "on the worthy message of President Cleveland, which, with so much courage, protects the dignity, sovereignty, and liberty of the American Nations." Similar forms of expression were issued by the Chamber of Deputies and by municipal political organs of the country. And with two notable exceptions, the *Rio News* and the *Jornal do Commercio*, both of which were dominated by British influences, the newspaper and periodical press commended the message. Interestingly enough, the message called forth the latent powers of one Brazilian publicist

[1] Communications of American ministers, Sept. 30, 1891, May 4, 1892, June 15, 1893, and Feb. 15, 1895, with the hundreds of pages of enclosures, in Despatches, LI, LII, LIV, LVIII; Instruction to Conger, July 2, 1892, in Instructions, XVII, 588 *et seq.*; President Deodora to President Harrison, Apr. 15, 1892, in Communications from the Brazilian Legation, VII; Mary W. Williams, "The Treaty of Tordesillas and the Argentine-Brazilian Boundary Settlement," in *The Hispanic American Historical Review*, Feb., 1922; A. G. de Araujo Jorge, *Ensayo de História Diplomática de Brazil*, pp. 53-84.

and jurist and inspired him to write a treatise on the necessity of maintaining the Monroe Doctrine. Entitled *Intervention and the Monroe Doctrine (A Intervençao e a Doutrina de Monroe)*, this seventy-page pamphlet was published the following year and widely distributed.[2]

The policy of the United States which flung defiance at European aggression in Latin America met approval in Brazil. But an aggressive policy on the part of the United States in the promotion of her own interests met with criticism in the same country. The criticism did not become severe, however, until Yankee and Brazilian interests clashed.

The outbreak of the war between the United States and Spain apparently occasioned little or no adverse comment in this South American country. The war provided an opportunity for Brazil to gather a few sheckles into her empty treasury by the sale of three war vessels to the United States, whose government was able to pay more than Spain could afford to pay. But the McKinley government declined at the very beginning to accept the proffers of Brazilian citizens to serve in the United States army and navy. The strictly neutral course which the Brazilian government claimed to pursue during the short conflict was deviated from in only one minor instance—when two United States war vessels, the *Oregon* and the *Marietta*, were permitted to remain in harbor at Rio de Janeiro eighty-four hours. Shortly after the termination of the fighting the Naval Club of the Brazilian capital sent a communication to the United States navy in congratulation of the latter's brilliant victory at sea. "Coming from a potent organization which, since the Revolution of 1894, has looked with disfavor on our government and people" because

[2] The author was Manuel Ignacio Carvalho de Mendonça. A copy of the book is to be found with the dispatch of June 14, 1898, in Despatches, LXII. See also dispatches of Dec. 23, 24, and 26, and the numerous excerpts from the Brazilian press enclosed with them, in *ibid.*, LXIX.

of the aid they gave to the government of Floriano Peixoto, this congratulatory message, thought the American minister, had special significance.[3]

On the other hand, the following year the visit of the U. S. S. *Wilmington* to the upper Amazon aroused considerable criticism in Brazil. While the vessel had permission to visit the *ports* of Brazil, it was later learned that she should have obtained special permission before ascending the "King of Rivers." As a result of failure to comply with the latter requirement, the American consul at Manâos was attacked by Brazilian residents soon after the vessel passed that city. After an exchange of a number of communications, the American minister and the Brazilian minister of foreign affairs arrived at an adjustment without serious difficulty. This matter of punctilio would have amounted to little except for its connection with American interest in rubber exploitation in the Acre territory.[4]

Excitement in Brazilian circles over Acre, an area on the borderlands of Bolivia rich in rubber, was the result of a contract between the Bolivian government and the Bolivian Syndicate, a concern composed of English and American capitalists—primarily the latter—making the syndicate the fiscal administrator in the territory. In order to make effective its responsibilities in the collection of revenue, the company was given the right to organize an armed force, including war vessels for operation upon the rivers. Moreover, the company was granted an option on the purchase of all government land in the region.

Knowledge of the existence of this contract aroused a great furor in Brazil. The most extreme newspapers—and

[3] Dispatches of March 7, Apr. 23, 25, and 27, and Sept. 5, 1898, in *ibid.*, LXII and LXIII.

[4] Dispatches of Apr. 25 and July 12, 1899, in *ibid.*, LXIII and LXIV.

they are more extreme than the most radical papers of the United States—expressed sympathy for unfortunate Cuba and the Philippines and warned Brazilians of the dangers threatening their country from the north. One paper averred that the *Wilmington* had ascended the Amazon the previous year in order to take arms to the Bolivian forces. What seemed ominous to the American minister was the fact that some of the alarmist newspaper accounts could have emanated from no other than official sources. When the minister took up the question with the Brazilian foreign office with a view to quieting matters, he learned that Brazil's specific objection to the broad concessions to the syndicate lay in the fact that they applied to a region which she claimed as a part of her domain. If Bolivia wanted to yield sovereignty over her own territory by conferring upon an alien body the right to protect it by military force, Brazil could not protest; but the region under consideration was not the undisputed property of Bolivia.[5]

The *communiqués* given out as a result of the first conferences between the American minister and the Brazilian foreign office, together with announcements from President Roosevelt that the United States had no intention of acquiring territory in the Acre, calmed the critical press of Brazil for a time. But receipt of reports from Washington—no doubt through the Brazilian minister there—that the Bolivian minister and the Roosevelt government were carrying on negotiations looking toward American intervention in the Acre dispute, and renewed activity of the Yankee minister at

[5] Indispensable in the study of this question is an anonymous and undated pamphlet entitled *The Acre Territory*. Among the many documents reprinted in the pamphlet is one giving the terms of the concession to the Bolivian Syndicate. See also Bryan, American minister at Rio de Janeiro, to Hay, Mar. 27, 1900, and Apr. 17, 1902, in Despatches, LXV and LXVII; *Gazeta de Noticias*, Apr. 10, 11, 12, and 16, 1902; *Jornal do Brazil*, Apr. 12-17, 1902; *Tribuna de Petropolis*, Apr. 15, 1902.

Rio de Janeiro in an attempt to comply with vigorous instructions from the Potomac, caused a renewal of the attack in more virulent form. The official organs vied with the unofficial in printing vituperative material.[6]

Meanwhile, the Brazilian government was not idle. The foreign minister held several conferences with the Bolivian representative at Rio de Janeiro in which he rebuked the Bolivian government for granting a concession that would prove a veritable Trojan horse to South American security. After the conference method failed to secure results, the Rio government put into execution a policy of retaliation which it had been holding over the head of its sister republic for some weeks. First of all, it withdrew from the Brazilian chamber of deputies a treaty providing for the free navigation of certain confluents of the Amazon which extended into Bolivia and which had never been relieved of restrictions. This was a stroke at the Bolivian Syndicate as well as at recalcitrant Bolivia, for at this very time the corporation was resorting to all available means to bring about the ratification of the treaty, erroneously thinking that defeat meant interference with its business. Interestingly enough, the American State Department was also using its influence to secure ratification, believing defeat meant interference with the syndicate's operation. Perhaps it made little difference that the president's cousin, W. E. Roosevelt, was among the New York capitalists who composed the organization.[7]

The next move of the Rio government was more effective. The minister of finance laid prohibitive transit duties on goods imported into or exported from Bolivia through the Amazon. This partial closing of the great natural high-

[6] See copies of the *Gazeta de Noticias* and the *Tribuna de Petropolis* for May, June, and July, 1902.

[7] Hay to Bryan, June 2, 1902, in Instructions, XVIII, 566.

way, which had been opened largely through the efforts of the United States thirty-five years before, brought a strong remonstrance from the American government. After spending several days in an unsuccessful effort to carry out John Hay's instruction of December 9, 1902, American Minister Seeger unburdened himself in an interesting letter to his superiors. Writing confidentially from Rio de Janeiro on January 30, 1903, he said in part:

In further explanation of this matter I beg leave to state that, the odious measure in question, although nominally directed against Bolivia is principally intended as a thrust against the United States, executed in deference to a clamorous public opinion.

As long as the Bolivians negotiated with a Brazilian syndicate for the leasing of the Acre district there was not a ripple in the political relations of the two countries.

Even the boundary question excited only benevolent remarks on the part of the Brazilian press and the Brazilian statesmen were almost ready to give to their Bolivian neighbor what, by general consent, belonged to them.

Bolivia's troubles began at the moment the so-called American syndicate appeared on the scene. From that time on, the insignificant "Acre revolution," an act of modern piracy directed by politicians and speculators in Manaos and executed by the basest kind of adventurers and cut-throats, received the assistance of the national government and thus became an influential factor in politics.

The rubber-robbers in Manaos donned the garb of outraged patriotism and declared violently against Bolivia for having sold out to the "Yankees," whose expansion policy was endangering Brazil and the rest of South America.

The Spanish adventurer Gomez—a man but recently discharged from a minor position in a commercial house here for stealing— loomed up in the foreground and from his place of refuge, Buenos Ayres, told the Argentine press startling tales about Yankee plots and Yankee conspiracies. The *Wilmington's* trip up the Amazon was the first step of the proposed annexation of the States of Amazonas and Para by the Yankees, the South Atlantic Squadron already had its orders for the same purpose and the "Acre Syndicate" was only a harmless name for a military outpost of the Yankee expansionists. Such were the rumors spread in Buenos Ayres, eagerly re-iterated here and seriously debated by the Brazilian press, which, with few exceptions, is very friendly to the United States.

The "Perigo Americano"—the American danger—became a standing article in the daily papers and the caricatures of Uncle Sam which appeared therein became more hideous from day to day.

The prohibitive transit duties prescribed by Brazil against Bolivia —in clear violation of the International Law and their own Constitution—were the result of this corrupt and morbid agitation.

The promulgators of this measure knew that they could kill two birds with one stone: they could injure the United States and Bolivia at the same time.

Mr. Magalhaes, the former Minister for Foreign Affairs here has—as the Bolivian Minister here, Dr. Pinilla, assured me—repeatedly declared the difficulties between Bolivia and Brazil could be settled the very moment Bolivia would get rid of the "American Syndicate," and at one time, Dr. Pinilla assured me, Mr. Magalhaes offered to procure the money to be refunded to the syndicate. Barao Rio Branco may be personally more just and liberal in his views and may think less of the "Perigo Americano" than his predecessor, but, if he wants to remain at his post he has to make concessions to the influential jingo-element, notoriously unfriendly to the United States and hostile to Bolivia as long as its government shelters that syndicate, which is generally supposed to be backed up—vi et armis— by the United States and to be pioneers of American aggressiveness directed against South America.[8]

It is unnecessary to examine the truthfulness of these accusations. In passing, however, it may be noted that the solicitor of the American Department of State, in reply to a

[8] Despatches, LXVIII; Instructions, XVIII, 584-585.

request for an opinion on the ground the United States government should take on the closing of the Amazon, said that the view taken by the Brazilian alarmists was precisely the view the United States would take if Canada should grant a concession of the disputed Alaskan district to a syndicate of German capitalists. This detached opinion of the legalist is nearer the truth than that of the American minister.[9]

Seeger's remonstrance at Rio de Janeiro availed little directly. Soon, however, the Brazilian government made a cash settlement with the Bolivian Syndicate, the Yankee capitalists relinquished their concessions in the Acre, and the Amazon was reopened to Bolivian commerce.[10]

While these negotiations were taking place, Brazil sent armed forces into the Acre and set up a temporary administration. On March 21, 1903, a *modus vivendi* was signed with Bolivia by which Brazil agreed to submit the disputed territory to arbitration unless an amicable settlement was reached within a period of four months. Before the expiration of the temporary arrangement the chief provisions of a permanent treaty had been agreed on by the contestants. By them, Bolivia relinquished control over a triangular region in the Acre valley much larger than that originally in dispute in consideration of a monetary payment of two million pounds sterling, a port on the Paraguay, and a railroad from San Antonio on the Madeira to a point on the Mamoré two hundred miles above.[11]

In all probability Bolivia would eventually have lost the rich rubber-producing territory of Acre to Brazil had the Bolivian Syndicate never come into existence. But there is

[9] Dispatches of May 6, 1902, and Feb. 14, 1903, in Despatches, LXVII and LXVIII.

[10] Dispatches, Feb. 12 and 22, and Mar. 3, 1903, in *ibid.*, LXVIII.

[11] Dispatches of Mar. 21 and 27, Nov. 19 and 21, 1903, Jan. 23 and Feb. 15, 1904, with enclosures, in *ibid.*, LXVIII and LXIX.

little doubt that the concessions to the Yankee capitalists hastened the transfer. They were the clubs with which the Brazilian rubber capitalists and the alarmists drove the Rio government into action.

Naturally, Brazilians had less interest in Roosevelt's policy in the Caribbean and its borderlands. While the press criticised his conduct in Panama, it did not succeed in arousing the people to public demonstrations as in the case of the Acre dispute.[12] With reference to the president's message of December, 1904, particularly that portion of it dealing with foreign affairs, the governmental organ at Rio de Janeiro made the comment that "this document shows once more the capacity of Mr. Roosevelt to look at questions from a purely American [meaning United States] point of view, and his profound faith in the future of his country and in its destiny."[13] On the new interpretation given the Monroe Doctrine in the cases of Venezuela and Santo Domingo, the comments were more caustic. One paper usually friendly to the United States said that Roosevelt, following in the footsteps of Cecil Rhodes, based his theory of American imperialism on the right of strong nations to annihilate the weak ones, and his method on hypocrisy.[14] Another paper carried an editorial under the caption "Effects of Monroeism" which, after describing the American policy in Cuba, Panama, Porto Rico, and Santo Domingo, had this added comment on it:

It is perceived that its great object is the conquest of markets for its agricultural and industrial products, and that the plan consists in improving the state of insolvency of the Iberian American Republics, to intervene in their internal government, under the pretext of pro-

[12] See *Jornal do Commercio*, Nov. 7-9, 1903.
[13] *Ibid.*, Jan. 14, 1905.
[14] *A Noticia*, Apr. 24, 1905.

tecting their sovereignty, but with the resolution of establishing over them the protectorate of the United States, and of extending its zone of commercial influence, creating special tariffs for North American products.

It is therefore clear that if Brazil desires to avoid complications with the great republic it only has one road to follow; that is, to open to the United States its internal markets, creating specific tariffs to favor the introduction of American commodities.[15]

On the other hand, there were evidences of cordiality between the two countries during the time that the carping critics were so vociferous. Brazil's government appointed a distinguished commission to represent it at the Pan-American Exposition held at Buffalo, New York, in 1901. Three years later it built a beautiful marble and granite palace for its exhibit at the St. Louis Exposition. Later, it removed the structure to Rio de Janeiro, where it was dedicated as a meeting-place for international conferences and similar gatherings. In 1905, the two nations complimented each other by raising their respective legations to the rank of embassies, an act which met enthusiastic approval in Brazil, despite the fact that one journal characterized it as "an unjustifiable luxury."[16]

There is other evidence that the two governments at Rio de Janeiro and Washington were making conscious efforts to promote cordiality between their peoples. In 1906, the former published a treatise entitled *Brazil, the United States and Monroeism* in an attempt to counteract the evil effects of numerous newspaper articles which had been scathing in their criticism of the United States and her recent policy. Although the work appeared under the *nom de plume* of J.

[15] *Tribuna de Petropolis*, Mar. 9, 1905.

[16] Despatches of Apr. 4 and May 8, 1900, and Jan. 31, 1905, in Despatches, LXV and LXXI.

Penn, there is little doubt that its real author was Baron Rio Branco, Brazil's very distinguished foreign minister. Emphasizing the incidents in the early history of the relations of the two countries which had stimulated friendships and good-will—intentionally omitting the jarring episodes—the author sought to summon the powerful influences of history and tradition to promote a cause he considered so important. As if to complement the efforts of Rio Branco, Elihu Root, secretary of state of the United States, went to Rio de Janeiro in the same year at the head of the American delegation to the Third Pan-American Congress. Brazilians, as well as all Spanish Americans, appreciated the fact that the first official visit of an American secretary of state abroad should be to Latin America. The memorable address of Secretary Root while acting as honorary president of the conference and the extraordinary wisdom and tact displayed at the numerous meetings held in his honor served to heighten the appreciation. Writing to his chief three weeks after his departure from Rio de Janeiro, the American ambassador said that "as a direct result of your visit to Brazil, the whole attitude of the Government and people of this Republic toward the United States has been revolutionized, and we may fairly count in the future that the assumption will be that we mean well, instead as it has been in the past that we mean harm." Following this compliment—which may be diluted according to age and taste—the ambassador pointed out three positive evidences of the influence of the New Yorker's visit, the most important of which was the immediate alteration of the Brazilian tariff granting a twenty per cent preferential treatment to United States goods.[17]

Any account of the diplomatic relations between the United States and Brazil since 1895 would be entirely in-

[17] *Foreign Relations of the United States*, 1906, I, 116-139.

adequate unless it included the commercial phase of the subject. During the early part of the period American agents were forced to concern themselves with proposals for remedying an unfavorable trade balance, which assumed the colossal proportions of five to one and which resulted from Yankee thirst for Brazilian coffee and Brazilian predilection for European manufactured goods.

Ignoring the complete failure of Blaine's reciprocity experiment in Brazil between 1891 and 1895, the McKinley government, soon after the passage of the Dingley Act in 1897, urged the South American country to try reciprocity once more. In the negotiations, Brazil was reminded that the United States was purchasing more than sixty million dollars worth of her products, ninety-five per cent of which were admitted without duty, whereas Brazil was buying from the United States goods to the value of only thirteen million dollars, eighty-seven per cent of which were subject to heavy duties. Moreover, American goods after entry into Brazil were subjected to further embarrassments, such as heavy freight rates from ports to the points of consumption.[18]

The "inequality in the burdens imposed upon imports in the respective countries" made less impression upon Brazil than the United States. To the overtures from Washington for a second reciprocity agreement, the Rio government for a time declined categorically to give serious consideration. The chief explanation for its attitude was the fact that the proposed changes in the tariff would involve a complete readjustment of the revenue laws of Brazil, for the tariff was the main source for funds. Such readjustment as the American proposals involved would be difficult in normal times; they were impossible when the country was in a bankrupt

[18] Dispatches of Apr. 15 and Oct. 22, 1895, and Aug. 11 and Sept. 8, 1897, in Despatches, LVIII, LIX, LXI.

condition already. After several refusals of the Brazilian government to make suggested modifications in her customs regulations, the American minister at Rio recommended that the president exercise his authority under the Dingley law and levy countervailing duties on Brazilian coffee imported into the United States. Made several times as a threat, this extreme measure was not resorted to, perhaps because it would have met resentment by millions of coffee drinkers in Yankeeland.[19]

Although the McKinley government did not resort to extreme measures, it kept up a continuous bombardment of the Rio government for favorable concessions. Representatives of American export trade, and shipping interests connected with it, pressed their bourgeois president to carry into execution his pledges.[20] The agitation finally bore fruit, though it was very little at first. The Brazilian tariff law which went into effect on January 1, 1900, provided maximum and minimum rates, and left their application to the chief executive. As a consequence of executive application, American flour and a few items of lesser importance received slightly more favorable treatment on entering Brazil. But protests from Argentina and from the Brazilian flour mills, which were operated primarily by British capital, caused the Brazilian Congress to repeal the adjustable act at the end of two years. After this, Yankee exports to Brazil—which had in spite of the law of 1900 declined from fourteen million dollars to ten million dollars during the decade from 1892 to 1902—fell off still more.[21]

[19] Dispatches, Oct. 15, 1897, Jan. 13, Feb. 1, Mar. 25, Aug. 10, 1898, May 16, Sept. 1, 1899, in ibid., LXI-LXIV; Secretary Hay to Minister Bryan, Mar. 4, 1899, in Instructions, LXIII, 420-425.

[20] Hay to Bryan, Mar. 4, 1899, in Instructions, XVIII, 420-425.

[21] Dispatches Nov. 29 and Dec. 14, 1899, Dec. 28, 1901, Jan. 3, 1902, Nov. 12, 1903, in Despatches, LXIV, LXVII, LXIX.

Still Yankee persistence continued. Toward the close of 1903 American Minister David E. Thompson worked out an arrangement with the Rio government whereby flour from the United States was to be given a forty per cent preferential treatment and other manufactured articles, such as rubber, paints, varnishes, condensed milk, clocks, and watches, a twenty to twenty-five per cent preference over similar articles from other countries. Unfortunately, the arrangement was subject to the approval of the Brazilian Congress, and the Senate refused consent. But, as frequently happens in Latin-American countries, an executive decree was called to the rescue and the arrangement was put into operation on April 20, 1904. Before expiring by constitutional limitation on December 31, Argentina had expressed strong resentment at the discrimination against her flour.[22]

The regular Brazilian Congress of 1905 ignored appeals from both the American minister and the Brazilian executive and declined to make it possible for a renewal of the agreement of the previous year granting preferential treatment to American articles. As a consequence, American flour especially was unable to compete with the products from Argentina and Austria. But on December 30, 1905, a law was passed which, though greatly increasing the import duties on most articles, restored the authority of the president to enter into preferential arrangements for one year at a time. This was the legal basis for the twenty per cent preferential agreement between the United States and Brazil which began July 1, 1906, and which included the items previously mentioned, in addition to typewriters, pianos, weighing machines, windmills, and a few other things. This agreement was renewed annually by presidential decree until 1911, when the prefer-

[22] Thompson's dispatches of Nov. 27, Dec. 27, 1903, Apr. 27, July 30, 1904, in *ibid.*, LXIX and LXX.

ential on flour was increased to thirty per cent. The last increase aroused fears in Argentina and caused her government to threaten retaliation through an increase in rates on petroleum, lumber, and other staples from the United States. The outcome of negotiations between Washington and Buenos Aires was a promise that the United States would not seek further preferential treatment from Brazil without giving Argentina six month's notice.[23]

As a consequence of the controversy over the valorization of coffee, the Brazilian government suspended the preferential tariff agreement with the United States toward the close of 1912. Fortunately, an early adjustment of the diplomatic differences brought a restoration of the commercial concession, and the outbreak of the World War found the total value of American trade with Brazil ($153,852,605) considerably larger than that of its closest rivals, though the balance was still in Brazil's favor by a margin of two to one.[24] The war, by practically eliminating European competition for a time, increased American-Brazilian trade about three hundred per cent; and with the increase the unfavorable balance against the United States was greatly reduced. After the return of peace in Europe, the old commercial channels to South America were gradually reopened, though the Yankee traders held the advantages they had gained remarkably well. In 1929, the annual trade between Brazil and the United States was still at the one-third billion mark,

[23] Ambassador Griscom was more diplomatic than truthful when, on August 31, 1906, he wrote Secretary Root that the preferential tariff agreement of July was a consequence of his visit. It was natural that American writers should take the ambassador's pill undiluted. See Graham H. Stuart, *Latin America and the United States*, p. 382. For Griscom's statement see *Foreign Relations*, 1906, I, 134ff. See also Minister Thompson to Root, Jan. 3, Feb. 11, 1905, Jan. 27, 1906, in Despatches, LXXI, LXXII; *Foreign Relations*, 1907, I, 90-118, 1908, p. 48, 1909, p. 40, 1910, p. 121, 1911, pp. 30ff.

[24] *Report of Second Pan-American Commercial Conference*, pp. 400-401.

with the balance in favor of the former because of Yankee taste for Brazilian coffee.[25]

Just as American traders sought assistance from their government in selling their wares in Brazil and elsewhere, so Brazilian merchants solicited governmental support in disposing of their products in the United States and in other markets; and just as the alignment between business interests and government has often led the northern republic into diplomatic controversies, so has the alliance between similar agencies led the southern republic into diplomatic dissensions. An example of the latter was the difficulty which Brazil had with the United States regarding the coffee valorization scheme.

The valorization scheme was an attempt to solve the problem arising from the production of enormous quantities of coffee in the Brazilian states of Minas Gerães, Espirito Santo, Rio de Janeiro, and São Paulo. At the opening of the present century, these states alone were producing more than four-fifths of the world's annual supply. In 1906, Brazil harvested twenty million bags of one hundred and thirty-two pounds each, estimated at three million bags more than the world's annual consumption. In the same year, other portions of the earth produced several million bags. Finally, it was estimated that about eleven million bags were already stored in the warehouses of the globe as a result of surpluses of former years. As a result of these enormous surpluses, prices fell far below the cost of production, and coffee planters faced financial ruin. Radical measures had to be taken to save foreclosures of mortgages on their plantations, held largely by European financiers.

Early in 1906 the presidents of the coffee states of Minas,

[25] *Pan-American Union Bulletin*, LIV, 48-49; LXI, 912; LXII, 1034; LXIII, 1022.

Rio de Janeiro, and São Paulo met and discussed plans for relief. The result of the conference was the valorization plan, which provided for the buying of surplus coffee upon the world market and holding it for higher prices. In order to put the plan in operation it was necessary to secure huge loans from foreign financiers. European bankers refused to be the first to make advances and the initial loan was secured from Herman Sielcken, a representative of the National City Bank of New York.

Before the close of 1906 the valorization committee of São Paulo, the largest coffee-producing state in the world, placed the system in operation. The following year the states of Minas Gerães and Rio de Janeiro joined São Paulo. Soon the national government began to give specific support to the plan, especially through loans to the state organizations; eventually it purchased at critical periods stocks of coffee on its own account. By keeping enormous quantities of coffee off the market when prices were low, the growers and dealers were saved from ruin. But the valorization system received much criticism from many portions of Brazil not engaged in coffee production, as well as from several foreign countries.[26]

Criticism of valorization dates in this country from 1911, when Congressman George W. Norris of Nebraska called for an investigation into the activities of the São Paulo valorization committee in the United States. A recent increase of about six cents per pound in the price of coffee was costing the American people, who consumed nearly a billion pounds annually, the huge sum of fifty-seven million dollars a year. It was alleged that such part of the committee's work as was carried on in the United States was in violation of the Sher-

[26] Department of Commerce, *Commerce Year Book*, 1926, I, 136, II, 611; P. Denis, *Brazil*, pp. 235-266.

man Anti-trust Act. An investigation by the Department of Justice followed and the attorney-general brought suit in the District Court of Southern New York against Sielcken and other agents of the valorization committee on the grounds that they were parties to a conspiracy in restraint of trade.

As the result of protests from the state of São Paulo, the Brazilian ambassador complained of the legal proceedings and requested that the suit be dropped. He claimed it was contrary to international law to direct action against a sovereign state. After the American ambassador at Rio de Janeiro reported that feeling throughout Brazil was sensitive on the matter and that continuation of the suit would embarrass American business enterprises, the Taft government reached a compromise whereby the United States promised to drop the legal action on condition that the committee sell the valorized coffee then stored in New York, amounting to about 932,000 bags, in open market before April 1, 1913.

At various times since 1913, especially in 1924 when the price of some grades of coffee advanced as much as fifteen cents per pound, caustic criticism has arisen in the United States against the restrictive arrangement under the valorization plan. In 1925 the Department of State requested American bankers to decline to give financial assistance to the state of São Paulo, which was again attempting to come to the relief of its coffee industry.[27]

The valorization controversy acted as a damper on Brazilian-American relations for a brief time. Mention has already been made of the temporary suspension by Brazil of the preferential tariff on Yankee goods, which entailed heavy losses for American exporters. No doubt in part as

[27] The available correspondence on the valorization controversy is in *Foreign Relations*, 1913, pp. 39-67; "Hearings on Crude Rubber, Coffee, Etc." p. 24. See also B. H. Williams, *Economic Foreign Policy of the United States*, pp. 400-402.

retaliatory measures Brazil also terminated the extradition treaty of 1897 and the protocols of 1898 and 1903, which had been negotiated with considerable difficulty.[28] But the Wilson administration undertook to repair the small breach made by the preceding administration and extended an invitation to Dr. Lauro Müller, Brazil's distinguished minister of foreign affairs, to visit the United States in reciprocation of Secretary Root's visit to Brazil seven years earlier. The invitation was accepted and Dr. Müller was cordially welcomed at Hampton Roads by a reception committee headed by Senator Root. Remaining in the United States more than a month, the Brazilian minister made an itinerary which took him from New England to the Pacific coast. While in Boston, Harvard University continued its historical rôle in Brazilian-American relations and conferred upon Dr. Müller the usual honorary degree. The visit seems to have been a factor in welding the broken chain of cordiality.[29]

The reception accorded Dr. Müller on his visit to the United States in the summer of 1913 is but one of many evidences of a conscious effort at Washington to allay a feeling of suspicion and mistrust toward the northern republic which had taken a rather firm hold in Brazil and the rest of Latin America. In one of his earliest statements after taking office, President Wilson outlined his Latin American policy by saying: "One of the chief objects of the new administration will be to cultivate the friendship and deserve the confidence of our sister republics of Central and South America and to promote in every proper and honorable way the interests which are common to the peoples of the two continents."[30] Many other statements of the chief executive and of his agents

---

[28] *Foreign Relations*, 1913, p. 25.
[29] *Foreign Relations*, 1913, p. 67-74.
[30] E. E. Robinson and V. J. West, *The Foreign Policy of Woodrow Wilson*, p. 179.

were similar in character, and apparently all were impelled by a desire to promote a common friendship.[31]

The Latin Americans were impressed with the sincerity behind the new policy and in general encouraged their governments to take advantage of the chance of coöperation with the government at Washington. Brazil was in the vanguard of the Latin nations which sought to promote the cause of co-operation and cordiality. During the period of greatest confusion in Mexico, her ministers and consuls did what they could to protect American life and property without offending Huerta and Carranza. Brazil also joined Argentina and Chile in proposing mediation between the United States and Mexico following the Tampico incident and the occupation of Vera Cruz by Yankee military forces. President Wilson's hearty acceptance of mediation inspired further confidence in the sincerity of his policy.

Brazil's attitude toward the World War likewise revealed her friendship for the United States. The latter severed diplomatic relations with Germany on February 3, 1917; Brazil took similar action on April 11 following. The United States declared war on Germany on April 6; on May 22 President Braz urged the Brazilian Congress to revoke the formal neutrality decree which had been announced on the outbreak of war between the United States and Germany. In his speech urging the revocation, President Braz pointed out that "the Brazilian nation, through its legislative organ, can without warlike intentions, but with determination, adopt the attitude that one of the belligerents [the United States] forms an integral part of the American continent, and to this belligerent, we are bound by a traditional friendship and by a similarity of political opinion in the defense of the vital

---

[31] See *ibid.*, pp. 180, 200-201; see also New York *Times*, Jan. 28, 1921.

interests of America and the principles accepted by international law."[32] The neutrality decree was annulled on June 1, and in announcing the fact to foreign representatives the Rio government set forth its reason: it was to give its "foreign policy a form of continental solidarity—a policy indeed which was that of the old régime on every occasion on which any of the other friendly sister nations of the American continent were in jeopardy."[33] Finally, on October 26 (1917) Brazil followed the United States into the war. Coöperation between the two largest nations was a strong factor in determining the attitude of the other nations of the Western Hemisphere toward the conflict.

Through the war and the peace negotiations Brazil and the United States stood side by side in upholding the ideals which President Wilson enunciated from time to time. That they failed to continue to stand together in the realization of the greatest of these ideals was no fault of the South American country, for she accepted the League of Nations and was elected to membership in its Council.[34]

The attitude of the Brazilian government in 1917-1918 toward two American companies which sought cable-landing concessions in Brazil, while not as liberal as some hoped it would be, was significant for the increasing friendship between the two countries. The executive decree of August 11, 1917, granting to the Central and South American Telegraph Company authority to lay two cables from Rio de Janeiro and Santos, respectively, to the Argentine Republic terminated forty-nine years of negotiations, for it was March 30, 1868, that William H. Seward first instructed J. Watson Webb to use his influence in favor of the concession advo-

---

[32] *Brazilian Green Book* (English edition), p. 40.
[33] *Ibid.*, p. 49.
[34] P. A. Martin, *Latin America and the War*.

cated by a Mr. Scrymser.[35] This concession, as well as those which followed, came after a bitter fight with the Western Telegraph Company, a British concern which possessed from 1893 to 1913 a complete monopoly on the route to Argentina. After meeting defeat in the Brazilian courts, the Western put in operation a system of rates from Brazilian points to Argentina which discriminated against messages destined for the United States over American-owned lines from Buenos Aires via the Pacific coast. Amounting to about twenty-four cents a word, this surtax was less for retaliation than for the purpose of forcing American messages via England, where the contents might become known to the British trader, in case they were of a commercial nature. The American government protested against the highly discriminating rates; but the Brazilian government replied that it could do nothing without cancelling entirely the concession of the British company.

On October 23, 1918, the president of the Argentine Republic signed a decree authorizing the Central and South American Telegraph Company to lay one or more cables between Argentina and Uruguay. This decree removed the last obstacle in the way of a direct, American-owned telegraph service between the United States and Brazil. The closing of the war made it possible to lay the cable which broke the long-existing British monopoly.

Once the monopoly was broken, events succeeded each other with great rapidity. On November 1, 1918, Frank Carney obtained a concession from the Rio government authorizing the same American company to connect by cable the Brazilian capital with Cuba. Meantime, Nelson O'Shaughnessy had obtained for the Western Union Tel-

[35] Seward to Webb, Mar. 30, 1868, in Instructions, XVI.

egraph Company the right to lay wires from Rio de Janeiro to both Argentina and the Greater Antilles. Owing to the influence of the Western Telegraph Company on the Brazilian government, many amendments to the concessions had to be secured; but the way had been opened.[36]

In addition to these, other evidences could be produced to show that America has gained over British influence in Brazil during the past few decades. But American influence has not advanced by methods similar to that used by the Hoover administration during the Brazilian revolution of October, 1930. If in the future an arms embargo is going to miss fire, as did that of the Hoover administration, the United States Congress would do well to repeal the joint resolution which sanctions its use.

[36] For the essential correspondence on this subject see *Foreign Relations*, 1918, pp. 35-82.

BIBLIOGRAPHY

Sources

Manuscripts

Department of State
    Communications from Brazilian Agents at Washington; from
        Foreign Legations.
    Notes to the Brazilian Legation; to Foreign Legations.
    Consular Letters from Bahia, Maranham (Maranhão), Mon-
        tevideo, Pará, Pernambuco, Rio de Janeiro (twenty vol-
        umes), St. Catherines, Santos, and Rio Grande do Sul.
    Instructions to Consuls.
    Despatches from Argentina, Bolivia, Brazil (seventy-two large
        volumes to August, 1906), Colombia, Ecuador, Paraguay,
        and Venezuela.
    Instructions to United States Ministers, to those in Argentina,
        Bolivia, Brazil, Colombia, Ecuador, Paraguay, and Vene-
        zuela.
    Miscellaneous Letters.
Library of Congress
    Jefferson Papers.
    Madison Papers.
    Monroe Papers.

Printed Sources

Official Documents
    Brazilian
        Annaes do Parlamento Brazileiro (Camara dos Srs. Depu-
            tados; Senado do Imperio do Brazil).
        Archivo Diplomatico da Independencia. 1922.
        Brazil, the United States and the Monroe Doctrine (Reprint
            from *Jornal do Commercio*, Jan. 20, 1908).
        Brazilian Green Book, English Edition, London, 1918.
        O Brazil e A Inglaterra ou o Trafico de Africanos. 1868.

Protest Against an Act of the British Parliament. 1845.
Relaçoes Exteriores do Brazil durante a Administraçao do Presidente Rodriguez Alves, 1902-1906. 1906.
Relatorio da Repartiçao dos Negocios Estrangeiros Apresentado á Assembléa Geral Legislativa (to 1889).
Relatorio Apresentado ao Generalissimo Chefe do Governo Provisorio dos Estados Unidos do Brazil (since 1891).
British
British and Foreign State Papers. 1812-1922.
Correspondence with the British Commissioners Relating to the Slave Trade. Compiled by the British Legation at Rio de Janeiro, 1837.
Hansard, *Parliamentary Debates.* 3rd Series.
Parliamentary Papers, Slave Trade Series.
Peruvian
Correspondéncia Diplomática Relativa a la Cuestión del Paraguay, Publicada por Orden de S. E. el Jefe Supremo Provisorio. Lima, 1867.
United States
American State Papers, Foreign Relations.
American State Papers, Naval Affairs.
Annals of Congress.
Congressional Globe.
Congressional Record.
Diplomatic Correspondence of the United States.
House Documents.
House Executive Documents.
House Journal.
House Miscellaneous Documents.
House Reports.
Papers Relating to the Foreign Relations of the United States. 1870-1918.
Report of the Second Pan-American Commercial Conference. 1919.
Senate Documents.

Senate Executive Documents.

Senate Journal.

Statutes at Large of the United States. 1850-.

Other Printed Sources

Benites, Gregório, *Anales Diplomática y Militar de la Guerra del Paraguay*. 2 vols. Asunción, 1906.

Cardoso de Oliveira, José Manoel, *Actos Diplomaticos do Brazil: Tratados do Periodo Colonial e Various Documentos desde 1493*. 2 vols. Rio de Janeiro, 1912.

Pereira Pinto, Antonio, *Apontamentos para o Direito Internacional ou Colleçao Completa dos Tratados Celebrados pelo Brasil com Differentes Naçoes Estrangeiros*. 4 vols. Rio de Janeiro, 1864.

Anonymous. *The Acre Territory: Documents Concerning the Controversy between Brazil and Bolivia over a Contract Made with American Citizens*.

SECONDARY MATERIAL

Books

Adams, Charles Francis (ed.), *Memoirs of John Quincy Adams*. 12 vols. Philadelphia, 1875-1876.

Agan, Joseph, *The Diplomatic Relations of the United States and Brazil*. Vol. I, Paris, 1926.

Agassiz, Professor and Mrs. Louis, *A Journey in Brazil*. Boston, 1871.

Araujo Jorge, A. G. de, *Ensaios de Historia Diplomatica do Brazil no Regimen Republicano, 1889-1902*. Rio de Janeiro, 1912.

Araujo, Oscar d', *L'idée Republicaine au Bresil*. Paris, 1893.

Armitage, John, *The History of Brazil, From the Period of the Arrival of the Braganza Family in 1808, to —— 1831*. 2 vols. London, 1836.

Assis Brazil, Joaquin Francisco, *A Republica Federal*. 6th edition, Rio de Janeiro, 1889.

Baker, George E. (ed.), *The Works of William H. Seward*. 5 vols. Boston, 1884-1887.

Barnes, J., *Commodore Bainbridge*. New York, 1897.

Benitez, Justo Pastor, *La Causa Nacional: Ensayo Sobre las Antecedentes de la Guerra del Paraguay (1864-1870)*. Asunción, 1919.

Bliss, Porter C. (?), *The Paraguayan Question: The Alliance Between Brazil, the Argentine Confederation and Uruguay, Versus the Dictator of Paraguay*. New York, 1866.

———— (?), *Revelations on the Paraguayan War, and the Alliances of the Atlantic and the Pacific*. New York, 1866.

———— (?), *General McMahon's Opinions in Regard to the Paraguayan War*. No date or place of publication.

Box, Pelham Horton, *The Origins of the Paraguayan War*. 2 parts. Urbana, Ill., 1927.

Brackenridge, H. M., *A Voyage to South America Performed by Order of the American Government in the Years 1817 and 1818 in the Frigate Congress*. 2 vols. Baltimore, 1819.

Buxton, Thomas Fowell, *The African Slave Trade*. New York, 1840.

Cady, John F., *Foreign Intervention in the Rio de la Plata, 1838-1850*. Philadelphia, 1929.

Candido Teixeira, J., *A Republica Brazileira*. Rio de Janeiro, 1890.

Carrey, Emile, *L'Amazone: les Revoltes du Pará*. Paris, 1857.

Carvalho, A., *O Brazil: Colonisaçao e Emigraçao*. 2nd edition, Porto, 1876.

Chandler, Charles Lyon, *Inter-American Acquaintances*. Sewanee, Tenn., 1915.

Christie, W. D., *Notes on Brazilian Questions*. London, 1865.

Cresson, W. P., *The Holy Alliance, the European Background of the Monroe Doctrine*. New York, 1922.

Denis, P., *Brazil*. New York, 1911.

Dunn, Reverend Ballard S., *Brazil, the Home for Southerners*. New York and New Orleans, 1866.

Expilly, Charles, *La Traité L'Emigration et la Colonisation na Brésil*. Paris, 1865.

Fabricatore, Carlo, *Il 15 Novembre 1889: La Revoluzione del Brasille*. Rio de Janeiro, 1889.

Foote, Andrew H., *Africa and the American Flag*. New York, 1852.

Freire, Felisbello, *Historia da Revolta de 6 de Setembro de 1893*. Rio de Janeiro, 1896.

Garcia, Manuel, *Paraguay and the Alliance Against the Tyrant Francisco Solano López*. New York, 1869.

Gleaves, A., *James Lawrence*. New York, 1904.

Gregg, W. R., *Past and Present Efforts for the Extinction of the African Slave Trade*. London, 1840.

Hamilton, James P., *A Biographical Sketch of Henry A. Wise, with a History of the Political Campaign in Virginia in 1855*. Richmond, 1856.

Hunt, Gaillard, *Writings of James Madison*. 8 vols. New York, 1908.

James, Herman G. and P. A. Martin, *The Republics of Latin America*. Revised edition, New York, 1924.

Jefferson, Thomas, *The Writings of Thomas Jefferson*. 20 vols. Washington, 1903.

Kennedy, Commander A. J., *La Plata, Brazil, and Paraguay, during the Present War*. London, 1869.

Malloy, William M. (comp.), *Treaties, Conventions, International Acts, Protocols, and Agreements between the United States of America and Other Powers, 1776-1909*. 2 vols. Washington, 1910.

Manning, William R. (ed.), *Diplomatic Correspondence of the United States Concerning the Independence of the Latin-American Nations*. 3 vols. New York, 1925.

Martens, G. F. de and Others, *Nouveau Recueil des Traités d'Alliance*. Dieterich, 1817-.

Masterman, George F., *Seven Eventful Years in Paraguay: a Narrative of Personal Experiences Amongst the Paraguayans*. London, 1870.

Mathieson, William L., *Great Britain and the Slave Trade, 1839-1865.* New York, 1929.

Mello, Custodia José de, *Apontamentos para a Historia da Revoluçao de 23 de Novembro de 1891.* London, 1895.

Melville, Herman, *Moby Dick.* New York [1928].

Morse, J. T., Jr., *John Quincy Adams,* in "American Statesmen," vol. XV. New York, 1892.

Mossé, Benjamin, *Dom Pedro II, Emperour du Bresil.* Paris, 1889.

Moore, John Bassett, *History and Digest of International Law.* 8 vols. Washington, 1906.

——, *History and Digest of International Arbitrations to Which the United States has been a Party.* 6 vols. Washington, 1898.

Nabuco, Joaquim, *Um Estadista do Imperio.* 3 vols. Paris, 1898-1900.

Núñez, Ignacio, *An Account, Historical, Political, and Statistical, of the United Provinces of Rio de la Plata.* Translated from the Spanish. London, 1825.

Oliveira Lima, Manoel de, *Dom João VI no Brazil.* 2 vols. Rio de Janeiro, 1908.

——, *Historia Diplomatica do Brazil: O Reconhecimento do Imperio.* Second edition, Rio de Janeiro and Paris, 1902.

——, *Nos Estados Unidos: Impressoes Politicas e Sociaes.* Leipzig, 1899.

Ouseley, William Gore, Esq., *Notes on the Slave Trade, with Remarks on the Measures Adopted for its Suppression.* London, 1850.

Page, Thomas Jefferson, *La Plata, the Argentine Confederation, and Paraguay.* New York, 1859.

Pereira da Silva, J. M., *Historia da Fundaçao do Imperio Brazileiro.* 6 vols. in 3, Rio de Janeiro, 1865.

——, *Historia do Brazil durante a Menoridade de D. Pedro II (1831-1840).* Rio de Janeiro, 1880.

Pitkin, Timothy, *A Statistical View of the Commerce of the United States of America.* Hartford, 1817.

Quesada, V. G., *História Diplomática Latino-Americana.* 3 vols. Buenos Aires, 1918-20.

Rangel, Alberto, D. *Pedro I e a Marquesa de Santos: a Vista de Cartas Intimas e de Outros Documentos Publicos e Particulares.* Rio de Janeiro, 1916.

Rebandi, Dr. A., *Guerra del Paraguay: la Conspiración contra S. E. el Presidente de la República, Mariscal Don Francisco Solano López.* Buenos Aires, 1917.

Reid, Samuel C., *The History of the Wonderful Battle of the Brig of War General Armstrong.* Boston, 1893.

Reid, Whitelaw, *After the War, a Southern Tour.* New York, 1866.

Richardson, J. D. (comp.), *A Compilation of the Messages and Papers of the Presidents.* 10 vols. Washington, 1896-1899.

Rio Branco, Barão de [José Mariada Silva Paranhos], *Brazil, the United States and the Monroe Doctrine.* Reprint from *Jornal do Commercio*, Jan. 20, 1908. Rio de Janeiro, 1908.

Rippy, J. Fred, *Rivalry of the United States and Great Britain Over Latin America (1808-1830).* Baltimore, 1929.

Robinson, E. E. and V. J. West, *The Foreign Policy of Woodrow Wilson, 1913-1917.* New York, 1917.

Rocha Yastrano, José da, *Inglaterra e Brazil: Trafego de Escravos.* Rio de Janeiro, 1845.

Russell, J., *History of the War Between the United States and Great Britain.* Hartford, 1815.

Saldias, Adolfo, *História de la Confederación Argentina.* 5 vols. 2nd edition, Buenos Aires, 1892.

Schuyler, Eugene, *American Diplomacy and the Furtherance of Commerce.* New York, 1886.

Smithsonian Institution, *Annual Report.* Washington, 1876.

Stuart, Graham H., *Latin America and the United States.* New York, 1923.

Tavares, Francisco Muniz, *Historia da Revoluçao de Pernambuco em 1817.* Pernambuco, 1840.

Vincent, Frank, *Around and About South America.* New York, 1890.

Walsh, R., *Notices of Brazil in 1828 and 1829.* 2 vols. London, 1830.

Washburn, C. A. *A History of Paraguay.* 2 vols. New York, 1871.

Webb, Gen. James Watson, *General J.(ames) Watson Webb, Late U. S. Envoy Extraordinary to Brazil, vs. Hamilton Fish and E. R. Hoar.* [1875.]

——, *Reminiscences of Gen'l Samuel B. Webb, of the Revolutionary Army.* New York, 1882.

——, *A Letter from His Excellency J. Watson Webb, U. S. Envoy Extraordinary and Minister Plenipotentiary in Brazil to J. Bramley Moore.* Rio de Janeiro, 1863.

Williams, Ben H., Economic Foreign Policy of the United States. New York, 1929.

Wise, Barton Haxall, *The Life of Henry A. Wise of Virginia, 1806-1876.* New York, 1899.

Newspapers and Magazines

A Noticia (Rio).
Alabama *State Journal.*
Anglo-Brazilian Times (Rio).
Aurora Fluminense (Rio).
Baltimore *News.*
Baltimore *Sun.*
Brazilian American (Rio).
Buenos Ayres Standard.
Charleston *Daily Courier.*
Charleston *Daily News.*
Charleston *Mercury.*
Chicago *Herald.*
Correio Mercantil (Rio).
Diario (Rio).
Flake's Semi-weekly Bulletin (Galveston).
Gaceta Official (Rio).
Gazeta de Noticias (Rio).

Jornal do Commercio (Rio).
Mobile *Daily Register.*
National Intelligencer.
New Orleans *Cresent.*
New Orleans *Daily True Delta.*
New Orleans *Picayune.*
New Orleans *Times.*
New York *Herald.*
New York *Sun.*
New York *Times.*
New York *Tribune.*
New York *World.*
O Philantropo (Rio).
Pan-American Union Bulletins.
Philadelphia *Press.*
Philadelphia *Public Ledger.*
San Francisco *Call.*
Saturday Evening Post.
Tribuna de Petropolis (Rio).
Voz da Juventude (Rio).

Periodicals

Adams, Jane Elizabeth, "The Abolition of the Brazilian Slave Trade," in *The Journal of Negro History*, X, No. 4.

Cleven, N. A. N., "Some Plans for Colonizing Liberated Negro Slaves in Hispanic America," *The Journal of Negro History*, XI, No. 1.

Cochin, A., *Laylor's Cyclopedia.*

Cox, I. J., "Pan-American Policy of Jefferson and Wilkinson," *The Mississippi Valley Historical Review*, I, 212-239.

Editorial, "The Regions of the Amazon," *De Bow's Review*, XVI, 231-251.

Hill, Lawrence F., "Confederate Exiles to Brazil," *The Hispanic American Historical Review*, May, 1927.

Hopkin's, E. A., "The Plata and the Parana-Paraguay," *De Bow's Review*, XIV.

"Inca," "Shall the Valley of the Amazon and Mississippi Reciprocate Trade?" *De Bow's Review*, XIV.

Manning, W. R., "An Early Diplomatic Controversy between the United States and Brazil," *The Hispanic American Historical Review*, I, No. 1.

―――, "Statements, Interpretations, and Applications of the Monroe Doctrine, etc., 1823-1845," *Proceedings of the American Society of International Law, 1914*.

Martin, P. A., "Causes of the Collapse of the Brazilian Empire," *The Hispanic American Historical Review*, IV, 4-48.

―――, "Latin America and the War," *The League of Nations Bulletin*, II, No. 4.

―――, "The Influence of the United States on the Opening of the Amazon to the World's Commerce," *The Hispanic American Historical Review*, I.

Maury, Lieut. M. F., "On Extending the Commerce of the South and West by Sea," *De Bow's Review*, XII, 381-399.

―――, "Direct Foreign Trade of the South," *De Bow's Review*, XII, 126-148.

―――, "Great Commercial Advantages of the Gulf of Mexico," *De Bow's Review*, VII, 510-523.

―――, "Valley of the Amazon," *De Bow's Review*, XIV, 449-460, 556-567; XV, 36-43.

Renaut, J. P., "Le Government Portugais à Rio de Janeiro," *Revue d' Histoire Diplomatique*, XXXIII.

Rippy, J. Fred, "Britain's Rôle in the Early Relations of the United States and Mexico," *The Hispanic American Historical Review*, VII, No. 1.

―――, "The United States and the Establishment of the Republic of Brazil," *The Southwestern Historical Quarterly*, III, No. 1.

Robertson, W. S., "South America and the Monroe Doctrine," *The Political Science Quarterly*, XXX.

Van Alstyne, Richard W., "The British Right of Search and the African Slave Trade," *The Journal of Modern History*, II, No. 1.

Williams, M. W., "The Treaty of Tordesillas and the Argentine-Brazilian Boundary Settlement," *The Hispanic American Historical Review*, February, 1922.

INDEX

Aberdeen Act, 114
Acre question, discussion of, 285-291
Acto Addicional, 76
Adams, President John Quincy, negotiations in *General Armstrong* case, 13-15; reproves Condy Raguet, 52 ff.
Adams, Robert, Jr., policy on recognition of Brazilian republic, 264 ff.
Agassiz, Louis F., visit to Brazil, 236-238
Agnes, the, as a slaver, 124-126
Alabama, the, in Brazilian ports, 152-153
Alley Law, 169-170
Allied and Paraguayan forces compared, 183-184
Amazon Company of Navigation and Commerce, 232
American-Brazilian relations, change in character of, 259 ff.
American commerce, status of in Brazil, 266 ff.
"American" policy, attempts to secure, 91-92, 104 ff.
American press, position on recognition of Brazilian republic, 265
Araujo Lima, as Brazilian regent, 75
Argentine-Brazilian alliance against Paraguay, 182-183
Artigas, José, program in Banda Oriental, 16 ff., 33 ff.

Bahia, American connection with insurrection at, 79 ff.
Banda Oriental, Argentine-Brazilian rivalry concerning, 33 ff.
Baron de Itajubá, 260
Baron of Rio Branco, 283, 292-293
Barrios, Colonel, invades Matto Grasso, 180-181
Benham, Admiral, and Brazilian naval revolt, 278 ff.
Benham, Rev. J. B., on the slave trade, 133

Blaine, James G., relation to First Pan-American Conference, 262; attitude toward recognition of Brazilian republic, 265-266; commercial policy of, 268 ff.; policy towards Deodora and Peixoto governments, 272 ff.
Bliss, Porter C., 199, 201, 204, 205
Blow, Henry T., policy as American minister, 259 ff.
Bocayuva, 242
Bolivian rivers, negotiations for opening, 225
Bolivian Syndicate, 285 ff.
Bowen, William, 251-252
Braz, President, and Brazilian-American relations, 302-303
Brazil, becomes independent, 26; recognized by the United States, 28-30; goes to war with Argentina, 35-36; complains of unneutral American course, 64 ff.; domestic problems, 74 ff.; attitude toward the slave trade, 112 ff.
Brazilian-American commercial relations since 1895, 293 ff.
Brazilian colonization agents in the United States, 242
Brazilian empire, causes for overthrow of, 263
Brazilian republic, establishment of, 263 ff.
Bright and Company, concessions in Brazil, 261
Buchanan, James, negotiates on Davis episode, 97 ff.
Buffalo Exposition, Brazil represented at, 292
Bureau of American Republics, 263
Buxton, T. F., author, 120-121

Cable concessions, 303-305
Canada, the, 207, 211, 212, 260
Caroline, the, 207, 208, 210, 211